READING HEGEL

THINKING LITERATURE
A series edited by Nan Z. Da and Andrea Gadberry

Reading Hegel

IRONY, RECOLLECTION, CRITIQUE

Robert Lucas Scott

The University of Chicago Press
Chicago and London

The University of Chicago Press, Chicago 60637
The University of Chicago Press, Ltd., London
© 2025 by The University of Chicago
All rights reserved. No part of this book may be used or reproduced in any manner whatsoever without written permission, except in the case of brief quotations in critical articles and reviews. For more information, contact the University of Chicago Press, 1427 East 60th Street, Chicago, IL 60637.
Published 2025

34 33 32 31 30 29 28 27 26 25   1 2 3 4 5

ISBN-13: 978-0-226-83808-3 (cloth)
ISBN-13: 978-0-226-83809-0 (paper)
ISBN-13: 978-0-226-83810-6 (e-book)
DOI: https://doi.org/10.7208/chicago/9780226838106.001.0001

Library of Congress Cataloging-in-Publication Data

Names: Scott, Robert Lucas, author.
Title: Reading Hegel : irony, recollection, critique / Robert Lucas Scott.
Other titles: Thinking literature.
Description: Chicago : The University of Chicago Press, 2025. | Series: Thinking literature | Includes bibliographical references and index.
Identifiers: LCCN 2024028964 | ISBN 9780226838083 (cloth) | ISBN 9780226838090 (paperback) | ISBN 9780226838106 (ebook)
Subjects: LCSH: Hegel, Georg Wilhelm Friedrich, 1770–1831. | Literature—Philosophy.
Classification: LCC B2919 .S35 2025 | DDC 193—dc23/eng/20240726
LC record available at https://lccn.loc.gov/2024028964

FOR BRONTË

We learn by experience that we meant something other than we meant to mean.

Contents

PREFACE: THESES ON READING HEGEL xi

INTRODUCTION · What Is Living-Dead in the Philosophy of Hegel? 1
- Everyone Has Become a Hegelian 1
- How to Read Hegel 8
- Critique beyond the Limits of Critique, Marx beyond the Limits of Hegel 13

Part 1 · Reading Hegel

CHAPTER 1 · Irony, or What Is 19
- "With What Must the Beginning of Science Be Made?" 24
- Hegel's Phenomenological Method 29
- The "Is" 35
- Woman: The Eternal Irony of the Community? 41
- From the Speculative Reading of the Proposition to the Speculative Reading of the *Phenomenology* 44
- Commitment Issues 50

CHAPTER 2 · Recollection, or The Gallery of Images 55
- The *Phenomenology* as a Gallery of Images 58
- The Fate of Representation 60
- *Er-Innerung* 66
- Some Examples 75
- Marx's Imagery: Difficult to Swallow 79
- Grey in Grey; Remembering and Repeating 80
- Suspicion or Trust? 84

CHAPTER 3 · The Spirit and the Letter, or A Series of Letters concerning the Spirit and the Letter within Hegel's Philosophy 89

- Letters against Letter-Bound Thinking 91
- God Is Coal 101
- Hegel and Luther 108

Part 2 · Hegel Reading

CHAPTER 4 · *Après la Lettre*: Hegel in a Postcritical Era 121

- *Hegel Contra Sociology* 121
- Hegel Contra Literary Theory 126
- Theory after *Kritik*? 129
- The Limits of Recognition 135
- Jameson's Hegelianism? 145
- Speculative Reading and the Critique of Political Economy 152
- The Remains of the Day 155
- Hegel's Defense of Poetry 158
- Knausgaard's Struggle 161

ACKNOWLEDGMENTS 167

NOTES 169

BIBLIOGRAPHY 199

INDEX 213

Theses on Reading Hegel [PREFACE]

The relationship between Hegel and literary theory is both severely contested and seemingly paradoxical. On the one hand, "theory" often names that which has established itself against figures like Hegel and all that he ostensibly stood for: the imperium of reason, systematicity, identity at the expense of difference, "absolute idealism," and the end of art. And yet, this opposition notwithstanding, it is also frequently claimed—and often by the same critics—that literary theory cannot escape Hegel. In spite of itself, it is argued, literary theory in practically all of its guises owes a profound debt to his philosophy and rests upon a number of concepts and ways of thinking that were prefigured by him. The critic Paul de Man states this claim most directly: "Whether we know it, or like it, or not, most of us are Hegelians.... Few thinkers have so many disciples who never read a word of their master's writings."[1]

It is the aim of this book, first, to complicate this account. It argues that while Hegel has indeed had a profound influence on literary theory, this influence can only be registered in how the latter has made use of certain concepts or arguments as abstracted from their more dynamic presentation in Hegel's writings. This "use" of Hegel has been very productive, with pivotal examples from the history of literary criticism ranging from György Lukács's theory of the novel to Jacques Derrida's deconstruction (the latter of which is not as anti-Hegelian as is often presumed). Such a procedure of abstraction, however, tends toward reducing "Hegel" to a series of propositions or positions, toward selectively rendering his thought as a methodology, or else toward taking a concept from Hegel (be it history, recognition, or difference) and assuming it as the quasi-transcendental precondition for its critical argument. As such, these attempts necessarily overlook what is perhaps the greatest innovation of Hegel's philosophy: a presuppositionless phenomenology that is both a theory *and* a presentation of experience. By abstracting from the presentation of the experience to its theory, you lose both. By beginning with a first principle, taken on authority, you do not begin at all. Thought is reduced, in Hegel's words, to a "monotonous formalism" and to "lifeless determinations," "like a skeleton with small bits of paper stuck all over it" (*PhG* §51).[2] It is on this point that Hegel's philosophy, particularly in the *Phenomenology of Spirit* (1807), itself approaches literature: its content cannot be simply abstracted from the singular experience of reading it. The mode of reading engendered by this *speculative* experience has been overlooked by literary theory; and it is for this reason that literary theory has never been truly Hegelian.

This book will also argue, then, that by reading Hegel "speculatively"— that is, by being alive to the experience of the content as it progressively (and sometimes regressively) unfolds—Hegel's phenomenology yields a literary theory of sorts, and more specifically, a theory and practice of reading. I say "of sorts" for, again, this is not a theory to be produced or taken possession of through the abstraction of certain concepts or else an instrumental method to be curated, packaged, and delivered over as a commodity to literary studies. Instead, it is a result to be achieved only through the experience of the incessant irony and disruption of the dialectic—that is, of reading Hegel. This is because Hegel's phenomenology is an innovation first in form, not content, whereby the reader is repeatedly led into accepting false certainties that are then comically undermined, forced to confront what was at first unwittingly excluded. While much has already been made of the importance of the reading experience for reading *Hegel*, particularly with reference to his development of the so-called speculative proposition, this book argues that the speculative experience of reading Hegel is productive of a mode of reading tout court.

It might be more accurate to say, then, that what this book offers is not a totally new literary theory but instead a theorization and defense of the experience of reading as essential to any work of critical interpretation. To mount this defense from an apparently Hegelian "position" may seem odd, given that Hegel perhaps more than any other is motivated to root out the complex mediations of any supposedly immediate experience— such as that of reading. And yet, it will be argued here that, while this is certainly the case, the novelty of Hegel's method is that he always immanently "follows the path" of this mediation from immediacy ("following the path" being the etymology of "method," *meta-hodos*).[3] Thinking, for Hegel, must always begin by risking the naivete, particularity, and "onesidedness" of immediacy, if only to follow it to its end to discover its disavowed mediation—for it is only by going through this immediacy that its mediation might be discovered. Too often in critical approaches to literature, it will be argued, this essential moment of critical naivete or attachment is rejected from the beginning for the comforting distance of critical detachment.

To defend immediacy and attachment as an essential moment not only of reading Hegel, but of critical reading more generally, may seem deeply irresponsible, or at the very least unwittingly instep with the contemporary cultural hegemony. As Anna Kornbluh has recently argued, immediacy can be confidently identified as the ruling category and aesthetic style of "too late capitalism." In twenty-first-century art, business, politics, relationships, and even critical theory, the immediacy of experience and its "payoffs" are what matters. We are who we are, we keep it real, with no filter. We want experiences, intense ones, but also vibes: "Buddha at the gas pump on the mindfulness plane of continuity."[4] Contemporary literature is characterized by a rejection of the mediations of fiction in favor of the immediacy of autofictional "first personalism";[5] contemporary film and TV increasingly spurns "the artifices of mediation" in favor of the authentic immediacy of Fleabag (for instance) winking at *you* through your screen; and even contemporary theory is increasingly characterized by a dismissal of the mediations of depth, structure, and critique itself, in favor of the apparent immediacy of the lived experience or cultural text *as it is*. To entertain, then, the idea that our immediate truth or immediate experiences are mediated (by history, economics, or the unconscious, for example), and therefore not as profound as they might seem, is understood by the Zeitgeist to be elitist, dismissive, obfuscating, and overcomplicating.

In resistance to this cult of the immediate, Kornbluh calls for a return, in both art and criticism, to mediation: to the detached, impersonal, and difficult "social process of making representations, connections, and meaning—which often reveals that the merely evident or intransitively existent does not already make sense."[6] For Kornbluh, mediation is the only medium for critical understanding, and immediacy must be rejected at the outset as an illusion which precludes this process.

This book shares Kornbluh's desire to ruthlessly critique immediacy as the style of too late capitalism, as well as her passion for the power of mediation as a critical force. Indeed, her book begins with an epigraph from Hegel: "Immediacy itself is essentially mediated."[7] However, where the present book departs from Kornbluh's argument is that it holds that to simply call for mediation, detachment, and impersonality risks being as abstract—and even as immediate—as immediacy itself. Hegel's crucial insight when it comes to the relationship between immediacy and mediation, overlooked in literary criticism and much critical theory (not to mention in much Hegel scholarship), is that mediation is not something that can be summoned in advance but is instead a result to be achieved or discovered by immersing oneself in and traversing the immediate. The idea that "immediacy is mediated" cannot be presumed and hypostasized in advance as a methodological principle. Instead the proposition that "immediacy is itself essentially mediated" must be read speculatively. We cannot say, for instance, "Immediacy is mediated so we can do without it and just skip to the mediation part"—for this is to critique immediacy, well, immediately.[8] In doing so, I will argue, Kornbluh obscures both the mechanisms by which apparently mediated critical and narrative modes emerge and the critical force of following the path of mediation from the intensities of immediacy. To achieve a style of mediation, it is not as simple as "speak[ing] impersonally without 'I.'"[9] For Hegel, it is only when immediacy is taken immediately, with full conviction and naive attachment, that it might give way to mediation. For the present book, this process is a matter of reading.

This argument will be conducted across three main chapters and one extended concluding chapter. The main chapters are organized conceptually around three essential yet overlooked modalities of Hegel's dialectic: irony, recollection, and "the spirit and the letter." They are chapters that take the form of extended readings of Hegel, while also taking the reading of Hegel as their central thematic question. The concluding chapter, meanwhile, equipped with these experiences of reading Hegel, turns more explicitly to literary theory by addressing recent and ongoing debates surrounding the "limits of critique" and the so-called postcritical in literary studies. It will end by defending the critical potential of lyric poetry and so-called autofiction (with reference to Karl Ove Knausgaard's *My Struggle* in particular), in spite of what Kornbluh identifies as their capitulation to the ideological conceit of immediacy.

* * *

On August 27, 1801, his thirty-first birthday, Hegel defended his doctoral dissertation "On the Orbits of the Planets." As part of this defense, he submitted twelve theses to debate with his examiners, the first of which was, "*Contradictio est regula veri, non contradictio falsi.*" Contradiction is the rule of truth, noncontradiction is false.[10]

The argument of the present work is also guided by a set of interrelated theses, the first of which also concerns the nature of truth. These three following theses do not correspond to the three main chapters. Rather, they guide and run through each of them.

Thesis 1: The truth for Hegel is ironic.

This first thesis argues that the truth, for Hegel, is ironic and can only be grasped and expressed as such. This thesis may seem eccentric, not least because, as we shall see, there is nowhere that Hegel is more incensed and scathing than when critiquing the ironic disposition of his contemporaries. Such a disposition, characterized in Hegel's view by a vain subjectivity, lazy relativism, and cynical indifference toward reality, consists, he claims, "in destroying and dissolving everything that proposes to make itself objective."[11] Unsurprisingly, then, the reception of Hegel, from Søren Kierkegaard to Robert Brandom, has usually taken it for granted that he was opposed to irony per se.

This book will argue, however, that this prevalent misconception has damaged our understanding of Hegel's philosophy and its import for literary theory. Far from representing the philosophical anti-ironist par excellence, Hegel is in fact a deeply ironic thinker. Crucially, this irony is radically opposed to that of the Jena Romantics whom Hegel so despised, as well as to the postmodern irony that still dominates much critical and cultural discourse today. Hegelian irony is not an intellectual disposition or a rhetorical figure. It does not pertain merely to an attitude or to language; of saying one thing when you mean another, for example. Rather, it describes the nature of truth itself.

One can have statements of fact that do not change, statements that are qualified once more information is acquired, statements whose meanings vary depending on their contexts, or else statements that turn out to be false. But such statements do not concern truth; this is because "truth," for Hegel, always refers self-reflexively to its own realization and development. Hegel is less interested, therefore, in asking "Is X true or false?" than he is in asking "What is the truth *of* X?" As Hegel argues in the introduction to *Phenomenology of Spirit*, it is precisely this former tendency to always be asking whether something is true or false that is itself false: "This fear of erring is already the error itself" (*PhG* §74). This claim does not affirm a kind of lukewarm compromise or relativism for which there is some truth in everything. Instead, the truth of X, in order for X to have any truth at all, must always be moving beyond itself, beyond its own apparent limits, and thus becoming something other than what it once was or how it first appeared—not relativism but extremism.[12] In order for a thing to stay true to itself, it must become something other; as it comes into itself, it at once becomes something different. This is the crux of Hegel's proposition that "essentially 'the true' is subject.... It is only the dialectical movement, this course of self-engendering, advancing, and then returning into itself" (*PhG* §65). It is also what he means when he writes, to introduce his dissertation, "*Contradictio est regula veri, non contradictio falsi.*" Without this absolute contradiction, there would be no truth, for truth is not a matter of fact, but is the activity of striving to become true.

Why, though, call this "irony"? Why not just stick to "contradiction," or else, perhaps, "dialectic"? Aside from one select comment in his lectures on the history of philosophy, in which he describes the dialectic as the "universal irony of the world,"[13] the word *Ironie* rarely appears in Hegel's vocabulary unless used with reference to the Jena Romanticism which he viewed as anathema to his own philosophical system. This book, however, will recover this notion of the dialectic as the "universal irony of the world" in order to highlight the *dramatic* nature of the dialectic. The ironic truth of something, for Hegel, can never be known in advance, but must be discovered and experienced. Truth must take us by surprise. To say, then, that the truth, for Hegel, is ironic and can only be grasped and expressed as such, is not to say that the truth must be grasped and expressed ironically. Hegel is insistent that one must never try to comprehend or communicate the truth with ironic distance, as if what is said is not really meant. On the contrary, the fact of Hegelian irony demands that we pursue the truth of something with absolute naivete and absolute conviction—if only, through experience, to confront and accept what our first impressions and intentions excluded. We must, in Hegel's words, "give force to what is"; we must "[set] aside every reflection, simply to take up *what is there before us*"—not as a capitulation to the status quo but, on the contrary, to realize the truth of what that apparent stability and stasis obscures.[14] Often the term "dialectic" is purged of this necessary experiential component, this necessary element of surprise. However, to understand the dialectic from the outside, to have the pretense of knowing in advance what the truth of something is or will turn out to be, without following and experiencing this truth as it unravels, is to merely formalize it as a rigid and inevitable schema. To truly grasp the irony of the dialectic, on the other hand, which is the irony of truth, Hegel asks only that we give ourselves up to it, in all its contingency and surprise, and go to the end. Hegelian irony is then a dramatic irony redoubled, in that we are the ones who, while assuming the position of knowing spectators observing the action, repeatedly find, but always too late, that we are the ones up on stage.

Essential to this understanding of truth is also the notion of recollection. To "go beyond" something, for Hegel, does not entail a simple departure or abandonment of it in order to make way for the new. Instead, the new always involves an interiorization and a recollection (the German word *Erinnerung* encapsulates both of these meanings) of its past. The truth is also ironic, therefore, insofar as it always stands in critical and contradictory relation to what it was before. Recollection is what is required to both suspend the irony of this contradiction between the past and its present iterations, and to have the resolve, the *Entschluß*, to intervene—that is, to realize the spirit in its progress. It is the task of isolating and taking to the end the truth of something, of conferring necessity and meaning on a contingent happening. Therefore, while the irony and surprise of the dialectic suggest the *passivity* of spirit—its inability to predict, prescribe, or proscribe its own future; "recollection" names the simultaneous work and *activity* of realizing the ironic truth of the past in the present.[15] Every sublation or *Aufhebung* is a labor of both systematic and selective memory which works through its own past in order to realize its specific determination and meaning. To give oneself up to the irony of the dialectic, then, paradoxically involves a constant and strenuous effort. This couple of passivity and activity cannot be divorced.

Thesis 2: The truth of Hegel is ironic.

The second thesis follows from the first. In a sense, it is the same as the first but with specific reference to Hegel himself. It therefore helps to illuminate the first as its prime example. If Hegel's conception of truth demands that it must be constantly going beyond itself—that in order to become more fully what it is, it must, ironically, become something else—then this conception must apply, in turn, to Hegel himself. In order to grasp the truth of Hegel today—or, put differently, to continue to pursue Hegelian speculative thinking—one must push Hegel to his extremes, even if that means going beyond any imagined authorial intentions or meanings. The efficacy of Hegel's thinking demands that it must be susceptible to its own workings. In other words, the philosophy of Hegel is itself subject to the irony of the dialectic and the irony of truth; or, to continue the theatrical metaphor from before, Hegel is not the theater director of spirit, orchestrating a drama he has plotted from the beginning, he is up on stage with us. This raises significant questions, which will be addressed, concerning the ethical and political stakes of authorship and its relationship to authority and autonomy, where Hegel represents perhaps the most extreme case. How can Hegel "author" the path of the dialectic without arrogating the authority to determine it? How can one "give oneself up to the dialectic" without dogmatically giving oneself up to "Hegel" as an absolute authority and author?

There can be no such thing as an orthodox Hegelian: To take "what Hegel said" as doctrine, to prioritize getting it absolutely clear in one's head, as though it were a puzzle to be solved or a body of work to be pinned down and mastered and applied, means that the truth of Hegel stops. To be a

Hegelian, then, which means to follow Hegel's thinking on his own terms, we must go beyond them. This is why Hegel's philosophy marks the end of philosophy only insofar as it affirms the speculative identity of philosophy with its own history and future. The history of philosophy is always complete and ended but always retroactively altered by each new radical development or interruption.[16]

Crucially, this is not to license interpretative liberties whereby the truth of Hegel can be whatever his reader wants it to be. On the contrary, just as the truth *for* Hegel can only be approached by setting aside every reflection and taking up what is there before us in its stupid immediacy, if only, through experience, to discover what this immediacy obscures, the truth *of* Hegel can only be approached by reading him with what Rebecca Comay and Frank Ruda call "a kind of mind-numbing literalism."[17] This is a totally different mode of reading from those who seek to modernize Hegel's thought by asking of it "what is living and what is dead" (as Benedetto Croce did in his eponymous study),[18] by rejecting in advance those elements of his thinking that now seem expendable, by trying to extract a spirit of Hegel from the embarrassing baggage that we have to sift through when reading him to the letter—be it God, metaphysics, or (perhaps the greatest offender) absolute knowing. To read in such a way is to read with critical detachment or ironic distance when, again, what reading Hegel demands is critical intimacy, to give oneself up to the drama of the experience of the dialectic. Similarly, however, just as to ask what is salvageable of Hegel can only ever end up with a deflated and truncated version of him, to read Hegel to the letter and the letter alone is merely to construct a partial account of what the historical Hegel intended. It reduces speculative thinking, again, to a series of fixed positions frozen in time to be merely learned and taken note of: Hegel's corpus—his dead body of work to be picked over.

How, then, to read Hegel with a "mind-numbing literalism" but without succumbing to the temptation of sticking with the illusion of immediate or literal meaning? This book will argue that it is only by first going through this dead letter and totally immersing oneself in it that the living spirit of Hegelian thinking might be realized. Only the most critically intimate or speculatively naive reading might animate the truth of the text. The dead letter of Hegel's text, then, is not (as claimed by poststructuralists from Derrida to Werner Hamacher) the troublesome material remains of the system preventing the final sublation into the heights of absolute knowing but rather the very condition of such knowing, a knowing that is "absolute" not because it is finally complete but because it is fully alive.

While these repeated references to life and death may appear to be merely metaphorical (as they are for Croce), my use of the terms "life" and "death" in this book will be in keeping with Hegel's own conception of life.[19] "Contradiction," Hegel writes in the *Logic*, "is the root of all movement and life; it is only in so far as something has a contradiction within it that it moves, is possessed of instinct and activity."[20] This is because to be alive is to experience the fundamental discrepancy between what I am and what I ought to be, a discrepancy which drives me beyond myself. This "ought" is not an externally prescribed purpose or imperative. Rather it is the internal purpose of life itself—that is, to be alive. The discrepancy, then, at its most fundamental is that life is mortal: life is indelibly marked by death. As Hegel writes of life in his *Philosophy of Nature*, it is "the disparity between its [life's] finitude and universality" that is the "original disease and the inborn germ of death."[21] Death is "life's inequality to (it)self," as Derrida puts it (apropos Hegel).[22] However, it is precisely this original disparity that is also life's condition. Certainly, to be dead is to be dead—death in and for itself is the only true tautology, and to be totally tautological is to be dead; but to be alive without the immanence of death to life is to be dead too, for without this fundamental antagonism a thing does not have the drive to move beyond itself. Hence, for Hegel to be alive, he must go beyond himself.

Thesis 3: A speculative reading of Hegel yields a speculative mode of reading.

This takes us to the third thesis, which argues that this way of reading Hegel, demanded by his presentation of the truth as ironic, yields, in turn, a Hegelian (dialectical, phenomenological, speculative) way of reading. This argument will be made first with reference to Hegel's idea of "the speculative proposition." The speculative proposition has traditionally been understood as Hegel's development of a new kind of writing by which he might better present the "plasticity" and dynamism of the dialectic (*PhG* §64). Indeed, this understanding encapsulates much of what is central to the argument of this book. Hegel's speculative proposition is fundamentally ironic, in that it must be misread before it can be actually read. This is not because it merely seems to mean one thing when in fact it means another, sneakily withholding its true interpretation until later. It is rather because it presents and actuates the impossibility of anything tautologically meaning what it means. By having the copula "is" affirming both identity *and* difference between the subject and predicate of the proposition, and thus by affirming that what the proposition means is always more than it meant to, "the dialectical movement, this self-engendering, advancing, and the returning into itself" is begun (*PhG* §65). It is only by first reading to the letter—by reading simply that "is" means "is"—that we are compelled to reread for the spirit—by which what "is" is brought to life.

This argument of the present book supplements this understanding, however, by arguing that the speculative proposition is always better understood as the speculative *reading* of the proposition, by which *any* proposition might be plasticized, dynamized, and brought to life. What has been neglected is that the speculative proposition is not only the product of a formal or stylistic innovation in philosophical writing; it is also the proposition (which could be any proposition) that has been animated by a dialectically and critically intimate mode of reading. Some have argued that "perhaps what is required now is the writing of new speculative propositions tracing the fate of subject and substance; perhaps philosophy and woman are one, and politics and woman are one."[23] This misses, however, that what is really required now is the reading of all propositions as speculative. Again, Hegel's propositional logic is concerned with asking what the truth of something is, not with asking whether it is true. Therefore, the speculative reading of the proposition, or reading as recollection, provides a model, for Hegel, for reanimating the ironic truth of the history of philosophy within the present. It is for this reason that Hegel could position himself as the ironic truth or "end" of all previous thought. By affirming for the first time a speculative identity between philosophy and the history of philosophy, the truth of the history of philosophy was for the first time recollected.

It will also be argued, finally, that the import of this mode of Hegelian reading is not limited to philosophy, nor even to propositions. In recent decades, literary criticism (and the humanities more generally) has been faced with an apparent crisis. Its prevailing critical paradigm—that is, the paradigm of critique itself—has been cast into doubt as a methodology for interpretation, and questioned concerning its once-assumed political and ethical efficacy. Principally, it has been accused of being overly detached and methodological; and of tending to excavate beneath the text to diagnose its disavowed symptoms at the expense of the text itself.[24] The speculative exposition of Hegel in this book, however, provides a different kind of reading: one which is critical but without succumbing to the pretensions of mastery or detachment, characteristic of what is often understood by the word "critique"; and one which prioritizes the singularity of the reading experience but without succumbing to the subjectivism or implicit conservatism of that which has called itself "postcritical." Following the work of Gillian Rose in *Hegel Contra Sociology* (1981), I will argue that the instrumental, methodologically detached, and diagnostic mode of much critical reading and theory remains stuck in an implicitly neo-Kantian critical paradigm, which favors explanation over truth. It will argue that it is therefore only by learning from Hegel's metacritique of Kant's critique, and from his corresponding development of the idea of speculative experience—the ironic experience that *contradictio est regula veri*—that we might make possible a renewal of critical thinking and reading in the moment of their crisis.

* * *

It must be conceded before moving on that to begin in this way, with an abstract statement of the work's theses, is already to risk the fallacy of what Hegel calls "shooting from the pistol" (*PhG* §16)—what we might describe in English as "jumping the gun"—prematurely assuming or prejudging the results to be achieved. One cannot simply assert that "truth, for Hegel, is ironic" and accept it as such. As already intimated, no truth for Hegel (not even this truth about truth itself) can be stated in advance, without following the drama of the experience of discovering it. As Hegel argues in the preface to the *Phenomenology*, any opening statement of aims or methodologies amounts to little more than an opening statement admitting to the succeeding work's failure. In assuming a beginning, the beginning goes unthought, thus throwing the validity of all that follows into question: "It would have shown itself to be incapable of grasping the truth" (*PhG* §1). Even to state *these* abstract claims about beginning is, in a way, to offer a "a stamped coin issued directly from the mint and ready for one's pocket"—to use another of Hegel's metaphors.

Hegel himself was afflicted by this apparent contradiction. For a thinker so averse to the illusion of immediate beginnings—beginnings which claim to be "not intervening" in or "not in the middle" (*in-mediatus*) of that which they ostensibly ground (to draw upon the word's etymology); beginnings not already caught up in the drama of experience—Hegel could not stop writing beginnings. Like the present book, the *Phenomenology* has two introductory chapters. The *Logic* has four. That this might not be a case of mere inconsistency, self-ironizing playfulness, or else tortuous defeatism is demonstrated by what comes after these repeated beginnings: yet more beginnings which reveal themselves to insufficiently certain. For Hegel, the repeated failure to begin is the only way to begin. In the case of the *Phenomenology*, for instance, even once we make it through the necessary preambles (themselves denouncing preambles as unnecessary), each of the succeeding sections may also be described as a kind of false start. Each "shape of spirit" that we occupy is a point of departure on the way to knowledge that considers itself to be immediate, but in each case, through experience, we discover what this certainty disavows: that this and every following apparently immediate beginning is always *mediate*, that each beginning has its own presupposition or law to be discovered and is therefore a beginning in the middle—literally "*in medias res.*" This discovery allows us to begin again with the knowledge of what we have learned, or else without the "knowledge" that we have successfully unlearned. It is only through the repeated failure to begin, through recognizing and re-cognizing each failed beginning, that we might repeat forward.

What Is Living-Dead in the Philosophy of Hegel?

[INTRODUCTION]

Everyone Has Become a Hegelian

The legacies of Hegel are often described less in terms of his reception or influence and more in terms of a haunting. While Croce's famous study inquires into this "undead" Hegel from an assumed position of detached critical hindsight, others allude to the ghost of Hegel far more ominously. The source of this omen is invariably located in Hegel's propensity to have seemingly anticipated every vain attempt to exorcise him. Michel Foucault, for example, warns, "We have to determine the extent to which our anti-Hegelianism is possibly one of the tricks directed against us, at the end of which he stands, motionless, waiting for us."[1] Similarly, Maurice Blanchot argues, "To read him, not to read him—to understand him, to misunderstand him, to reject him—all this falls under the authority of Hegel or doesn't take place at all."[2] This is because, in the words of Hamacher, "Every new reading of Hegel's writings finds itself confronted by the dilemma of ... already being grasped by what it seeks to grasp"; of finding that it has "already been caught up within its circling coils."[3] In each case, the persistence of the dialectic is personified as Hegel himself, presented as a menacing spectral presence. Despite being apparently dead—both literally and, others might argue, in terms of his philosophical viability—there is always the uncanny sense when reading Hegel that he is reading you back, that every imaginable opposition is a trap which he has laid, that every time we think we are in control or know where we are going, he (or, more properly, the ironic truth of the dialectic) pulls the rug from beneath us. As Slavoj Žižek frequently puts it (paraphrasing Adorno), to ask whether Hegel is dead is the wrong question; perhaps we should instead be asking whether we are dead in the eyes of Hegel.[4]

Even Derrida, who heralds his own concept of *différance* as "the limit, the interruption, the destruction of the Hegelian *relève* [*Aufhebung*, sublation] *wherever* it operates"[5]—as the remains of writing which resist being swallowed by the Hegelian system—also concedes that "we will never be finished with the reading or rereading of Hegel" and that in essence he, Derrida, "does nothing other than attempt to explain [himself] on this point."[6] This may seem like a contradiction. If the Hegelian *Aufhebung* is destroyed, why can we never escape it? The answer is that there are always two Hegels for Derrida. As he puts it in the opening chapter of *Of Grammatology* (1967), Hegel is "the last philosopher of the book and the first thinker of writing," the thinker of the logos, the absolute, and presence but "*also* the thinker of irreducible difference."[7] He marks "The End of the Book"—the "idea of the book" being that "which always refers to a natural totality, ... the encyclopedic protection of theology and of logocentrism"— both as its highest point and therefore as its self-negation.[8] Hegel, for Derrida, is the arch-antagonist of the enterprise of deconstruction but also its essential condition.

It is because of this apparent inescapability that some of the most significant proponents of Hegel in recent decades have been those who have exposed the prematurity of any declaration of his "death." Rose's *Hegel Contra Sociology*, for instance—which will become especially important to this book in its concluding chapter—shows that recurrent issues in twentieth-century social theory (from Durkheim to Weber, Simmel, Adorno, Lukács, Althusser, and Habermas) demonstrate an insufficient engagement with Hegel, and in particular a failure to have come to terms with his critiques of Kant and Fichte. Rose is at pains to insist that this does not constitute an attempt to establish the "contemporary relevance" of, or else an "ingenious and ahistorical 'return'" to, her subject but rather, that she is attempting "to retrieve Hegelian speculative experience for social theory, ... first of all, by recognizing and discussing the intellectual barriers which stand in the way of such rereading."[9] Judith Butler's *Subjects of Desire* (1987), meanwhile, takes a similar approach, with a specific focus on Hegel's twentieth-century French reception. While this reception "may be read as a succession of criticisms against the subject of desire, that Hegelian conceit of a totalizing impulse," Butler demonstrates that Hegel himself was implicated "in the construction of this conceit, and that his vision is less 'totalizing' than presumed."[10] Similarly, Catherine Malabou's *The Future of Hegel* (1996) challenges the reading of Hegel by Heidegger (which had a great influence on this French reception) for its insistence upon the reassuring certainty that "Hegel does not have a future"—in the double sense that Hegel does not have an adequate concept of futurity and that therefore he is a thing of the past. Malabou shows, however, that Hegel's dialectic is far more open-ended, "plastic," and difficult to elude than that of the straw man who has been constructed (only to be summarily "deconstructed") in his place, that the future of Hegel is not only possible but inevitable insofar as his speculative thinking, by definition, is constantly moving beyond itself.[11] Žižek describes his defense of Hegel in the same way, again. The "reassertion of Hegel's speculative thought," he writes, is not "a denial of the post-Hegelian break—but rather a bringing forth of that very dimension which sustains the post-Hegelian break itself." He claims that the historical rejection of Hegel (from Schopenhauer to Kierkegaard, Nietzsche, and Deleuze, almost always on the grounds of his ostensibly totalizing rationalist holism) has attacked a straw man and thus amounts to a spurious and premature proclamation that he has been overcome: "a desperate attempt to *go on thinking as if Hegel had not happened*."[12] Each add credence to Foucault's worry that at the end of every anti-Hegelianism, Hegel waits.

There is another reason, though, why the signs of Hegel's legacy seem so ubiquitous and inescapable—and, in this case, overdetermined. While traditionally oppositional accounts of Hegel may be described (as above) as failed attempts to escape him, more recent approaches are better thought of as attempts to accommodate him to contemporary philosophy and theory in spite of his more eccentric ambitions; as concessions that there is some "truth" there despite the alleged failures. As Comay and Ruda have remarked, there is a sense today that "everyone has become a Hegelian": "Having been cured of his metaphysical sickness, Hegel has suddenly become compatible with an unexpected variety of contemporary philosophical projects. From radical theology to Anglo-American pragmatism, from liberal democratic theory to radical anarchism, from speculative realism to psychoanalysis, a plethora of diverging positions have set out to prove that Hegel was actually not so bad."[13] While in every case it is Hegel's alleged totalizing holism that is explicitly rejected, it is paradoxically this drive toward encompassing everything that makes Hegel so easy to pick and choose from. Whether one is looking for a proto-Marxist critique of private property or a conservative defense of monarchism, a discourse of universalism or Eurocentric racism, a radical theology or a radical atheism, an anarchist conception of a voluntaristic and mutually policing society or a defense of the bourgeois state and its institutions, as long as we have the liberty to decide what of Hegel is living and what is dead, then he can end up being all things to all people.

Perhaps the most common attempts to save Hegel in recent decades have been those projects which have aimed, implicitly or otherwise, to recruit and mobilize certain concepts from Hegel for the development of theories of democracy, civil society, and public life. In each case, such projects can be described quite uncontroversially as selective readings that (following Croce) divide the living from the dead. Jürgen Habermas, for example, finds value in Hegel's conception of intersubjectivity but criticizes his emphasis on the state and other political institutions. For Habermas, the Hegelian *Geist* is the realm of societal norms which are conceptually shaped and developed through discursive practices, a realm which is in turn shaped and developed through intersubjective relations of mutual recognition. This conception of spirit is central for Habermas's own theorizations of democratic public life, particularly in *Knowledge and Human Interests* (1968). However, in his subsequent work (especially *The Theory of Communicative Action* [1981] and *The Philosophical Discourse of Modernity* [1985]), while retaining and intensifying this central focus on discursively constituted norms, Habermas more explicitly criticizes Hegel's stress on their political and institutional embodiment.[14] Similarly, Axel Honneth (a former student of Habermas) insists upon "recognition," conceived as the ground of all political struggle and identification, as the most important contribution of Hegel's philosophy for political thought, while regretting Hegel's later demotion of recognition to a mere stage in spirit's development from its original status as spirit's transcendental and existential basis.[15] Both of these accommodating and selective approaches to Hegel abstract a concept from his thought for its utility and give it the status of a quasi-transcendental precondition for their arguments. They therefore preclude from the beginning the requisite speculative naivete and irony of a presuppositionless philosophy, producing instead a kind of Hegel-synecdoche, where a severed part stands in for the truth of the whole.

Robert Brandom's *A Spirit of Trust: A Reading of Hegel's "Phenomenology"* (2019), meanwhile, reads Hegel through the lens of analytic philosophy, and pragmatism in particular—that is, Brandom *rereads* Hegel's *Phenomenology* through the lens of another, later development in philosophical thought. As we shall see, it consists in what Brandom calls a *"de re"* reading, defined as an "attempt to say what *really* follows from the claims made, what is *really* evidence for or against them, and so what the author has *really* committed herself to, regardless of her opinion about the matter."[16] This may on the face of it seem more like a Hegelian recollection, or *Erinnerung*, which reconstructs the truth of Hegel for today. However, Brandom conducts his reading, like Habermas and Honneth, by elevating a component of Hegel's thought to the level of a quasi-transcendental, identifying and prioritizing a master theme which can be utilized for its import at the expense of the rest. In his own words, "The defining subject that serves as both lens and filter for the present account is *conceptual content*"[17]—what he takes to be Hegel's nonpsychological account of concepts progressively acquiring determinate content through relations of incompatibility (the coin is pure copper and not pure aluminum) and consequence (and therefore the coin is an electrical conductor). (The example is Brandom's own.)[18]

The limitations of this reading are conceded from the first page by Brandom himself:

> The narrative I retrospectively discern within Hegel's is by no means the only one that can correctly and productively be recollected from the intricate and far-ranging story that he tells. Indeed, what is offered here is in many ways a severely selective reading. I am really concerned only with what he has to say insofar as it bears on *one* of the many topics he addresses. I believe it is an axial, organizing topic, and that focusing on it provides a useful perspective on all the rest. But the sharp focus involves real restrictions.[19]

Through this "lens and filter" ("selective" and "restrictive"), Brandom's "*de re*" reading argues that the primary concern of the *Phenomenology* is to discover and describe "the transcendental conditions of the possibility of determinately contentful conceptual norms"[20]—basically, the conditions of possibility for things we can all agree on in spite of our differences. This belies again a precommitment to the political and ethical value of recognition as an instrumentalizable tool for realizing a more liberal and democratic society—without grasping the phenomenological development of its ironic truth. For Brandom, this is not a problem. Although he concedes that his reading is "severely selective," he excuses himself by arguing that there is always a "context" of interpretation—in particular, the prior learning and perspectives of the reader.[21] The reader must always when reading be referring back to the facts "*as she takes them to be*; that is the best any of us can do."[22] Brandom's *de re* reading attempts to say, then, "what *really* follows from the claims made" but only by assuming in advance the commitments that he has held before reading. In the case of Brandom, these commitments might be said to include liberal democracy (politically) and "semantic pragmatism" (philosophically). As Stephen Houlgate has forcefully argued, and as I will later develop, by licensing the assumption of such preconditions and prior commitments to the reading of Hegel, Brandom ignores Hegel's *phenomenology*, the essential experiential modality of speculative thinking. Although Brandom produces what he calls a "semantic reading" of Hegel's *Phenomenology*, such a "reading" (which reads through a particular lens with an assumed set of prior commitments) means that he does not actually read it at all.[23]

Just as Hegel has been recently accommodated by a range of philosophers and sociologists, a similar trajectory can be traced in literary studies. There has, on the one hand, been a marked, welcome increase in explorations of the question of Hegel and the literary. These have often concerned

Hegel's literary references or employment of literary modes and how an understanding of such appeals to the literary might illuminate the particular passages in question and Hegel's philosophy as a whole. One example is Allen Speight's *Hegel, Literature and the Problem of Agency* (2001) which reinterprets Hegel's *Phenomenology* with reference to each of Hegel's literary allusions (from *Antigone* to *Hamlet* and *Rameau's Nephew*), demonstrating that literature, for Hegel, gives the reader unique access to the aporias of ethical agency, its retrospectivity, its theatricality (that is, its sociality), and its need for forgiveness.[24] Another is Katrin Pahl's *Tropes of Transport: Hegel and Emotion*, for which Hegel's *Phenomenology* provides an experience of truth as temporal through the intertwining temporalities of "the syncopating measure of poetic rhythm, the virtual present of theatrical enactment, and the folded sequence of narrative."[25] Both studies describe the *Phenomenology* as "quasi-literary,"[26] cutting through its traditional reception as a systematic catalog of different possible approaches to knowledge and truth, for which any literary reference would function merely as an example or illustration.

In other such studies of the status of literature in Hegel's *Phenomenology*, particular attention has been paid to Hegel's curious decision to end the *Phenomenology* with a quotation (or rather a misquotation) from a poem by Schiller—curious because it comes at precisely the moment when Hegel claims to have surpassed the need for such "picture-thinking" (*Vorstellung*). (I will provide my own answer to this conundrum in chapter 2.)[27] In the past ten or so years in particular, there has also been a flurry of studies which have explored how a comparative reading of Hegel with particular authors or literary movements might elucidate both of them, whether they read Hegel or Hegel read them or not—with authors ranging from Edmund Spenser to William Shakespeare, Molière, William Wordsworth, Giacomo Leopardi, Hermann Melville, Thomas Mann, Franz Kafka, Samuel Beckett, Elizabeth Bishop, and J. H. Prynne.[28]

Of particular interest here, though, are two works that have asserted the Hegelian character of literary theory itself. As stated at the beginning of this book, this may seem like a surprising claim given that "theory" is often the name given to that which established itself against Hegel. Particularly in the poststructuralist tradition (from Derrida to Foucault, Deleuze, Hélène Cixous, Paul de Man, Geoffrey Hartmann, J. Hillis Miller, and Homi Bhabha), theory is contra all that Hegel (ostensibly) stood for. And yet—in a move that again implicitly confirms Foucault's warning that Hegel stands waiting at the end of every professed anti-Hegelianism—M. A. R. Habib, in his book *Hegel and the Foundations of Literary Theory* (2018), makes the historical and conceptual case that literary theory finds its "foundation" in a kind of dialectical thinking inaugurated by Hegel. The concepts and modes of reading which have been the mainstay of a broad range of theoretical approaches were originally articulated by Hegel, whether these theories know it or not. Habib argues that literary theory follows the Hegelian dialectic as far as "its second stage, the stage of 'difference,'" while "refusing to admit progression from this to a third stage, which might effect any kind of metaphysical closure." In doing so, it "retracts Hegelian content into the status of *form*, of 'method,' or 'strategy.'"[29]

There is always something problematic about the drive to identify a "foundation" or origin of something, and the ascribed authority implied with such a designation; but it is particularly problematic when it concerns Hegel—a philosopher whose commitment to be without presupposition complicates and undermines every notion of origin, of a pure beginning, or of first principles. A historical justification of the truth of something, for Hegel, is no justification at all. As we shall later see, for example, Hegel was particularly irritated by what he took to be facile arguments concerning the truth of Christianity and its doctrines which used the historicity of Christ and the early church as its evidence. "It is still primarily immaterial," Hegel says, "where that doctrine came from. The question is solely whether it is true in and for itself."[30] Importantly, though, in the same way that I have just made recourse to evidence of the historical Hegel's position to justify the claim that such evidence for speculative thinking is not a measure of truth, Habib's claims are not useless. His book compellingly argues for a renewed engagement with Hegel from those who have traditionally distanced themselves from him (such as literary theorists) and expands our understanding of theory through an engagement with its hidden contexts. However, what such an approach cannot succeed in doing is identifying the *truth* of Hegel in the sense that I have begun to develop, which can only arise from an engaged and even naive experience of *reading* him. Instead, Habib identifies how various literary theorists, wittingly or otherwise, have abstracted and made use of some concepts from Hegel's writing (be they difference, recognition, history, or the arbitrariness of the linguistic sign) as the quasi-transcendental conditions of their theoretical frameworks.

Andrew Cole's *The Birth of Theory* (2014) makes a comparable argument to Habib's concerning Hegel and literary theory, with the added qualification that while the birth of theory can be traced back to Hegel, the moment of conception can be located in the Middle Ages. In contrast to Habib's work, however, Cole does capture something of the truth of Hegel beyond any putative abstractable "content"—and this is because he *is* receptive to the way in which this content is presented and experienced. Hegel, for Cole, is a fundamentally medieval thinker, and by reading Hegel within the tradition of medieval thought and of medieval history and culture more broadly, we can both better understand him and subsequent developments in philosophy and theory. For example, Cole argues that Hegel's dialectic should be viewed within the medieval lineage of Plotinus and Nicholas of Cusa, rather than solely within the classical lineage of Plato and Aristotle. What is distinct about this kind of dialectic is its stress on the interplay between concept and figure, and the notion that thought itself has a shape and a rhythm. This allows Cole to make the case that even thinkers like Nietzsche and Deleuze, despite their professed anti-Hegelianism, should be read as "part of a specialized dialectical tradition" from Plotinus to Hegel; that, in spite of being contra Hegel in terms of manifest content, in terms of style, Deleuze in particular inhabits a distinctly Hegelian-phenomenological (and by extension medieval-figural) style.[31] By retrieving the dialectic of concept and figure for Hegelian phenomenology, Cole emphasizes the formal innovation and experiential content of Hegel's work, and thus its essential literary character. Moreover, by realizing this essentially literary character, we are reminded of the impossibility of adequately reducing Hegel (or the dialectic more generally), as Habib seeks to do, to any hypostasized "position," method, or abstracted, prefigured concept.

How to Read Hegel

To emphasize what may already be apparent: Both Hegel's ubiquity in theory, philosophy, and political thought, and the contested nature of his reception, can be accounted for by the question of how to read him—and the extent to which this question is emphasized or else neglected as incidental. The question of "how to read" is not the same as "what it means." "How to read" does not ask for an interpretation or an explanation or a content. It instead asks how a reader should orient themselves, what they should presuppose, what they should prioritize, what they should look out for. One way of putting it is that it asks for a method. This question has proved so uniquely fruitful in the reception of Hegel precisely because it is so uniquely essential, and yet unanswerable, with it often being the case that the more an answer is attempted, the more likely it is to be wrong. This impossibility gets to the heart of the speculative character of Hegel's philosophy, by stressing the corresponding notions of presuppositionlessness and of experience: Hegel's reader must be without presuppositions in their reading, including the presupposition of an instrumental method, in order to have the speculative experience of the irony of truth. Such a reading of Hegel does not have speculative experience as its presupposition or precondition, because "speculative" names the experience which is acquired precisely through not having a presupposition or precondition.

The question of how to read Hegel is therefore both the most important but also the most superfluous. Important because it is through the speculative experience of reading Hegel that the ironic truth of his dialectic is set in motion; and superfluous because there is no method for such a reading other than the commitment to suspend all such methods. The only answer to the question of how to read Hegel is to resolutely commit to refusing all positive answers. In short: The question cannot be merely neglected as superfluous but must be repeatedly emphasized for its superfluity.

The most influential account of the question comes from Adorno's *Hegel: Three Studies* (1963), particularly the third: "Skoteinos, or How to Read Hegel" (which will be more fully addressed in chapter 1). Crucially for this book, Adorno explicitly positions his readings of Hegel in contrast to the selective "living or dead" readings licensed by Croce. The truth of Hegel, for Adorno, "lies in the *skandalon*—in the stumbling blocks, in the traps and snares—and "not in its plausibility. Hence rescuing Hegel—and only rescue, not revival, is appropriate for him—means facing up to his philosophy where it is most painful and wresting truth from it where its untruth is obvious."[32] The "spirit of Hegel" cannot be realized by ignoring Hegel "to the letter"; instead the spirit must be wrested from the letter.

An example of such an Adornian reading, at least in this sense, can be found in Susan Buck-Morss's *Hegel, Haiti, and Universal History* (2005), which argues that the 1791 Haitian Revolution is the overlooked point of reference for Hegel's famous master-slave dialectic. While this may sound like a straightforwardly historicist recovery of a forgotten context, the essential contribution of Buck-Morss's reading is her argument that, in a certain sense, Haiti represents the ironic truth of Hegel—the spirit of Hegel wrested from his letter. While, as a child of the French Revolution, Hegel decried the "slaveries" of dogma and ignorance, he was conspicuously silent regarding the literal slavery which dominated the colonies. The literal crushing of the masters by the slaves is, then, the truth of a dialectic which Hegel himself could not fully articulate or bring to bear. "There is no doubt," Buck-Morss writes, "that Hegel and Haiti belong together."[33] It is this asserted speculative identity—the simultaneous distinguishability and affirmed inseparability—of these two apparently wildly heterogeneous terms which leads Žižek to conclude, apropos Buck-Morss, that "Hegel and Haiti" represents "the most succinct formula of communism": the formula of a theory and historical practice of universal freedom.[34]

To return to Adorno: The particular focus in his third study of Hegel is what he calls Hegel's *skoteinos*—his darkness. To read Hegel, for Adorno, is not to translate the obscurity into clarity but to dwell in the obscurity and suffer it; the difficult form has a content, performatively instantiating the difficult nonidentity and identity between thought and language.

To capitulate instead to the Cartesian ideals of clarity and purity of expression spuriously presupposes the abstract identity of thought and language, and thus settles for an approximation. The advice Adorno gives to Hegel's reader is therefore simultaneously comforting and troubling: "At times one literally does not know and cannot conclusively determine what is being talked about.... There is no guarantee that such a judgment is even possible."[35]

While there are many similarities between Adorno's account of the question of how to read Hegel and my own, the crucial difference spawns from Adorno's relationship to Kant. For Adorno, Hegel is ultimately "untrue in the face of Kantian discontinuities," and can only be read consistently by "sacrificing consistency" altogether.[36] In short, Adorno retreats from Hegel to Kant at the last minute, whom he takes to have more resolutely insisted upon the nonidentity between thought and things in themselves (or, perhaps, words and their referents), where Hegel's privileging of identity spuriously resolves this difference. I will argue, on the other hand, that the Kantian theory of reading implied by Adorno here, which insists upon upholding discontinuity, inconsistency, and revel over repose, is to neglect the resolve and the simplifying work of recollection which are essential modalities of speculative reading. Here we find a curious similarity between Adorno and Derrida. Both Adorno with his "negative" dialectics, and Derrida with his conception of *différance* at the limit of *Aufhebung*, retreat to an implicit Kantianism which insists upon the irreducibility of nonidentity, apparently out of a fear of the totalitarian implications of resolve. I will argue, however, that a speculative reading of the proposition does not finalize meaning once and for all, nor dictate its signification; but nor does it refuse meaning, or laterally, indefinitely defer it. Instead it affirms the reading of the proposition (and of writing more generally) as a site of the ironic realization of spirit and truth: of contest, commitment, and surprise; of meaning and a logos which is always actual, even "present," but also always subject to its own revolution.

Another influential account of reading Hegel, or of Hegel and reading, comes from Heidegger. One of the great merits of Heidegger's lectures on the *Phenomenology* lies in his alertness to the *Phenomenology* as a phenomenology—that is, as both a theory and a presentation of the experience of consciousness. In these lectures, Heidegger avoids giving *a* reading of the text; he avoids merely interpreting it, as if it was an external object to be analyzed and picked over by the detached critical observer. He instead immanently works through it as an example of how a speculative reading must actualize itself through its own development, without recourse to external presuppositions or expectations. Heidegger also insists upon the importance of *re*reading. He is firm with his students: "We can begin to understand the work only if we have already reached its end. In this lecture course I presuppose such a first reading of the entire work. If such a reading has not taken place or does not take place in the next few weeks, there is no sense in sitting here: You cheat not only me but yourselves."[37] He argues, then, that the *Phenomenology* itself must be read as a speculative proposition: misread to the letter and reread for its spirit.

Paradoxically, however, it is on this same topic of reading and rereading that Heidegger underestimates Hegel's radicality—particularly concerning Hegel's conception of recollection. The *Phenomenology* must be reread, for Heidegger, principally because "The end of the work does not escape its beginning, but presents a return to this beginning.... The standpoint of one who grasps it and thinks it through is, from the beginning to the end and from the end already in the beginning, one and the same standpoint, namely, that of absolute knowledge."[38] The *Phenomenology* must be reread in order to be read, for Heidegger, because it is only at the end that we realize the absolute standpoint which governed the movement from the beginning, and that therefore it is only by returning to the beginning and repeating the journey that the content can be properly understood with the clarity that this standpoint delivers. This presents the reading of the *Phenomenology* as a closed circle of reference, with no possible progression beyond itself within itself, and thus without a future. Like Hegel's philosophy, the reading of Hegel, for Heidegger, is always looking backward. Hegel only "speaks about having been," he says, "but never about the future. This accords with his view of the past as the decisive character of time: It is a fading away, something transitory and always bygone."[39] For Heidegger, the *Phenomenology* must be reread because it can only be understood as something that has already happened. As this book will demonstrate, however, although Hegel is a thinker of recollection, this does not commit him, as implied, to *anamnesis*—to the notion that all knowledge is already implicitly known; that the new is always already old since it is plotted from the beginning. Instead, it will be argued that it is precisely through the process of recollection, of rereading, that speculative thinking opens itself up to the future.

It is on this question of Hegel and the future that Malabou bases her riposte to Heidegger's Hegel, a riposte which climaxes, in its final chapter, with another account of Hegel and reading. This is perhaps the best account of Hegel and reading we have, for its argument that it is in the act of reading as recollecting that the novelty and the future of thinking is made possible. For Malabou, the unique resistance to reading posed by the speculative proposition—the disruption of the linear progression from subject to predicate—not only forces the reader to reread it differently from an "absolute" (for Heidegger, final) standpoint; it also transforms the reader into "the author of the enunciation. The reader rewrites what he or she reads."[40] This kind of reading, which Malabou, after Hegel, describes as "plastic" (*PhG* §64), is what really designates the absoluteness of knowledge for Hegel: not its total mastery or finality but its fully living, self-actualization. Heidegger therefore has an inadequate conception of Hegelian irony. He understands that the proposition must be reread, as it is only recursively that its ironic truth is realized. However, he underestimates that *this* truth may in turn have an as yet unrealized ironic truth: not only must the proposition be reread, even once it has been reread it must be read again. If the second reading offers a final resting place, then it is just another letter that kills.[41]

This demand for incessant rereading may seem like a guise of what Hegel calls the "bad infinite," in which the movement to overcome finitude always remains the same, an interminable lateral progression of just-one-mores for which the true infinite is always deferred. Malabou's account of plastic reading, however, can be used to demonstrate how it avoids this pitfall. What defines the true infinite, for Hegel, is the infinite that is not negatively affected by finitude, and therefore one that contains the finite within it. Therefore, if a "bad infinite" reading is one that either rereads the proposition to the letter again and again but always defers its meaning, or else one which rereads for the spirit without going through the letter, thus licensing arbitrary and creative interpretations of "infinite" possibility, then a truly infinite reading is one that experiences the ironic truth of the proposition as a tension—opposed in its unity—between the finite letter and its infinite spirit. This, once again, is the definition of life, for Hegel. To be alive is to be afflicted by finitude, to tarry with it, and yet also to resist it.

This will also be essential for demonstrating how Malabou's theory of plastic reading does not "legitimate arbitrary exegesis" or "interpretative violence"—in spite of its invalidation of "any idea of readerly 'objectivity' if by 'objectivity' we mean the attempt to bring to light, once and for all, what the text 'means.'"[42] Against the common prejudice that "the validity of an interpretation relies on the effacement of *all* subjectivity," Malabou demonstrates how "Hegel's great originality is that he shows exactly how an interpretation that aims at nothing more than universality ... would be in reality particular and arbitrary."[43] Such a spuriously "universal" interpretation is analogous, again, to both reading merely "to the letter" and also reading for the spirit of the text without first going through the letter. In each case, it dismisses from the beginning the possibility of speculative thinking by insisting upon its own objective certainty without the requisite contingency of experience. Equally, however, to defend an element of subjectivity in interpretation does not amount to a defense of subjectiv*ism*—

of making recourse to one's own preexisting subject position or prior commitments as evidence or justification, as "the best any of us could do" (as Brandom puts it). Hegel's insistence on the essential place of experience in interpretation does not refer to affect, nor to one's own personal experiences or perspectives that they bring to the text. In fact, Hegel insists, it is only by relinquishing any personal intrusions that the reader's subjectivity might be formed through the irony of experience: the "refusal both to insert one's own views into the immanent rhythm of the concept and to interfere arbitrarily with that rhythm by means of wisdom acquired elsewhere, or this abstinence, are all themselves an essential moment of attentiveness to the concept" (*PhG* §58). Subjectification, then, names merely the total immersion of the reading subject in the substance. The reading subject starts to read as an "accident" (that is, as a subject in all its particularity and arbitrariness), but through the recursive rereading of the speculative proposition they are transformed into the substance of the text—they substitute their own subjectivity for the subject of the proposition. The reader not only follows the movement, they "adopt" it. The resulting experience is an experience which is not limited to the "letter" of the text, but it is also not one which is spuriously liberated to interpret it arbitrarily. It is instead one which is formed by submitting itself absolutely to the "letter" precisely in order to realize what that initially apparent objectivity obscured: its spirit. "Progressively," Malabou writes, "in the course of reading, the reader's subjectivity is formed into a substantial accident, a style, a plasticity.... Plasticity, informing the self-determining movement of substance and establishing the identity of contingency and necessity, is experienced in the act of reading. This is precisely what Absolute Knowledge knows."[44]

Critique beyond the Limits of Critique, Marx beyond the Limits of Hegel

While Malabou's notion of plastic reading developed in *The Future of Hegel* is applied to the reading of Hegel specifically (and the future of philosophy which, she argues, will be written in a speculative idiom),[45] the concept of reading developed throughout this book will be recovered in its concluding chapter for the critical reading of literary works. While the critical paradigm of literary theory has been criticized in recent years by writers such as Rita Felski, Heather Love, Sharon Marcus, and Stephen Best for its alleged critical detachment, elitism, chronic suspicion, and for its drive to excavate beneath the text for its disavowed conditions of possibility at the cost of the text itself, it can be demonstrated that their proposed "postcritical" alternatives all have recourse to a precritical subjectivism.

By addressing the question of "the limits of critique" from a Hegelian perspective, however—and in particular by following Hegel's critique of Kant's critique—a different mode of critical reading is possible: one which is immanent to the text yet open to realizing its ironic truth.

This will draw substantially upon Rose's work in *Hegel Contra Sociology* to "retrieve Hegelian speculative experience for social theory"[46]—a work which demonstrates how Hegelian speculative experience (the ironic experience of contradiction as the truth) might yield a theory which is critical not in spite of but because of its aversion to the pretensions of critical detachment. In accordance with some postcritics, I will contend that Marxist literary criticism in particular has had a tendency to neglect the experiential content of reading for the text's material and ideological conditions of possibility. In resistance to postcritique, however, I will argue that the retrieval of Hegelian speculative experience for literary theory might provide a critical Marxist model of reading which is both alert to a text's conditions of possibility, but also to the critical potentials of the text itself. In particular, this critical potential will be located in literature's ability to provide a speculative experience not of the text's reducibility to its sociopolitical determination but of the contradiction between the text and its determination. The critical force of such an experience is that it sustains the contradiction or the irony of life lived under the ascendency of real abstraction—that is, of life lived under capital.

This will inevitably raise the question of Marx's relationship to Hegel. Without addressing this as an intellectual-historical question, however, I will approach it as a question of the spirit and the letter—and the different modalities of this question as developed throughout the book: irony, recollection, and resolve. I will contend, as such, that a critical Marxism might represent the ironic truth or recollection of Hegelian speculative thinking under contemporary capitalism. Marxism is essential to Hegelianism. Neither can be thought without the other. While this may seem anachronistic, conceding the obvious point that Hegel preceded Marx, it will be argued that the birth of the spirit of Marxism marks the point at which the spirit of Hegelianism reaches its limit and moves beyond itself, that the condition of the continuation of the spirit of Hegel is the spirit of Marx. This is not because of any inherent failures or weaknesses of Hegelian speculative thinking; it rather represents its tenacity and its ready adaptability to comprehend its "*own time*."[47]

In the preface to this book, I wrote that, for Hegel, the truth of spirit, in order for spirit to have any truth at all, must be constantly moving beyond itself. This could suggest a sense of inevitability, of progress without resistance. But what if it does not move beyond itself? What if the place of spirit is usurped? This is the problematic of Marxism, which only turns Hegelian dialectics on its head insofar as it recognizes that the self-actualizing absolute subject of history and freedom has been substituted for that of capital, with the real life of humanity reduced to a "dot-like" isolation, to the real abstraction of a living death.[48] This is the crux of Adorno's dictum (taken from Ferdinand Kürnberger) that what passes for living is not really life: that "life does not live."[49] Life is instead alienated and wasted in the involuntary activity of labor for the creation and accumulation of value—that is, for the reproduction of the absolute subject qua capital. It does not move beyond itself—it is not the true infinity of dynamic self-actualization—but is instead gelatinated into a bad infinity of socially necessary labor time.[50] It is not then the collective spirit which actualizes itself, moving beyond itself and its own limits, becoming other to become more fully what it is, but capital. This develops an argument that has been made in recent years by Keston Sutherland, who reads Marx's *Capital* (1867) as "an ironic interpretation of Hegel that spells out the socially true meanings of Hegel's philosophy.... Not only is the individual now, in ironic truth, the abstraction to which Hegel was earlier accused [by Marx] of reducing him—nothing more than a disposable predicate, *Menschenmaterial*—but capital, on its side, is the subject actualized by the universal into infinite self-actualisation."[51] Lenin describes this self-actualization of capital, this drive to be exceeding its own limits which is a condition of its own survival, when he argues that imperialism represents the highest stage of capitalism.[52] This could be rephrased in the terminology of this book by saying that imperialism is the ironic truth of capitalism. However, as global temperatures hurtle toward and possibly beyond a point of no return, and yet carbon emissions continue to be spewed into the atmosphere for the extraction of yet more profit according to capital's own unrelenting logic and insatiable appetite, we are faced with the irrefutable fact that the imperialism which is this highest stage of capitalism will not stop with countries or people but with life itself.

To retrieve Hegelian speculative experience for a Marxist literary theory, then—which is to sustain, intensify, and tarry with the contradiction between what passes for living and life—is not to neglect the prime Marxist goals of comprehending the world through a ruthless critique of political economy, and of changing it through revolution. On the contrary, following Rose, this book will conclude that "a presentation of the contradictory relations between Capital and culture is the only way to link the analysis of the economy to comprehension of the conditions for revolutionary practice."[53] While "man has lost himself in the proletariat," in Marx's words[54]—that is, while the life of humanity is now withdrawn into the deathly real abstraction of its economic function—the speculative experience of this contradiction is, to use Hegel's, the condition of an "imminent change. This gradual process of dissolution, which has not altered the physiognomy of the whole, is interrupted by the break of day, which in a flash and at a stroke brings to view the structure of the new world" (*PhG* §11).

Reading Hegel

[PART ONE]

Irony
Or What Is

[CHAPTER ONE]

As already noted, the word *Ironie* rarely appears in Hegel's work except when discussing the ironic disposition of his Romantic contemporaries in Jena—and rarely is Hegel more incensed, more polemical, and more damning than at these moments. In his lectures on aesthetics he describes Romantic irony, variously, as "morbid," "wishy-washy," "annihilating," "mediocre," "feeble," "grotesque," "false," and "trash."[1] He even seems to ascribe Novalis's early death to his irony, to which he assigns literally pathological characteristics.[2] Irony, for Hegel, is consumptive and self-consuming: an eternally interiorizing self-reflection, both self-indulgent and self-destructive. It yearns for the infinite so intensely that it overlooks everything finite—that is, everything else—and can therefore only ever achieve the most arbitrary and particular existence. Even worse, for Hegel, it is destructive of reality itself. It is an antiphilosophy which elevates itself above, or else turns itself against all objective content, the difficulty and messiness of phenomena, and in doing so posits a world without the possibility of truth; it consists in nothing less than "destroying and dissolving everything,"[3] it is "the art of annihilating everything everywhere."[4] For Hegel, as Kierkegaard puts it, "irony is anathema."[5]

To say this sounds melodramatic, as well as vague, would not be unreasonable. Hegel's reaction to Romantic irony in his lectures on aesthetics is quite exceptional in his body of work for its virulence, and notable for its lack of rigor, nuance, and textual justification. As Jeffrey Reid writes in the introduction to his book on Hegel's critique of Romanticism:

> Let it be said right away that Hegel's interpretation is unfaithful, to the extent that it is strongly critical and even polemical. As such, the Hegelian interpretation is far from demonstrating or presenting a comprehensive knowledge of the theories and works of the Jena Romantics, but rather

shows itself to be highly selective regarding them. Hegel hardly ever refers directly to the actual works of the Romantics. When he does highlight a key expression in their writings, in order to make it the pivotal point of his critical enterprise, we notice, looking closely at the texts that Hegel might have been familiar with, that the expression only appears in a marginal fashion and in a context alien to the one evoked in the Hegelian critique.[6]

In de Man's succinct formulation: "What he says about it whenever he talks about it is just about always the same, and isn't very much."[7] With Schlegel in particular, de Man continues, Hegel "loses his cool, which doesn't happen very often."[8] This, again, echoes Kierkegaard's assessment: "He takes every opportunity to talk about these ironists and always in the most unsympathetic manner.... Explanation is often lacking—but Schlegel is always reprimanded.... By his one-sided attack on post-Fichtean irony he has overlooked the truth of irony, and by his identifying all irony with this, he has done irony an injustice."[9]

While Hegel certainly appreciates some of the important differences between the various guises of Romantic irony—between Schlegel and Novalis, for instance—he argues that these differences merely represent different moments of the same thing. While the irony of Schlegel represents a pretense to complete subjective mastery over objectivity, where reality is conceived of as the plaything of the creative genius, and a field of infinite possibility; the irony of Novalis represents a radical skepticism concerning objectivity and reality and a correspondingly self-indulgent yet self-destructive retreat into the abject loneliness of the pure self. "Frightened of being polluted by contact with finitude," this form of irony winds "down as it were into a spiritual decline," a sickly nihilism which, like Novalis dying of consumption, collapses under the weight of its own ironic self-critique.[10] These apparently distinct positions—of radical hubris, on the one hand, and radical humility, on the other—are in fact the same, Hegel argues, because of this shared ironic relation to objectivity: "The *vanity* of all *things* is its *own* vanity, or it *is* itself vain" (*PhG* §525). In other words, the vanity (that is, the egomaniacal conceit) of the subjective mastery over the objective, must itself become vain (that is, futile, worthless, null); the Romantic genius, having ironized everything in existence, has nothing left to ironize but itself. Schlegel and Novalis are thus two sides of the same dialectical coin. This follows, for Hegel, from their fundamental, even crude, adherence to the Kantian logic of the understanding, whereby objectivity is bracketed beyond the understanding and comprehension, and therefore, Hegel argues, destroyed, dissolved, annihilated.

One of the questions that will be addressed in the next chapter is whether such a mode of critique—"unfaithful," "unsympathetic," and without "cool"; with a drive toward reduction, exaggeration, and even caricature—can and should be justified, and what it might suggest about Hegel's philosophy as a whole. The object of this chapter, in the meantime, is not ultimately to examine Hegel's opposition to Romantic irony but rather to complicate the resultant, tacit assumption that Hegel is opposed to irony *per se*—the perception that, "in his eyes, irony is anathema," in all cases and always. This is the perception that one might get from readings of Hegel since Hegel (and especially since Kierkegaard). While a relationship between irony and the dialectic has been acknowledged since Plato (and not least by Hegel himself, as we shall see), the vast majority of the discussions dedicated to the topic of Hegel and irony only discuss the question of Hegel and *Romantic* irony. From Kierkegaard's *On the Concept of Irony* (1841), to de Man's "The Concept of Irony" (1977), Claire Colebrook's *Irony in the Work of Philosophy* (2002), Reid's *The Anti-Romantic* (2014), Fred Rush's *Irony and Idealism* (2016), and Robert Brandom's *A Spirit of Trust* (2019), significant discussion is dedicated to Hegel's critique of Romantic irony, but no consideration is given to the possibility of a Hegelian irony.

A Hegelian irony has been invoked in passing by some other critics. Judith Butler, for instance, emphasizes the "permanent irony of the Hegelian subject"—the irony that, in order to know itself, the subject "requires mediation" and "knows itself only as the very structure of mediation." Hegel, for Butler, shows that the irony of the subject is that it "cannot know itself instantaneously or immediately, but requires mediation to understand its own structure."[11] This is another way of saying, as intimated in the introduction, that in order to truly know itself, the subject must know itself as something other than itself. Butler later describes this irony of the Hegelian subject as "the irony of Hegel's incessantly myopic traveler" in the *Phenomenology*, who always finds himself "mocked by the metaphysical domain which seemed always to exceed his understanding."[12] The "traveler" of the *Phenomenology*—both reader and subject—is repeatedly afflicted by the ironic discovery that the final destination, absolute knowing, has not yet been reached. Richard Rorty describes a similar irony in Hegel, an irony which he finds to anticipate "that tone of belatedness and irony which is characteristic of the literary culture of the modern day." Hegel "made unforgettably clear," Rorty argues, "the deep self-certainty" of "each new dialectical synthesis"—while also making "unforgettably clear why such certainty lasts but a moment."[13] This is also the "Hegelian irony" described by John McGowan as "a hermeneutic which focuses on the illusion of intention, the illusion that the individual by himself can be said to choose what to do and to exercise some control over what is achieved by that doing. It is the totality, the 'cunning of reason' or Oedipus' fate, that rules; Hegelian irony reveals that rule to individuals who continually make the mistake of believing their own independence."[14]

Rose, finally, also refers in passing to Hegel's irony, albeit with a crucial difference to those above. For Rose, as with Butler, Rorty, and McGowan, Hegel's phenomenology expounds the "drama of experience as intrinsically ironic," realizing "the inevitable subjectivity of our positings, and of the ever-painful shifts to further positings of the relation between 'subjectivity' and 'objectivity,' which always fail to guarantee a sustainable reality." Experience is thus "expounded as the changing configurations of the inevitable collision between concepts of self and reality, between concepts of subject and object."[15] The difference, here, however, is that while irony is conceived by Butler, Rorty, and McGowan as melancholic, relativistic, or tragic, and thus prompts a reversion to a place of ironic detachment, assuming once again an ironic relation to objectivity, a sense that we can never truly know or be sure of something, and that modernity consists only in the "bewildering variety of vocabularies from which we can choose, and the instability of each,"[16] Rose's Hegelian irony only functions insofar as the subject repeatedly and boldly stakes itself anew with complete commitment as the only way to approach such knowledge and certainty, in spite of such inescapable mediation, myopism, uncertainty, and illusion. In Rose's words, the irony of speculative experience "reopens the way to conceive learning, growth and knowledge as fallible and precarious, but risk-able."[17] Hegel's irony, therefore, for Rose, does not anticipate the irony of postmodernism, as argued by Butler, Rorty, and McGowan, but instead provides an antidote to it: the justification and the means both for radical commitment and action, and also for the necessary courage and adaptability to move forward when things inevitably and sometimes painfully do not go as expected. McGowan argues that Hegelian irony reveals the rule of the cunning of reason "to individuals who continually make the mistake of believing their own independence," who believe that they can "choose what to do" and "exercise some control over what is achieved by that doing"—an admonishment to any would-be radical bent on putting their principles or beliefs into practice. But Rose demonstrates how Hegelian irony in fact reveals that it is only by making such "mistakes" that any progress, be it in knowledge or in action, is possible at all.

In resistance to the prevailing narrative of Hegel as an anti-ironist, this first chapter will build upon Rose's account of Hegelian irony in particular, in order to provide a more substantial articulation of irony and its central place in Hegel's work. With reference to his conceptions of method, beginning, and propositional form, it will demonstrate that we have been so overwhelmed by the extremity of Hegel's attack on Romantic irony that we have been blinded to the centrality of irony to his own thought. This irony is neither a stylistic choice nor a rhetorical strategy nor an incidental personal disposition. Nor does it have a "performative function," as de Man theorizes—it does not console or promise or excuse.[18] It is rather a necessity borne from what Hegel discovers as the intrinsic irony of truth—of what is in-itself. That is, in discovering the irony of truth, Hegel discovers the irony of irony: that irony is not merely a subjective disposition in relation to the truth, but an essential modality of the truth itself. Without grasping the irony of truth, Hegel's conception of truth (and by extension the truth of Hegel's philosophy) is merely described as a process, development, or movement, without being realized or experienced as such.

It will be argued that it is for this reason that the act and experience of reading, for Hegel, is essential to the truth of what is read. Often, the speculative nature of Hegel's philosophy has been attributed to his speculative mode of exposition, as epitomized by his innovation of the so-called speculative propositional form. As Günter Wohlfart writes at the beginning of his extensive study *Der spekulative Satz*, "The problem of the speculative proposition is the problem of the linguistic presentation of the speculative"; "the problem of the presentation of the speculative idea as the philosophical content of the proposition is, in the end, identical to the problem of the speculative method."[19] Stephen Houlgate writes on a similar note that Hegel "employ[s] a special kind of proposition" capable of "aritculat[ing] or unfold[ing] what the subject [of the proposition] actually is in truth."[20] While agreeing that the speculative proposition is essential to an understanding of the presentation of the speculative, I will argue that such accounts do not go far enough toward grasping the role of the *reader* in realizing the speculative truth of Hegel's philosophy, and speculative truth as such. The problem of the presentation of the speculative is not one that can be resolved through a formal innovation in writing or exposition alone—that is, in the employment of a special kind of proposition. Hegel's speculative proposition should therefore also be understood as the speculative reading of the proposition, for the former yields the latter: a mode of reading by which any proposition may be made speculative, which might realize an ironic and developing truth beyond the fetters of its apparently fixed form.

Contrary to Kierkegaard's claims, then, not only does Hegel perceive the "truth of irony," he thinks that truth itself is ironic. To reformulate Kierkegaard's above critique of Hegel: By focusing on his one-sided attack on post-Fichtean irony, we have overlooked the irony of truth, and by identifying Hegel's critique of Romantic irony with a critique of irony as such, we have done both irony and truth an injustice.

"With What Must the Beginning of Science Be Made?"

In Fred Rush's account of the relationship between irony and Hegel's dialectic, he writes:

> The two parts of irony that are implicit and explicit (i.e. withheld meaning and the apparently plain meaning) seem correlative to the two components of forms of consciousness that Hegel takes it to be so (i.e. the in-itself and the for-itself). But there is a significant—one might say definitive—difference. For, in the Hegelian case, the former is converted to the latter on account of intolerance to contradiction, conveying an overall impression of earnestness to the conceptual work. In the romantic case, there is no such conversion, for irony works just to the extent that it is not translated into flat declaration.[21]

And shortly afterward: "For Hegel ... *Geist* or Logic progresses in a necessary and *univocal* way toward a final form of understanding .... For Schlegel, by contrast, the individual human being progresses *equivocally* by advancing ironically various self-understandings."[22] These passages concern the apparent methods and *teloi* of Hegel's idealist philosophy and Schlegel's Romantic antiphilosophy. "In the Hegelian case," Rush argues, that which is implicit is always made explicit, withheld meaning is made plain, equivocation becomes "flat declaration," and that which is in-itself (i.e., that which is implicit, potential, relational, and unreflective) becomes for-itself (i.e., explicit, actual, and self-comprehending). In this teleological translation of conceptual tension into conceptual harmony, *Geist* progresses methodically and necessarily in a straight line toward its final goal of absolute knowing where all contradiction is overcome and all reality is conceptually mediated and thus subsumed within the mind. The "definitive difference," Rush claims, is that Schlegel is content with suspending thought ironically within these contradictions and indeterminacies of meaning and exploring the supposedly infinite lateral progressions that they might bring. Hegel is conceptually "earnest"; Schlegel is conceptually promiscuous. For Hegel, contradiction is anathema; for Schlegel, it is possibility. In Schlegel's own words, it is "eternal agility, of the infinitely abundant chaos."[23] Rush argues that the discrepancy which defines consciousness, on the one hand, and irony, on the other, may "seem correlative," but while consciousness resolves this disparity, irony suspends it.

There are a number of problems with this distinction that Rush draws. However, I will aim only to correct what is claimed of Hegel, for it is through his definition against Schlegel's irony that Hegel has been misconstrued. First, anyone who has read Hegel's written work and claims to have found "flat declarations" is, ironically, not reading hard enough. They can only have retreated from the text to a presupposed overall conception or spuriously abstracted a positivistic account from the presentation of the work. Adorno writes on reading Hegel, "At many points the meaning itself is uncertain";[24] and later: "The person who retreats to Hegel's overall conception when faced with Hegel's elaboration of his thoughts ... has already renounced rigorous understanding, has capitulated because Hegel simply cannot be understood rigorously."[25] While Adorno could be making this claim sarcastically—that "Hegel simply cannot be understood rigorously" (*Hegel strikt gar nicht zu verstehen sei*)[26]—satirizing through free indirect discourse the philistine who is content with getting the overall gist of Hegel's philosophy because its specificity is just far too complicated for anyone to possibly make sense of, he at the same time means it quite sincerely. This is owing not to some logical ineptitude or argumentative inconsistency on Hegel's part, nor to some necessary intellectual inferiority on the part of his reader. On the contrary, "Hegel simply cannot be understood rigorously" because of his reproach to the very notion or possibility of a rigorous understanding—at least where "rigor," or *die Striktheit*, is understood etymologically as "stiff," "restrained," or "tight." That the "meaning *itself* is uncertain," that "*der Sinn selbst ist ungewiß*,"[27] means, for Adorno, that the obstacle to understanding is not just epistemological but rather logical, even ontological—that is, the obstacle is inherent *in* the meaning as such, and so to remove the obstacle is to destroy the meaning. When reading Hegel we are sometimes met with words, propositions, even whole passages, where the meaning simply cannot be translated from its difficult presentation into an easier, more digestible idiom. It is there to be suffered as uncertainty as such, a present marker of that which resists "flat declaration." Hegel consistently rejects and subverts the prevailing philosophical expectation and presupposition that the true or "reality" can be grasped in any immediate sense; from a particular, single, positive statement; or from simple, linear argumentation. Obscurity follows obscurity; even in a moment when Hegel seems to capitulate to formal declaration, when a moment of clarity or place of anchorage seems to be offered, our reading on compels us to return to this statement and confront what it withheld, to confound the clarity which came before. (I will return to this point later.)

Rush overlooks this necessity because he has not grasped the even more fundamental point that when consciousness in-itself becomes for-itself, this cannot be described as or through a "flat declaration," nor any other stable entity. "The former is" *not* simply "converted to the latter on account of intolerance to contradiction." This does not mean, however, that the difference between the in-itself and the for-itself is merely suspended. Rather, consciousness in-*and*-for-itself, for Hegel, arises out of consciousness being first for-itself: in defining itself against its own content, it recognizes its own content as its other, and this minimal yet radical discrepancy which eludes flat declaration or abstract identity, produced by this self-othering, drives it beyond itself. Rush is therefore correct to imply that the idea around which Hegel's phenomenological method revolves is this distinction but wrong to suggest that the *telos* of this method is this distinction's collapse. This is not what absolute knowing is. This point will prove essential to grasp, for it is what dictates the specificity and the necessity of the ironic experience of Hegel's speculative philosophy.

This rather abstract account can be clarified with reference to the introduction to the *Phenomenology*, in which Hegel describes the method of his inquiry into the science of the experience of consciousness, and how one might begin to undertake such an investigation. For Hegel, both the truth of method and of beginning only come to be through the ironic experience of their impossibility—of the failure of their actuality to correspond to their concept. "It might be useful," he writes,

> to recall something about *the method of the way it* [the science of the experience of consciousness] *is carried out*. This exposition, represented as the *conduct* of *science* in relation to knowing *as it appears* [erschienenden Wissen], and represented as the *investigation* and *testing of the reality* of cognition, seems incapable of taking place without some kind of presupposition which underlies it as a *standard*. For the testing consists in the application of an accepted standard, and in the resulting equality or inequality between the standard and what is tested lays the decision as to whether what is tested is correct or incorrect. (*PhG* §81)[28]

In this passage we are told what we have come to presuppose of philosophy, even if we have not yet realized it: that we presuppose a presupposition as such—a standard, be it the ground or principle upon which a philosophy is built (such as Descartes's *cogito*, or Fichte's *Ich bin Ich*), or else an adequate method of procedure. Both the preface and the introduction begin with similar invocations of the same expectation:

> In the preface to a philosophical work, it is customary for the author to give an explanation—namely, an explanation of his purpose in writing the book, his motivations behind it, and the relations it bears to other previous or contemporary treatments of the same topics ... (*PhG* §1)

> It is a natural supposition [*Vorstellung*] that, in philosophy, before one gets down to dealing with what is at issue, namely, the actual cognition of what,

in truth, is, it is first necessary to come to an understanding about cognition, which is regarded as the instrument by which one seizes hold of the absolute or as the means by which one catches sight of it. (*PhG* §73)²⁹

However, in each case, this "custom" or "natural supposition" is not adhered to. We are told what we are "seem[ingly] incapable" without, and then refused this very object through a demonstration of its logical impossibility. Our expectation is dictated then denied:

> But for a philosophical work, this seems not only superfluous, but in light of the nature of the subject matter, even inappropriate and counterproductive. For whatever it might be suitable to say about philosophy in a preface ... none of these can count as the way to present philosophical truth. (*PhG* §1)

> But here, at the point where science first comes on the scene, neither science itself nor anything else has justified itself as the essence or as the in-itself, and without something like that taking place, it seems that no examination can take place at all. (*PhG* §81)

Where we expect to find an introduction to the instruments and methods required for our inquiry, we are forced to think again. The introductory exercise, traditionally conceived, can only "bring us back to where we were before"; "the thing—here, the absolute—[would be] again for us exactly what it was prior to this consequently superfluous effort." "If the testing of cognition which we suppose to be a *medium* made us acquainted with the law of its refraction, it would be just as useless to subtract this refraction from the result, for it is not the refraction of the ray but rather the ray itself through which the truth touches us that is cognition, and if this is subtracted, then all that would be indicated to us would be just pure direction or empty place" (*PhG* §73). This last criticism is directed implicitly at Kant and his followers (but could also be attributed to Locke and Descartes, for example), those who approach thought as an "instrument" or "medium" and are therefore bound to the idea that our cognitive faculties stand between us and reality, "between cognition and the absolute," and therefore render the in-itself (conceived here in the Kantian sense) as fundamentally inaccessible. Hegel spells this out most explicitly and most humorously in his *Encyclopedia Logic*: "To want to know *before* one knows is as incoherent as the Scholastic's wise resolution to learn to *swim, before he ventured into the water*."³⁰ Just as we can't know how to swim before entering the water, without having first swum, we can't know how to think without having first done a lot of thinking—only then, long after any putative first beginning, does the "how" begin to emerge. The question of "how" to swim, cannot be merely "subtracted" from the activity of swimming.

These introductions to method are at once denunciations of the notions of introductions and methods, and therefore suggest a certain irony. But what is the nature of this irony? Donald Phillip Verene writes that the presentation of Hegel's introduction "follows an ancient principle that he does not state: to say what a thing is, say what it is not and say what it is. In the first eight paragraphs Hegel says what method is not; in the following nine paragraphs Hegel says what method is."[31] This is correct in a sense but does not go far enough. Not only does Hegel say what method is by saying first what it is not and then what it is: he articulates what method is by assuming the logic of "method" in its immediacy in order to draw out its immanent contradictions. It is through this articulation of "method" in its simplicity and the coming to know of its present impossibility or deadlock that method is driven beyond itself and becomes something other—and actual.

It is this articulation of method that epitomizes Hegel's method as such: assuming a thing in its immediacy and "following its path" (for this is the etymology of "method," *meta-hodos*) to discover its disavowed mediation. Perhaps the most emblematic and succinct example of this is in the opening of Hegel's *Science of Logic* where "*Being, pure being*—without any further determination" turns out to be *nothing* precisely because of this very purity.[32] It is only through the force of the purity of being—that is, through trying to grasp being immediately in its pure and simple being-ness *without* any irony—that it is revealed, ironically, to be identical with its opposite. The irony then is not in the articulating or the expositing—that is, in the subjective stance or disposition of the author or speaker—but in the articulation or exposition itself. This is not an irony of detachment but rather attachment; not mastery but naivete or submission.

This is emblematic of the ironic nature of the dialectic. It does not mean that the introduction to science is simply an introductory statement rejecting introductions. An ironic gesture such as this would be representative of a kind of irony that Hegel hates, following the structure of fetishistic disavowal, an irony which acknowledges its own shortcomings precisely in order not to address them—*je sais bien, mais quand meme*, or "I know very well (that introductions are necessarily abstract and rest upon presuppositions outside the science and therefore undermining of science as such), but nevertheless (I must start somewhere)." Instead, the introduction and method to science only comes to be through the ironic discovery of their own constitutive impossibilities. This first misstep—of accepting the need for an introduction or a "first step" as such—is therefore ironically revealed as the necessary first step, the first lesson learned in the education of our philosophical consciousness. As Rose notes: "The need ... for an introductory abstract statement at the beginning of a phenomenology, is itself justified as one of the determinations of substance.... The abstract rejection of abstraction is the only way to induce abstract consciousness to begin to think non-abstractly."[33] For Rose, then, a formative misstep is therefore not only found in the introductions and prefaces that we have come to expect and which Hegel denies us but also in the introduction and the preface that do indeed introduce and preface the *Phenomenology*. Even these are necessary missteps in the "path of despair" (*PhG* §78)—determinations which are necessary and yet undone by the determinations that follow.

Hegel's Phenomenological Method

So what, then, is this methodless method which arises from the realization of the contradictory nature of method as such—implicit in this articulation of the failures of introductions and prefaces to introduce and preface? One popular stereotype of Hegel is that he is the most methodical of thinkers, with every thesis being countered by its own antithesis which prompts the resolution of a new synthesis that is faced by a new antithesis, and so on; or else with every positing being negated and then negated again to produce a new position—a rigid protocol to apply to everything.[34] But now we know that "the testing of the reality of cognition" can never proceed by the "application of an accepted standard," not even the hallowed "dialectic," how are we to proceed? What method can we assume without presuppositions, and without falling into a mechanism? Certainly not "the unmethod that bases itself on either vague sentiments or on inspiration" nor "the capriciousness of prophetic chatter," both of which "despise not only the science of the necessity of the concept; they despise scientificity altogether" (*PhG* §49).[35] Furthermore, how can such a methodless method be prescribed without itself becoming methodical, or, inversely, without the need for so many apologetic qualifications and caveats that it can never get going in the first place? And finally, why does this methodless method necessitate the ironic exposition of both itself and of the task to which it is directed?

Hegel starts by "remind[ing]" us of "the abstract determinations of knowing and truth as they come before consciousness." These are not presuppositions as such, but rather descriptions of the passive and immediate experience of consciousness: "That is, consciousness *distinguishes* itself from something while at the same time it *relates* itself to it" (*PhG* §82). We recognize a thing (*every* thing) as something which exists independently of us. But also that, in recognizing it, it is represented to us in our mind, and so consciousness relates itself to it. It does not matter yet what the determinations of this thing are, or even if it actually exists; nor does it matter the validity of our relating to it. Hegel is just describing the general passive activity of consciousness, "look[ing] on" (*reine Zusehen*) (*PhG* 85).[36] He describes this same procedure in the *Logic* as "setting aside every reflection,... tak[ing] up *what is there before us*."[37] We begin only by passively looking onto or taking up something in its simplicity and immediacy. "This something," Hegel writes, "is something *for consciousness*, and the determinate aspect of this *relating*, or of the *being* of something *for a consciousness*, is *knowing*. However, we distinguish this being-for-another from *being-in-itself*. That which is related to knowing is just as much distinguished from knowing and is posited as *being* also external to this relation. This aspect of this in-itself is called *truth*" (*PhG* §82). Our relating to an object—"something"—is what defines our knowledge of it. But the truth of the object—its "being-in-itself"—stands outside this relation. This, at first, seems broadly in line with Kant's critical philosophy, for which ontology is bracketed beyond knowledge, whereby (the truth of) the thing in-itself exists outside epistemology, to which all nondogmatic philosophy is limited—with the important difference that Hegel seems to assume on authority the de facto intelligibility of the in-itself.

Some readers of Hegel stop here; they read this as "flat declaration"—to use Rush's phrase. They define Hegel's phenomenological method as the progressive comparison of what we hold to be true with the actual truth, whereby we methodically adjust our knowledge to fit what we can glean of its objects. Brandom, for example, illustrates the relationship between what a thing is in-itself and what it is for consciousness, and the process by which the two are progressively reconciled, with the example of a straight (in-itself) stick which, when half submerged in water, appears (for consciousness) bent.[38] The truth (the stick in-itself) does not change. What changes is our representation of the truth (of the stick) in-itself *for* consciousness—that is, our knowledge of it.

> The "new, true object" is the bent-stick representation revealed *as* erroneous, as a *mis*representation of what is now *to* the subject the way things really are: a straight stick. This representing is "true" not in the sense of representing how things really are, but in the sense that what is now to consciousness is what *it* really is: a mere appearance, a misrepresenting.... What alters is the status of the bent-stick representing, what it is to consciousness. It had enjoyed the status of being to consciousness what the stick is in itself. But now its status has changed to being *to* consciousness only what the stick was *for* consciousness: an appearance.[39]

He puts it more succinctly later on: "The object that was taken to be in itself reveals itself, via incompatibilities, as in fact ... only what it was for consciousness."[40] In presenting the process of knowledge like this, the *Phenomenology* itself is presented as an attempt to grasp the process "by which concepts evolve. It is the process in and through which more and more of how the world really is, what is actually materially incompatible with what in the objective alethic sense becomes incorporated in material incompatibilities deontically acknowledged by subjects."[41] It becomes something like a correspondence theory of truth, whereby progress is defined by the development of concepts adequate to their objects; whereby the progress of knowledge is defined as the methodical approach toward the nature of reality independent of our consciousness of it. I say "something *like* a correspondence theory of truth" because with Brandom (as with Kant) what is in-itself, this nature of reality independent of our perception, is ultimately fundamentally unknowable—or, at least, in the case of Brandom's Hegel, it is fundamentally unknowable whether our knowledge has finally grasped it. For Brandom's Hegel, even our revised knowledge of the apparently bent stick as straight is still just the *appearance* of an in-itself for consciousness, albeit an improved appearance developed through a process of determinate negation and mediation.

This is where the pragmatist and normative element of Brandom's reading comes from. Intersubjective agreement, for Brandom's Hegel, overcomes correspondence as the criterion of objectivity. The truth is not that which corresponds to an object beyond any correlation of subject and object (for such an object for Brandom's Hegel, after Kant, cannot be finally known) but instead that which can be broadly agreed upon through the use of an instrumental (that is, scientific) method. Brandom would probably not agree with this account. Indeed, he argues that Hegel "understands the objective world"—that is, what is in-itself—"as always already in a conceptual (and so ultimately thinkable, intelligible) shape," and so "it does not owe to any activity by the thinking subjects to whom it is in principle intelligible."[42] Nevertheless, by Brandom's own account, there is always the chance that what we take to be objective or in-itself, even the stick that we discovered to be straight, may—and, in the case of more scientifically complex objects (a black hole, or a virus, or an ecosystem, for example), probably will—reveal itself again to be merely for consciousness; that is, our knowledge may again be revealed retrospectively in its incompleteness or even its error, and therefore qualified and improved. Therefore, even if we presuppose that the in-itself is in a conceptual shape and therefore thinkable in principle, that does not guarantee that it is actually thought. Our knowledge of the in-itself remains residually uncertain, and the ultimate criterion for objectivity, then, remains its normative status for consciousness as acknowledged by the consensus of a community.

A perhaps crude but nonetheless crucial point to make concerning Brandom's account of Hegel's method is that such material empirical objects such as sticks which exist independently of consciousness are not principally the objects of the *Phenomenology of Spirit*, and so this method described by Brandom cannot adequately describe that of Hegel's phenomenology. The primary object of the *Phenomenology*—as suggested by its original title, "*The Science of the Experience of Consciousness*"—is consciousness itself; and, as Hegel explicitly states, consciousness, when taken as an object for consciousness, is an object unlike all others, and the discovery of its uniqueness dramatically destabilizes the hard distinction which was previously drawn between that which is in-itself and that which is for consciousness. While Brandom of course stresses the importance of consciousness, in the above example describing Hegel's method he still seems to treat the formation of consciousness primarily instrumentally, merely as the medium through which to know external objects. In contrast, for Hegel,

> the nature of the object which we are investigating goes beyond this division, or to this semblance of division and presupposition. Consciousness in its own self provides its own standard, and the investigation will thereby be a comparison of it with itself, for the difference which has just been made falls within consciousness.... Precisely because consciousness knows of an object at all, there is already present the difference that something is, to consciousness, the *in-itself*, but another moment is knowing, or the being of the object *for* consciousness. It is upon this difference which is present that the testing depends. (PhG §§84–85)

The crucial point is that, when consciousness takes itself as its object, "the difference which has been made [between (1) the object in-itself which exists outside any relation to consciousness and (2) the object as it exists for consciousness] falls within consciousness" itself. In short: there is not only an opposition between consciousness and its object but rather the fact of this opposition divides consciousness itself. Hegel goes as far as to say that "consciousness itself is their comparison" (PhG §85). When consciousness takes itself as its object, therefore, it realizes that what it is in-itself is the speculative unity—that is, the inseparable but distinguishable coupling—of these two moments, in-itself and for-itself. It can never finally grasp what it is in-itself in a positive or static way, for the way in which it appears to itself—that is, its own self-conception, for-itself—is a constitutive part of what this "in-itself" is. This moment of being for-itself inherent in what consciousness in-itself is, is the minimal contradiction which guarantees that what is in-itself is always both itself and not; and it is the repeated attempts of consciousness to articulate this contradiction which guarantees that consciousness is dynamic or "plastic," a process or movement which is always forming itself through its own development. As soon as it grasps it, what it is has changed. This apparent failure of consciousness to be fully itself is then at once the very condition of its possibility. And it is therefore "this difference which is present," which is always present, upon which the methodless method rests—upon which "the testing depend"—methodless because its standard is not external nor presupposed but itself and therefore self-disputing, self-responsive, self-reconstructive: Consciousness takes itself as its object and compares itself with itself, but in doing so what "itself" is progresses. This retrospectively clarifies Hegel's earlier statement that "the inequality which takes place in consciousness between the I and its substance which is its object is their difference, the *negative* itself. It can be viewed as the *defect* of the two, but it is their very soul or what moves them" (*PhG* §37). The self-inflicted wounding of consciousness is its own healing.

One must state clearly, at this early stage, that this does not mean that Hegel's idealism is, as it is again often caricatured, the radical preoccupation of the individual consciousness with its own self at the expense of thinking about reality. Granted, Hegel is not too interested, in the *Phenomenology* at least, in the external reality of empirical objects like sticks or facts indifferent to consciousness. What distinguished the object of the *Phenomenology*—the historical realization of consciousness (in reason, morality, art, religion, and so on)—is that it *does* change in itself when it changes for itself because they are products of the truth of consciousness. That is, in the unfolding of the truth of the *Phenomenology of Spirit*, consciousness in the individual sense is revealed to be merely a moment in the determination of spirit. Unlike sticks, spirit has no existence in itself unless it exists for-itself—but it does not only exist for-itself; it exists in-itself (as truth) in history. Like consciousness, then, what spirit is in-itself is defined by a contradiction between these two irreducible moments, opposed in its unity. What is in-itself is defined by a split.

For Brandom, however, the in-itself is by definition noncontradictory. Contradiction (what he labels as "material incompatibilities") always falls on the side of cognition—a contradiction which must be overcome: "It is *impossible* for one object simultaneously to exhibit materially incompatible properties (or for two incompatible states of affairs to obtain), while it is only *inappropriate* for a subject simultaneously to endorse materially incompatible commitments.... Finding oneself with materially incompatible commitments obliges one to *do* something, to revise those commitments so as to remove the incoherence."⁴³ Brandom, then, has what Hegel disparagingly calls with reference to Kant "a tenderness for worldly things." He cannot entertain the possibility that the world itself might bear "the blemish of contradiction" which is assumed to "fall to thinking alone."⁴⁴ For Hegel, on the other hand, the gap between consciousness and its object (the gap which defines consciousness) is redoubled in the object qua substance as subject. Continuing from where we left off in paragraph 37, we can see that "however much this negative now initially appears as the inequality between the I and the object, still it is just as much the inequality of the substance with itself. What seems to take place outside of the substance, to be an activity directed against it, is its own doing, and substance shows itself to be essentially subject" (PhG §37).

What spirit is for-itself must change to account for what is spirit in-itself. This is the task of comprehension, of grasping the truth. But in realizing what spirit is for us, it changes spirit in-itself, as what spirit is in-itself is also for-us. These two moments of spirit then reciprocally influence one another but they never converge upon an abstract or tautological self-identity. Spirit, in order to remain true to its meaning, changes its meaning. The methodless method of the *Phenomenology of Spirit* rests upon this redoubled gap, where spirit compares itself with itself—that is, between its concept and its realization or externalization in history—and it is through this comparison that spirit moves. Every stage of the *Phenomenology of Spirit* is characterized by a different attempt to articulate the gap between these two particular moments which will never be resolved, at the levels of individual, moral, and religious experience, and it is precisely the repetitive failures of spirit to articulate this gap that propels its self-movement and self-development. Absolute knowing, therefore, is not the final "successful" attempt but the ironic realization of the necessity of this gap as such.

Rush claims that "the former [i.e., the in-itself] is converted to the latter [the for-itself] on account of intolerance to contradiction," but now we can see that the opposite is the case. There is no final conversion, and certainly not on account of an intolerance to contradiction. As Hegel emphatically states in his *Logic*, echoing his much earlier thesis that *contradictio est regula veri, non contradictio falsi*:

> Internal self-movement, self-movement proper, *drive* in general ... is likewise nothing else than that something is, *in itself,* itself and the lack *of itself* (*the negative*), in one and the same respect.... If ... a concrete existent were not capable of overreaching its positive determination and grasping the negative one at the same time, holding the two firmly together; if it were not capable of harboring contradiction with it, it would not then be a living

unity as such, not a ground, and in contradiction it would founder and sink to the ground. — *Speculative thought* consists only in this, in holding firm to contradiction and to itself in the contradiction.[45]

Truth is thus characterized by a constitutive, ironic contradiction. It "is, *in itself*, itself and the lack *of itself* (*the negative*)." If it ceased to harbor this contradiction within it, it would cease to be at all; it would be inanimate and dead, like a stick. Reconciliation is, therefore, not the reconciliation of contradiction but rather the reconciliation *with* contradiction: it is "looking the negative in the face and lingering with it" (*PhG* §32).

The "Is"

The ironic presentation of Hegel's philosophy is necessitated by the discovery of the ironic nature of truth, where "irony" refers to that which is never fully (or at least tautologically) what it is. If truth is in some sense constitutively incomplete—that is, if what it is in-itself is both itself and the lack of itself—then it cannot be adequately presented positivistically, as "flat declaration," as if what it is is just that. Hegel rejects this use of language with his critique of sensuous certainty, the first stage of the *Phenomenology* that follows the preface and introduction. Sensuous certainty is that which "expresses what it knows as this: It *is*" (*PhG* §60). In other words, what it dogmatically claims to be certain about is that there is complete identity without difference between what it expresses and its object. However, in doing so, it omits all of its object's determinate characteristics. It affirms its object's *being* but nothing else: "Its truth only contains the *being* of the item." Like the speaker of Samuel Beckett's poem "What Is the Word," all it is able to do is point stupidly at the thing ("this this — / this this here — / all this this here —") without concretely grasping any of its determinate qualities.[46] If Hegel's great discovery, as described above, is that abstract identity, so often taken to be real identity, is in fact illusory, the correlate of this in Hegel's critique of language is that the copula "is," taken as the marker of identity, is in fact a metaphor which has forgotten that it is one.

In what way, then, can irony as truth or the truth as irony be realized in a philosophical work? If "is"—the most ubiquitous of verbs, backbone of propositional logic, and the primary bearer of affirmation, veracity, and truth in language—is revealed to be and to have always been an obfuscating metaphor, how can we go on using it without the kind of ironic distance that Hegel so despised? It is not as simple as saying one thing when you really mean another. This would suggest that the reader would have to "see through" the irony to the truth "beneath." The point is, on the contrary, that there is nothing to see through at all, and that the truth is ironic as such. But if this is the case and the truth is as it is stated, then how is this ironic at all?

For Hegel, it is precisely the ubiquity and familiarity of this word "is" that makes it not only emblematic, but the crux of speculation. He writes in his *Encyclopedia Logic*: "What is ... familiar is usually what is most unfamiliar. Thus, for instance, *being* is a pure determination of thought. And yet, it never occurs to us to make the 'is' the object of our consideration. We typically believe that the absolute must lie somewhere far yonder. But it is precisely that which is wholly present and which we as thinking beings always carry with us and make use of, even if without explicit consciousness of the fact."[47] But how, precisely, to "make the 'is' the object of our consideration"? As argued in the previous section, it is only by setting aside every reflection and presupposition and taking up what is there before us in its immediacy that the ironic truth of the thing might be realized. It is only by first making and learning from the mistake of thinking abstractly that consciousness might begin to think concretely, speculatively. Therefore, the irony of irony is that, at the level of the proposition, the speculative nature of the "is" is only realized by first using it totally literally—that is, naively, and without ironic distance, where "is" just means "is."

As we saw with Wohlfart, Hegel's notion of the speculative proposition is often taken to be a formal innovation in philosophical writing capable of presenting the speculative, the ironic truth that what is in-itself is both itself and its lack, which drives itself beyond itself. Indeed, this is the idea of the speculative proposition suggested by Hegel when he writes that: "only the kind of philosophical exposition which rigorously excludes the ordinary relations among the parts of a proposition"—subject, copula, and predicate—"would be able to achieve the goal of plasticity" (*PhG* §64). But the suggestion that the speculative character of a philosophy is guaranteed only by its philosophical style, by the writer or authorship, does not entirely grasp the importance of Hegel's speculative proposition. To state the obvious, there is nothing formally distinct about Hegel's propositional form. Instead, it is the reading consciousness which must repeatedly discover for itself that what *is* is always also what it is not; that "is," too, is in-itself itself and its lack. This denotes the essential experiential content of Hegel's philosophy. Hegel does not need to develop a totally new propositional logic, therefore, but rather takes this propositional logic to its end so that it might by itself bring to light what it had disavowed. "Is" is thus the most speculative word in Hegel's corpus, perhaps even more than "*Aufhebung*," as that which signifies the identity of identity and nonidentity. (As Hegel writes elsewhere, this speculative identity is not only absolute, but is *the* absolute.)[48] Crucially, however, this "is" which is as much an "is not" cannot be affirmed as both in advance, but must be repeatedly discovered as such. For it is only through the repeated discovery and experience of this contradiction that the reading of the proposition drives it beyond itself. To use "is" "literally" as speculative thinking demands it, then, is to assert it abstractly, if only to realize what that abstract identity left obscured, and so bring it to concretion. One approaches *what is* without irony, to realize the irony inherent in what is. Hegel's speculative proposition teaches us how to read in this way and thus opens up the possibility of reading all propositions speculatively.

Before going into Hegel's exposition of the speculative proposition in the preface to the *Phenomenology*, it may be helpful first to draw on Hegel's description of Socratic irony and its relation to the dialectic in his lectures on the history of philosophy. Hegel says:

> The irony of Socrates has this great quality of showing how to make abstract ideas concrete and effect their development, for on that alone depends the bringing of the Notion into consciousness.
>
> In recent times much has been said about the Socratic irony which, like all dialectic, gives force to what is taken immediately, but only in order to allow the dissolution inherent in it to come to pass; and we may call this the universal irony of the world.[49]

While the German reads "*Alle Dialektik läßt das gelten, was gelten soll, als ob es gelte*," the succinct English translation—"all dialectic, gives force to *what is* taken immediately"—is felicitous (even in spite of its omission of Hegel's *détournement* of the Kantian *als ob*, or "as if").[50] The dialectic gives force to "what is" in terms of what is immediately present or apparent, if only to facilitate its sublation—and this is true of the word "is" itself. All dialectic gives force to what *is*. Likewise, Hegel's propositional logic gives force to what "is" is, "taken immediately"—but only in order to allow the dissolution inherent in "is" to come to pass—to realize, through reading, the speculative and ironic nature of the "is" itself; to make its abstract identity concrete and therefore effect the development of the proposition beyond the fetters of its abstract form.

Hegel develops this peculiar propositional logic most extensively in the preface to his *Phenomenology*. Again, what is particularly unique about this exposition is that it presents the speculative nature of the proposition, and thus speculation itself—what he calls "the goal of plasticity"—as something that can only be achieved through the experience and the act of reading. The "rigorous exclusion" of "the ordinary relations among the parts of a proposition" is a necessity which must first be discovered and then performed by the reading subject (*PhG* §64). This is why, despite being a "distinct" propositional form, the speculative proposition is formally indistinct from ordinary propositions. It follows the traditional grammatical logic of *S* is *P*, where the *S* refers to the subject of the proposition, and the predicative *P* refers to its determinations. The novelty of the speculative proposition lies, therefore, not in some extraordinary linguistic or formal device but in the dramatic, even comic, realization of a notion of identity that retains difference within it, of an "is" which includes an "is not," an "is not" which only becomes apparent upon a compelled rereading after a necessary misreading, and thus leads the assumed stability of the subject-predicate relation awry. This "realization" is meant in both senses of the word: the reader at once *becomes aware* of the dialectical nature of the "is" and in doing so, *makes it so*. A proposition is only speculative by being read as such.

For this reason, the speculative proposition is better understood as the speculative *reading* of the proposition. Understood this way, "the kind of philosophical exposition which rigorously excludes the ordinary relations among the parts of a proposition which would be able to achieve the goal of plasticity" does not only have to be sought and found in Hegel but may be realized and actualized through the speculative reading of any proposition. That is, the truth of any proposition may exceed its abstract self-identification. This does not mean that any proposition *must* yield speculative truths but that in the act of reading there is always the potential for the animation or realization of an ironic, dynamic, and possibly explosive truth which otherwise eludes the "flat declaration" as suggested by its form. This will become increasingly important in the later chapters of this book where it will be argued that the methodless method of "giving force to what is" and "following the path" (*meta-hodos*) provides a model of critical reading in which the truth of a work may be repeatedly and ironically realized anew.

Hegel's first example of such a speculative proposition is "*God is being*" (Gott ist das Sein) (*PhG* §62).[51] This proposition is true. However, its truth lies not in the abstract identity it seems to assert, nor in the exhaustion of the second term in the first, but precisely in that it resists such a ratiocinative and "flatly declarative" reading, which would spuriously resolve, rather than harbor the contradiction that it renders. As Catherine Malabou puts it, "The linear *transition* between subject and predicate, although it is immediately suggested by both the philosophical statement and its own form, encounters resistance."[52] When Hegel uses the word "subject" in the following passage, it is a pun. It denotes both the subject of the proposition and the reading subject. In traditional propositional logic, the subject is fixed, and the predicate proceeds to tell us something about it; the reading subject is fixed too, "the knowing I" that synthesizes or collapses the predicates into the subject and declares it to be so ("It expresses what it knows as this: It *is*."): "At first, it is usually the subject as the *objective* fixed self which is made into the ground. The necessary movement advances from here to the multiplicity of determinations, or the predicates. It is here that the knowing I takes the place of that subject, and it is here that it is both the binding together of the predicates and the subject supporting them" (*PhG* §60). An analogous example of this is Brandom's aforementioned *de re* reading where the reader refers back to the facts "as she takes them to be," "as the best any of us can do"; one takes on authority their own subjectivity (or else the subject of the proposition) "as the *objective* fixed self which is made into the ground"—the fixed anchor of all subsequent predication.

In reading propositions like "God is being," however, the stability of the subject of the proposition and the subject qua reader is disrupted and undermined. The subject, here, is "God"; the predicate is "being." But (and here Hegel ventriloquizes the internal monologue of the reading subject)—but "'being' is not supposed to be a predicate. It is supposed to be the essence"; that is, it is supposed to be a subject; a ground. The reading subject then assumes "being" as a subject and reads backward, "but, as a result, 'God' seems to cease to be what it was through its place in the proposition, namely, to be a fixed subject." We read a proposition expecting a linear transition from subject to predicate or predicates but, in having this expectation undermined, by finding a subject in the place of the predicate, we are "thrown back to the thought of the subject," and find it changed. The predicate "being" is expressed as subject, "as the *essence* which exhausts the nature of the subject [God]," but in doing so "it finds the subject [God] also to be immediately present in the predicate [being]." "Thinking, instead of getting any further with the transition from subject to predicate, feels instead inhibited" (*PhG* §62); it (the thinking subject and the subject of the proposition) oscillates from subject to predicate and back again, it becomes stuck in the proposition it had expected to merely take note of and pass by. "This conflict between the form of a proposition per se and the unity of the concept ... destroys that form" (*PhG* §61). And thus speculative propositional form comes to be through the ironic discovery of the impossibility of propositional form as such (just as the notion of "method" and its introduction came to be through the ironic discoveries of these presuppositions' self-defeating internal logics). In this form, subject and predicate are not affirmed as identical with nor exhaustive of each other, but are left circling around the copula between them—"is"— which is revealed to affirm an "identity of subject and predicate [which] does not abolish their difference" (*PhG* §61), an identity of identity and nonidentity. The tension created by this identity and nonidentity is not merely suspended, however. It is instead this tension that drives the meaning of the proposition beyond the abstract self-identification as suggested by its form; that drives it beyond simply and tautologically "meaning what it means." "God," before assumed to be the fixed subject par excellence, is revealed instead as being, in-itself, itself and the lack of itself, and thus dynamic, "self-engendering, advancing" (*PhG* §65). As Rose puts it, "The subject of the proposition is no longer fixed and abstract with external, contingent accidents, but, initially, an empty name, uncertain and problematic, gradually acquiring meaning as the result of a series of contradictory experiences."[53] This, for Hegel, does not undermine the subject (even if the subject is God) but rather makes the subject *true*.

On encountering such propositions, our "knowing how to read" is checked and undermined; the usual way of interpreting and understanding proves insufficient: "Common opinion ... learns from experience that it means something other than what it took itself to have meant, and this correction of its opinion compels knowing to come back to the proposition and now to grasp it in some other way" (*PhG* §63). In order to be read properly, therefore, speculative propositions—and even the word "is" itself—must first be misread, for it is only in the *Gegenstoß* (translated by Pinkard as both "counter-punch" and "counter-stroke") (*PhG* §§60, 61),[54] in being "thrown back" (*PhG* §62), upon encountering resistance and retreating, that what is returned to (the true, not as abstract identity, but as a concrete speculative identity of identity and nonidentity) comes to be. The speculative identity only arises through the failure of its abstract identity; the possibility of reading arises only from misreading. It is only though this reversal that the ironic truth comes to be realized.

Hegel acknowledges how irritating this is: "For the most part, this unfamiliar impediment forms the basis for the complaints about the unintelligibility of philosophical literature even when the individual has otherwise met the conditions of cultural formation for understanding such philosophical writing. In what is said about this, we see the reason behind the specific reproach which is so often levelled against such writings, namely, that so much has to be read over and over again before it can be understood" (*PhG* §63). But for Hegel this irritation borne from the necessity "to be read over and over again" is a necessity which must be endured as a condition of true knowledge. The truth of philosophy, and thus the true itself, can only be accessed indirectly, through the ironic experience of first having missed the mark. The assumed fixity of the subject as a stable notion in-itself must be repetitively undermined in order to realize the subject in its dynamism. This is why, in a letter to his friend, the poet Karl Ludwig von Knebel, Hegel contrasts the argumentative or propositional style of his journalism with that of his philosophy, saying of the latter that the "subject matter does not permit that clarity of exposition which discloses the object in a finished state and clear light at first approach, and which is possible in the case of a concrete subject matter."[55] The object of reportage may be disclosed "at first approach" because its subject matter is constituted by facts—time, place, circumstance, statistics—which do not change what they are in-themselves when they change for us, where all besides the facts are opinion and rhetoric. On the other hand, the object of philosophy to be grasped and expressed, that is the true, cannot be disclosed on first approach, for what it is in-itself must be revealed, retrospectively and ironically, in its incompletion, in order for it to drive beyond itself.

Woman: The Eternal Irony of the Community?

This understanding of the irony of the dialectic may help us to grasp Hegel's infamous description, from later in the *Phenomenology*, of "woman" as "the eternal irony of the community"—as the "internal enemy" that threatens to bring about the downfall of serious government and statecraft with frivolous feminine concerns such as pleasure, enjoyment, and the family (*PhG* §474). At the very least, this passage provides an opportunity for a speculative reading of Hegel against himself, "to wrest truth" from where its "untruth is obvious."[56]

"Human law," for Hegel in this passage, "*is* in its activity itself the manliness of the polity and *is* in its actual activity the government"—an activity, however, which is constantly disrupted by the individualism of women which the polity must otherwise rely upon for the reproduction of the family:

> By intrigue, woman—the eternal irony of the community—changes the government's universal purpose into a private purpose, transforms its universal activity into this determinate individual's work, and it inverts the state's universal property into the family's possession and ornament. In this way, woman turns to ridicule the solemn wisdom of maturity, which, being dead to singular individuality—dead to pleasure and enjoyment as well as to actual activity—only thinks of and is concerned for the universal. Woman turns this mature wisdom into an object of ridicule for immature, high-spirited youths and into an object of contempt for those youths' enthusiasm.[57]

This presents a classic misogynistic metaphysics of subjectivity by which only men are capable of transcending their particular sensuous self to achieve rationality and to conceive of universality, while women are always subject to irrational and particular passions which constantly threaten to disrupt this universal interest. Women, for Hegel, are essential for the reproduction of the family, which makes up the "elemental unit" of the polity, but they are equally the eternal enemy of the polity, for their exclusive focus on their own particular familial concerns at the expense of the community at large. Hegel then goes on to argue that the only way to suppress or compensate for this frivolous immaturity and thereby save the polity is through war. War alone can negate through sacrifice on the battlefield the "singular personalities" of youth cultivated by doting mothers, while at once harnessing this bravery for the greater good.

To a contemporary reader this argument might read as a piece of Swiftian satire: the war machine as a conspiracy orchestrated by the establishment to rid society of overindulged boys raised on excessive maternal praise, lured into battle (and certain death) by promises of glory, allowing the seasoned statesmen (and only men), relieved of this distracting influence, to quietly attend to the mundane work of government. And yet, this account reflects a relatively accurate account of the historical Hegel's view on the "woman" who, as he puts in the *Philosophy of Right*, "has her substantial vocation [*Bestimmung*] in the family"—"her ethical disposition consists in this [family] *piety*." "Man," meanwhile, "has his actual substantial life in the state."[58] This is the dichotomy or even the aporia which Hegel finds crystallized in the opposition between Antigone (who safeguards the law of the family) and Creon (the ruler assigned to protect the law of the state) in Sophocles's tragedy—where Antigone's moral obligation to bury her brother Polynices comes into conflict with Creon's decree forbidding it.[59] The "solution" of war to this contradiction may seem farcical, but perhaps Hegel thought it was the best one could hope for.

Can this description of woman as eternal irony and internal enemy be "rescued" (to use Adorno's word—for "only rescue, not revival, is appropriate for him")?[60] Some feminist readings of this passage have attempted to do so. Julia Kristeva, for example, says in an interview: "I am very attached to the idea of the woman as irrecuperable foreigner.... And to try to preserve this part as unreconcilable permits us perhaps always to be what Hegel called the eternal irony of the community. That is to say, a sort of separate vigilance that keeps groups from closing up, from becoming homogeneous and so oppressive."[61] In all likelihood this is how the historical Hegel intended woman-as-irony to be understood—woman as permanent foreigner, outsider, nuisance—though Hegel of course did not view it so positively. Kristeva "rescues" the idea of woman as "irony" and "enemy," then, by reclaiming Hegel's sexist designation.

But doesn't such an acceptance of an "eternal" contradiction to be "preserved" fall short of the true irony of speculative thinking? To be "attached" to such a position, like Kristeva, is to hypostasize exclusion and otherness, characteristic of a more Romantic conception of irony as self-edifying distance. Equally, to call for permanent or at least regular war as the only solution to "suppress this spirit of individuality" (*PhG* §474), like Hegel, is violently exclusionary, and evidence of the worst tendency in vulgarly dialectical thinking which rounds up any troubling particulars which won't assimilate, and sends them off to their death, either in thought or (in this case) in reality.

To realize the ironic truth of Hegel's proposition that "woman is the eternal irony of the community" against whatever he meant to mean, it must be reread speculatively. Again, it is what Adorno calls Hegel's *skandalon*, those obstacles to reading or sense, that "[compel] knowing to come back to the proposition and now to grasp it in some other way" (*PhG* §63). In contrast to Kristeva, who embraces the identity designated by what she reads as an abstract identity claim, we must reread it as a speculative identity claim. Far from threatening or undermining the *truly* universal community, what women actually do in Hegel's story, through their exclusion and limitation to a predesignated role, is demonstrate that the community's claims to universality are in fact merely formal, empty, and abstract. In a sense, women are critics, living exemplars of the fact that the "universality" of a society predicated on the exclusion of women from public life (and yet totally reliant upon women for its sustenance and reproduction) is of course no universality at all, a universality which can only sustain itself through denial and arbitrary self-destruction.

We need not limit ourselves to women. All who could be called "inexistent" to use the terminology of Alain Badiou, those unrepresented in "the situation," the disruptive element from which true "eventual" change could emerge, are in this sense "the irony of the community." The irony of the community "testifies, in the sphere of appearance, for the contingency of the being-there"[62]—it is that which testifies that that which "is" is neither natural nor necessary. The inexistent are derided and even destroyed for apparently representing partial and especially corruptive interests, when in fact, insofar as they represent that which is not represented by the "universal," they are the excluded part whose particular emancipation would involve the universal emancipation of everyone. We see hegemonic states everywhere behaving like the historical Hegel: impatient with the intransigence of groups they consider to be fundamentally incommensurable with the community at large. How else, for instance, are we to understand the apartheid in Israel where, since at least 1948, there has been an ongoing attempt to violently exclude the "inexistent" Palestinian element from the community, the "void set" which testifies to the contingency of the given ontological order. The founding of Israel was predicated on the inexistence of the Palestinians. Israel was terra nullius, "a land without a people for a people without a land." And yet the Palestinians are there, the eternal irony of Israel qua Zion, the disruptive excess which must be neutralized. Since October 2023, this has been taken to its end with the move to totally purge or annihilate the people of Gaza.

The woman *is* the irony of the community (the Palestinian *is* the irony of Israel) insofar as she represents a point of impasse for the community's claims to universality. But the revelation of the ironic truth of this empty, formal universality urges us not to stamp out these particularities or to simply and glibly celebrate their "difference" (the temptations of fascism and liberal democracy, respectively) but to transform social and political life in order to establish the conditions for their genuine inclusion. Marx calls this transformed life communism. As he writes apropos the proletariat, that troublesome eternal irony and internal enemy whose particular interests and passions disrupt the universality of capital: their alienation cannot be overcome "without abolishing all the inhuman conditions of life."[63]

From the Speculative Reading of the Proposition to the Speculative Reading of the *Phenomenology*

One possible objection to all this is that not every proposition in the *Phenomenology of Spirit* appears to function in this way. Not every couple of subject and predicate circle wildly around an "is," with the speculative reader repetitively thrown between the two, realizing what is read in its motile configuration by encountering resistance from what is first misread as a flat declaration. This is evident from the fact that some of the best exegetes of this passage—for example, Malabou and Hamacher—while making much of its importance for a reading of Hegel in general, do not give any examples of speculative propositions from the body of the *Phenomenology* beyond Hegel's own examples from the preface of "God is being" and "the actual is the universal." Rose locates a few more examples of such propositions in Hegel's lectures and the *Philosophy of Right* whose copulae have been misread as affirmations of an abstract identity between the related terms: "In general religion and the foundation of the state is [*sic*] one and the same thing; they are identical in and for themselves"; and "What is rational is actual and what is actual is rational"; and "To comprehend *what is*, this is the task of philosophy, because *what is*, is reason."[64] These deceptively declarative statements have indeed caused much confusion due to their being understood as a defense of, for example, a quietist justification of the status quo, due to their being read as if the ordinary relations between subject and predicate persist, as if they were ordinary propositions. Even Adorno, for example, claims that the thesis that the actual is rational is "indistinguishable from apologetics."[65] However, such deceptive statements from Hegel are relatively few and far between.

Perhaps Hegel's most radical speculative proposition—most radical in terms of the resistance it presents to linear, ratiocinative reading; in terms of the intensity of its self-contradiction—is the infamous so-called infinite judgment from the section on phrenology in the *Phenomenology*: the proposition that the *"being of spirit is a bone"* (PhG §343). This speculative proposition is important for Lacanian readers of Hegel such as Mladen Dolar and Žižek for illustrating avant la lettre Lacan's theory of the simultaneous incommensurability and inseparability of the subject ($) and its unobtainable object of desire (*a*) which sets in motion the process of signification.[66] In Hegelian terms, the bone represents the material remainder of spirit which both resists and guarantees the economy of sublation. Importantly, the way that Žižek describes the proposition that "spirit is a bone" and its relation to this simultaneous failure and possibility of subjectivity epitomizes the experience of speculative reading as elaborated by Hegel above, and the status of this experience as a condition for realizing the speculative truth of a proposition:

> The proposition "the Spirit is a bone" provokes in us a sentiment of radical, unbearable contradiction; it offers an image of grotesque discord, of an extremely negative relationship.
>
> However, ... it is precisely thus that we produce its speculative truth, because *this negativity, this unbearable discord, coincides with subjectivity itself*, it is the only way to make present and "palpable" the utmost—that is, self-referential—negativity which characterizes the spiritual subjectivity. We *succeed* in transmitting the dimension of subjectivity *by means of the failure itself*, through the radical insufficiency, through the absolute maladjustment of the predicate in relation to the subject. This is why "the Spirit is a bone" is a perfect example of what Hegel calls the "speculative proposition," a proposition whose terms are incompatible, without common measure. As Hegel points out in the Preface to the *Phenomenology of Spirit*, to grasp the true meaning of such a proposition we must go back and read it over again, because this true meaning arises from the very failure of the first, "immediate" reading.[67]

But speculative propositions such as "spirit is a bone," and such as Hegel describes them in the preface, are exceptional—at least in terms of this radical sense of an "unbearable contradiction." This is not, however, because Hegel sets up the speculative proposition as an expository ideal, which he then fails to realize, but because he sets up the speculative reading of the proposition as an analog and a microcosm of speculative reading as such.

"The *proposition*," as Hegel writes, "ought to express *what* the true is" (*PhG* §65). In this sense, the *Phenomenology of Spirit* should be read as one long speculative proposition, as an attempt to express what the true is as a whole (or as *the* whole). The importance of the reading experience of the speculative proposition, then, is that it represents the reading experience of the *Phenomenology* in microcosm. As Hamacher remarks, it is the "paradigm of the whole speculative movement" in which "the grammatical logic of subsumption characteristic of 'representational thinking' [*vorstellendes Denken*]"—in this case, the formally logical predication of a fixed subject—"is replaced by the circular logic of dialectical thinking."[68] It also graphically and syntactically represents the *Phenomenology*'s central concern—that of identity—through its own central term: the "is." Finally, Hegel's exposition of the speculative proposition is important because it reveals that speculative thinking is realized most intensely as an experience and act of reading.

Far from every stage of the *Phenomenology* neatly transitioning into the next, overcoming the logical and conceptual tensions of the previous one, each presents itself as a new hurdle; every synthesis or rational achievement which is approached appears, upon arrival, as yet further conceptual tension and contradiction. It is, then, ironic in the sense of a dramatic irony to which the reader is not privy until it is too late, as the means by which they might be confronted with the disparity present in the true as such. This is why Butler is right to claim that "as readers of [the *Phenomenology*], we undergo the drama of accepting false certainties and then being rudely and, indeed, comically confronted by that which they unwittingly exclude."[69] Hegel's reader is never passively witnessing the comedy of the text unfold, or enjoying the dramatic irony from the outside. Instead, they are wholly implicated as a character within it, afflicted by incessant confusions and false conclusions, producing the reading's content and form by being compelled to read differently, speculatively. This is what characterizes an immanent as opposed to a transcendental reading of the dialectic, which is the difference between experiencing and therefore realizing the truth of the dialectic in all its irony, plasticity, and surprise, and merely formalizing it as a schema or method (in the instrumental sense, where the method is distinct from the object to be apprehended). "Indeed," as Butler goes on, "the narrative journey of Hegel's emerging subject in the *Phenomenology* is marked by a repeated and insistently premature proclamation that the absolute has been achieved."[70] Absolute knowing *is* of course achieved at the end of the *Phenomenology*, but this absolute knowing is itself ironic: it is not, as the reader might have expected, a fullness and immediacy of knowledge and experience, or a complete conceptual mediation of reality, but rather the moment of return, the ironic reversal, where we are "thrown back to the thought of the subject," and are compelled to reread what we had first misread: where we reread the gap between us and the in-itself as a gap *in* the in-itself; where we reread the apparent disparity between us and the truth of absolute knowing, as a disparity inherent in the truth of absolute knowing itself.

This complicates the idea, advanced by Josiah Royce and later developed by the likes of Jean Hyppolite and M. H. Abrams, of the *Phenomenology* as a bildungsroman—as documenting a teleological process of (self-)realization and demystification toward maturity and reconciliation.[71] It may seem that this reading is not without some textual justification. Hegel's chosen metaphor for the *Phenomenology* is, after all, a "ladder" (*PhG* §26). He also describes the dialectic as "unrelenting" in the *Phenomenology* (§80); as "the universal, irresistible power which nothing, however secure and firm it may feel itself to be, can withstand" in the *Encyclopedia*; and, in the *Logic*, as "free of restrictions, and as the absolutely infinite force to which no object that may present itself as something external, removed from reason and independent of it, could offer resistance."[72] However, perhaps these grandiose claims, upon rereading, might reveal their own ironic truth. As Comay notes, "What he describes [as a ladder] is actually more like a game of snakes and ladders, where the snakes vastly outnumber the ladders, where at any moment you might find yourself sliding back to the beginning."[73] Rush claims that Hegel's dialectic "involves sequential progressive change from one world view to another, measured in terms of coherency that overcomes conceptual tension."[74] But this is asserted without textual justification beyond an insufficiently literal reading of Hegel's own claims—that is, Rush's reading does not "give force" to literal-mindedness in order to bring about its own transgression but instead retreats from the letter to a hypostasized and lifeless "flat declaration." Where is this "coherency that overcomes conceptual tension" actually to be found in the *Phenomenology of Spirit*? While it does indeed progress, this progress is always, at once, obstruction. It documents a process of "coming to know and knowing about that coming to know"[75]—as Isobel Armstrong puts it—but essential to this process are the disruptive revelations of the *wrongness* of knowledge, and the repetitive, incessant undoings of what we had come to know (and known about that coming to know), which are at once constitutive elements of what that very knowledge is.

That the *Phenomenology* is not a work of linear formation does not signal it either as an unequivocal work of destruction, nor absolute knowing as a standpoint of absolute loss. Instead, read properly (that is, in surrender to the dialectic, following the path), the *Phenomenology of Spirit* at once documents and engenders the progressive challenging and undermining of the coordinates of "common sense" and established knowledge on and in their own terms. This is its negative work. On the other hand, it is this very reading experience, which immanently negates itself, that engenders the (negated negation of) the receptivity to the contingencies of reality that allows thinking to be adaptable, critical, progressive, and without presupposition—that is, speculative.

Another way of putting it, perhaps, is that the *Phenomenology* is a work of mourning, not melancholia. This conception of mourning should be distinguished, however, from the postmodern conception of Derrida, for example. Derrida ironically reformulates Descartes: "I mourn, therefore I am." For Derrida, mourning is an endless, "impossible" process, and it is only this mourning that drives us on.[76] The speculative work of mourning, on the other hand, is one that takes the risk of completing itself. This does not mean that the gap inherent in absolute knowing is finally overcome but rather that knowing, in spite of this gap, continues to take the risk of staking itself, and even of abstraction, of making more propositions with naive commitment—not with the delusional hubris of the fundamentalist or zealot who cannot be falsified but with the revolutionary courage of the historical actor who knows that the ironic truth of their position can only be realized by repeatedly putting it into action and going to the end, learning from their mistakes, and risking action once again. "Experience will only accrue if the angel discovers the violence in its initial idea," as Rose puts it.[77] "No one who puts a hand to the plow and looks back is fit for the kingdom of God."[78] This, of course, is a painful process. It is for this reason that even in completing the work of mourning one is not freed from the path of despair.

Consequently, although I have suggested that Hegel's description of the *Phenomenology* as a "ladder" should be read ironically, this does not merely mean that it should be read as if the total opposite is true. Like Hegel's speculative proposition, on first reading this metaphor seems to affirm a simple or abstract identity between its object and the chosen image; but as we read on, (to repeat) we "[learn] from experience that it means something other than what it took itself to have meant, and this correction of its opinion compels knowing to come back to the proposition and now to grasp it in some other way" (*PhG* §63)—that is, we are forced to understand it as affirming both identity *and* nonidentity, ladders *and* snakes. The speculative truth, the vital dialectical twist or ironic reversal of this is that, for Hegel, it is only by being rudely confronted with these obstructions and obstacles to reading, when we were promised a path to knowledge without resistance, that the only path to knowledge becomes possible. In other words, it is only by encountering snakes when we expected a ladder that a ladder appears.

If this conception of the true that I have been rehearsing here seems untenable for its irreconcilability with more acceptable conceptions of the true, that is, in a sense, because this untenability and unacceptability are integrally constitutive elements of such a conception. Truth for Hegel is necessarily dialectical and thus necessarily self-disputing. It stands for a direct confrontation with contradiction in the very substance of reality and thought. Our first reaction to the revelation of this nature of truth is therefore one of self-defense. As Sutherland describes it: established knowledge "acts up, squirms, revels in phlegmatics, grabs for what it already owns or contains, eulogises over abstractions, asserts the unarguableness and even the divinity of its institutions; above all, it 'recount[s] conventional ideas as if they were established and familiar truths.'"[79] But at once, the intense unacceptability of this unresolved encounter presents the only possibility for the generation of further thought from thought, of staking ourselves once again. The inherently contradictory nature of truth stands as both its interminable obstacle and its interminable possibility; and the strenuous effort with and against this contradictory truth (of contradictory truth) is what gives definition to speculative thought.

The reason that Hegel so detests the Romantic irony of his contemporaries in Jena—Schlegel, Novalis, and Schleiermacher—therefore, is not because of its inimical difference to his system and method but its uncanny closeness. Romantic irony amounts to an inadequate reflection of his own ironic dialectic. Both are characterized by self-consciousness, the deployment of contradiction as a positive resource, and a self-reflexive awareness of the limitations of one's own ideas, actions, and language. But while Romantic irony is aloof with respect to the world and announces a self-reflexive awareness of its own limits and inadequacies in order to expiate and cynically distance itself from these limits and inadequacies and the damage they might do—a self-reflection which is at once indifferent to the world and yet paranoid of its judgment—the ironic as dialectic at once acknowledges and operates within these inadequacies and limits, repeatedly staking itself and embracing the risk of activity, as the only way to move forward. It is deployed not to spuriously escape such limits, but to configure them as such, on and in their own terms (despite the risk, the inevitability, even the necessity, of being misread), for the true for Hegel is found not despite brokenness but in brokenness itself. The dialectic "only wins its truth by finding its feet in absolute disruption" (*PhG* §32).

Commitment Issues

The Adornian question, then, of "how to read Hegel," is revealed as the most fundamental question. It is also revealed as the most unnecessary. There is no schema or trick or hermeneutic method that is required to discern the thought of the *Phenomenology*. Rather, all that the *Phenomenology* asks of its reader is a kind of active passivity, or a willed abnegation of one's own will.[80] This is not because "Hegel" is an authority with whom we should not quibble, who knows better. Hegel is also, like us, merely "looking on" at the movement of spirit, ignorant of where it will go. (He was, after all, "in the habit of calling this piece ... his voyage of discovery."[81]) Of course, Adorno is conscious of this irony. It is rehearsed in miniature by the title of his third study on Hegel: "*Skoteinos*, or How to Read Hegel." "*Skoteinos*" (σκοτεινός), Greek for dark, mysterious, shady, and untrustworthy, seems to point to Hegel's obscurity—that is, the difficulty of reading him. As such, this seems to be set up as a problem. Adorno's choice to render this quality of Hegel's writing in Greek, a language reserved for the learned and initiated, seems to performatively and indeed ironically embody this obstacle to understanding. The subtitle, on the other hand, "How to Read Hegel," seems to point descriptively to the following study as a solution; its clarity and straightforwardness, and the simplicity of its vocabulary, seem to leave no room for confusion: this is a guide, a "Hegel for dummies," which will provide you with the know-how necessary to come to grips with this famously difficult philosopher. The ironic reversal is that the content of the essay, directed, as is typical of Adorno, against these Cartesian ideals of clarity, certainty, and method, argues that a programmatic statement of "how to read" is itself the obstacle to reading, and that σκοτεινός must be confronted as a necessity. *Skoteinos* itself is the criterion for how to read Hegel. To repurpose Hegel's own words: the reader learns from experience that the title means something other than what it took itself to have meant, and this correction compels knowing to come back to it and grasp it in some other way (*PhG* §63).

We have determined that Hegel's philosophy does not explain or argue or posit abstract propositions, "flat declarations." But if this is the case, where does its content lie? If it still *thinks*, what is the precise nature of this cognition? The answer is suggested in this phrase "learns from experience" and by what Adorno calls the "experiential content of Hegel's philosophy." This experiential content does not denote affect or feeling, nor "prosody as cognition";[82] its motivation, as Adorno notes, is neither biographical nor psychological nor physiological;[83] nor is it intended to render the contours of phenomenological experience in its fundamental determinations (as attempted by subsequent works in phenomenology, such as those by Heidegger, Henry, Husserl, and Merleau-Ponty). Instead, what Hegel calls experience is concerned merely with the animation of the contradiction present in the true: "This *dialectical* movement which consciousness practices in its own self (as well as in its knowing and in its object), *insofar as, for consciousness, the new, true object arises* out of this movement, is properly what is called *experience*" (*PhG* §86). Experience is then nothing but the passive witness (which nonetheless requires a constant strenuous activity) of the conceptual movement of the true, surrender to its incessant ironic twists and turns; it is the holding fast to the contradiction of the in-itself with itself, which is its very soul and movement, and the following of this movement to its apogee. This is the form and content of speculative thought, epitomized in the activity of reading.

This is why, as soon as one tries to bring a particular mode of interpretation to bear upon this experience, interpretation itself becomes impossible, because we bring a presupposition. One must, again, challenge Brandom on this point, who prescribes two "equally valid"[84] interpretative modes for reading: *de dicto* and *de re*.[85] The former, *de dicto*, aims to discern how Hegel himself would have answered particular questions regarding his text, given his particular historical commitments:

> One engaged in this sort of interpretation is trying to specify the contents of commitments in a way that would be recognized and acknowledged *as* specifications of those contents *by* the one whose commitments they are.... One seeks to know so thoroughly what an author actually said, how his thought developed over his lifetime, what the rhetorical strategy of each work is and how it was understood by its author as fitting into the oeuvre, what his extraphilosophical concerns, attitudes, and experiences were that one can answer questions on his behalf in something like his own voice.[86]

It asks, in short: what did Hegel mean to mean?

The latter, *de re*, aims to discern what "*actually* follows" from Hegel's claims, regardless of his intended meanings, where the reader provides the context for interpretation. The reader "assesses the inferential significance of the ascribed claim from the inferential context provided by her own commitments."[87] In other words, such specifications "attempt to say what *really* follows from the claims made, what is *really* evidence for or against them, and so what the author has *really* committed herself to, regardless of her opinion about the matter."[88] Brandom's own pragmatist semantic interpretation of the *Phenomenology* in *A Spirit of Trust* represents such a reading: it depends upon claims that Brandom himself holds to be true in advance.

Both of those "readings" of Hegel prevent a reading of Hegel altogether, for they approach the question of "how to read" as a traditionally hermeneutic one, and, in doing so, sacrifice the essential notion of experience, as described above, as philosophically contentful. In fact, one of Brandom's own apparent "commitments" upon which his *de re* reading depends is that experience is beneath philosophical consideration: "'Experience' is not one of my words," he states proudly. "I do not find it necessary to use it in the many pages of *Making it Explicit* ... and the same policy prevails in this book [*Articulating Reasons*]."[89] While in *A Spirit of Trust*, Brandom presents Hegel's concept of experience as essential, defined as the "process that determines conceptual contents," he abstracts this notion of experience *in* the *Phenomenology* from the experience *of* phenomenological thinking and reading. He thus sacrifices experience in spite of professing its central importance. Brandom acknowledges that he undertakes his particular reading of Hegel based upon his own personal commitments, and does so "without claiming that Hegel would have acknowledged them."[90] There seems little point, therefore, in complaining that "Hegel wouldn't agree"—this would be a *de dicto* rebuttal, anyway. What I do want to argue, however, is that by reading in these ways, one is not and cannot read Hegel speculatively and therefore cannot grasp its truth. If there is a speculative *de re* reading of Hegel—that is, a reading of Hegel which grasps what actually follows from the words on the page according to the immanent movement of the dialectic—it is possible only by pursuing and radicalizing the claims of consciousness within the singular experience of consciousness itself, in spite of consciousness's presupposed "commitments."

First, prior "commitments" are just presuppositions, and presuppositions are anathema. As Houlgate argues against Brandom, "The only commitment of his own the phenomenologist may bring to bear on the study of consciousness is the commitment to *set aside* any determinate commitments of his own and to work out what experience is made necessary by the commitments of consciousness alone."[91] To read *de dicto* can only perform a kind of historicism. The attempt to reconstruct the singular perspective of a historical individual, "Georg Wilhelm Friedrich Hegel," by attempting to discern the wealth and nuance of his historically contextual commitments, is, as Brandom himself states, basically intellectual historiography.[92] What Brandom does not concede is that such a reading, while certainly interesting and valuable in its own right, prevents a reading of the ironic truth of what is read (of which speculative experience is not only essential but the essence). This is why, as argued in the introduction, there cannot be such a thing as an orthodox Hegelian. To read with an aspiration to grasp Hegel's "intended meaning" is to be un-Hegelian. But to read *de re* is to read with ironic distance, to try and discern the work's "relevance" or "insight," to divide the "living" from the "dead," or else to reconstruct the text as a series of "claims" and "commitments" to be judged for their present veracity and utility.

The enfranchisement and empowerment of the reader suggested by Brandom's description of *de re* interpretation—whereby the reader provides their own context—is opposed, therefore, to my own insistence on the importance of the reader in the realization of the speculative, ironic truth of the proposition. Hegel's irony functions, ironically, only insofar as there is no ironic distance to our reading, only insofar as we assume absolute naivete. It is only when we read with naivete, "suspending judgment and leaving understanding and explanation to another day" (in the words of Comay and Ruda), that we discover the deviation of what is in-itself from itself, which animates this contradiction, and is thus its self-movement. To experience this self-movement is to think speculatively. Comay and Ruda describe this naivete by way of analogy to psychoanalysis:

> Hegel demands of his readers a properly psychoanalytic attitude. The absolute method is the equivalent to the "fundamental rule" of analysis—the annoying obligation to speak "freely"—to communicate whatever comes to or "falls into" the mind, *Einfälle*, without selection, omission, or concern for connection, sequence, propriety, or relevance. Like a passenger on a train (that's Freud's own somewhat Proustian analogy), you're to report the changing mental scenery as it passes by, merely "looking on [*reine Zusehen*]," suspending judgment and leaving understanding and explanation to another day (or person). Our task is simply to "take up *what is there before us* [aufzunehmen, *was vorhanden ist*]."[93]

This should be emphatically distinguished from other kinds of possible passivities of thinking. One can imagine, for example, a New Age guide on "how to read Hegel." In recognizing, like Hegel, the necessity of passivity, the necessity for a suspension of presuppositions, and the absence of a positive self as a substantial psychical agent, it prescribes that, before each engagement with the text, the reader must undergo a ritual of mind clearing of these illusions and obstacles. Admittedly, the "psychoanalytic attitude" described above, which is required to "read Hegel"—"looking on," "speaking freely," "suspending judgment"—does sound analogous to a practice of meditation—"letting oneself go," etc. The essential difference is that while a meditative passivity establishes a distance between itself and the source of negativity, so that what changes is not this source but rather the way in which we relate to it, an elevation above it for the purposes of calm and contentment (and thus another guise of Romantic irony), Hegelian passivity surrenders to this negativity and the disruption that it entails, it continues down the path of despair. The former dismisses the negative as a transitory illusion. It is "a life that is fearing death and austerely saving itself from ruin." The latter, on the other hand, "looks the negative in the face and lingers with it." "It bears death calmly, and in death, sustains itself" (*PhG* §32).

* * *

In this chapter I have tried to demonstrate that one cannot grasp Hegel's notion of the true without appreciating its irony. Not that we should, like the Romantics, assume an ironic relation to the true, but that by pursuing the true without presuppositions and with absolute commitment, we realize that the true itself is ironic. It is only through this repetitive experience of the irony of truth that speculative thinking becomes possible, abstraction is made concrete, and the truth of the proposition moves beyond itself.

I have also argued that the presentation of this speculative thinking is not just limited to the way in which it is written down—that is, in the innovation of a special kind of propositional form—but that speculative thinking is also made present through the act and experience of reading. By generalizing the idea of the speculative proposition to one of the speculative *reading* of the proposition, we may begin to intimate the outline of a theory of speculative reading as such, by which what is read is speculative not by merit of the way in which it is composed but rather through the way in which it is read. The meaning or ironic truth of a text might be realized by a critically intimate mode of reading which, on rereading, *recollects* it anew. It is this theme of recollection which will be the focus of the following chapter, which is the active counterpart to the passivity of the reader's "looking on."

Recollection
Or The Gallery of Images

[CHAPTER TWO]

> *But none of the feelings which the joys or misfortunes of a real person arouse in us can be awakened except through a mental picture of those joys or misfortunes; and the ingenuity of the first novelist lay in his understanding that, as the image was the one essential element in the complicated structure of our emotions, so that simplification of it which consisted in the suppression, pure and simple, of real people would be a decided improvement.*[1]
>
> MARCEL PROUST

In the final paragraphs of the final chapter of the *Phenomenology of Spirit*, Hegel looks back on and describes the preceding narrative of spirit's "coming-to-be." On the one hand, he writes, this coming-to-be can be considered as "*nature*"—as a "*free contingent event*." "Nature" refers here to what spirit "is" in its stupid, conceptless, and unthought immediacy. Spirit's development is thus conceived as something which just happens, beyond spirit's control. Spirit is completely passive in the face of the ironic twists, turns, and dramatic reversals of the dialectic. Thought of in this way, spirit's "immediate coming-to-be"—the *Bildung* narrative of the *Phenomenology* presented over the preceding pages—is "nothing but this eternal relinquishing [*Entäußerung*] of its *stable existence*," a displaced agency of meandering contingency, a bad infinity of merely living on, for which spirit can only sit back and observe (*PhG* §807).[2] "Coming-to-be," in this sense, spirit's nature, is then something that happens to spirit, and not something that spirit does or itself participates in.

"However," Hegel continues, "the other aspect of spirit's coming-to-be, *history*, is that *knowing* self-*mediating* coming-to-be." Conceived in this way, spirit's coming-to-be is reclaimed, not as a random series of events beyond its control that merely happened and continue to happen to it, but as its own history—a history upon which it can confer meaning and significance. As Timothy Bahti succinctly puts it: "The relation between *Geschehen* and *Geschichte*"—between the "free contingent event" of nature and history—"is one between *Geschehen* and *das was geschehen ist*"—between the immediacy and indeterminacy of a happening and the subsequent mediated and determinate knowledge of what happened. *Geschichte* is then "necessarily *nach Geschehen*"—an after-happening. "It is retrospective, and thus reflective, *nach-denkend*"—an after-thought—the consolidation and comprehension of what happened, after the fact.[3] It is an *inwardiza-*

tion and a *recollection*. Hegel's word *Erinnerung*—which he hyphenates on a couple of occasions (*Er-Innerung*) to emphasize this notion of the inner (*das Innere*)[4]—encapsulates both of these meanings.

This act of spirit's recollection of its own history—the moment when it looks back on its own coming-to-be and reclaims it as its own—is at once, then, the condition of its entrance *into* history. It is for this reason, Hegel continues, that although spirit's coming-to-be is "relinquished into time … this relinquishing is likewise the relinquishing of *itself"* into time (*PhG* §808).[5] In other words, this relinquishing, this *Entäußerung*, is not merely the excretion of the inessential waste that follows the subject's digestion of its substance (the gastroenterological metaphors are Hegel's own), but this externalization is spirit's excretion *of itself* from the purity of logic into the messiness of phenomena.

As Terry Pinkard notes, "*Entäußerung*" has explicitly religious and in particular Christological connotations. It is "the term that Luther used for his translation of *Kenosis*, the act of God 'humbling' himself (as the King James translators had it) or of 'emptying' himself (as some more modern translators have rendered it), so that, for Christians, God became flesh":[6] Christ is God relinquished into time, which is at once the relinquishing of himself, as the precondition for the life of his (holy) spirit in the community of believers. God "forsakes [his own] existence and gives [his] shape over to recollection [*seine Gestalt der Erinnerung übergibt*]" in Hegel's words (*PhG* §808).[7] This explains the apparent paradox of Christ on the cross crying out to the God who is, in a sense, himself, "*Eli, Eli, lema sabachthani?*" (My God, my God, why have you forsaken me?).[8] It is only by "forsaking" himself and giving himself up to recollection that the (holy) spirit (of God, of Christ) is brought to life—hence the inwardizing-recollection of the *Gestalt* of Christ at the Eucharist: "Take, eat,… do this in remembrance of Me."[9]

This is why, as Hegel goes on, "the *aim*, absolute knowing, or spirit knowing itself as spirit, has its path in the recollection [*Erinnerung*] of spirits as they are in themselves and are as they achieve the organization of their realm" (*PhG* §808).[10] As we shall see, this has been interpreted as emblematic of Hegel's voraciousness—his desire to consume everything within the economy of his system, "the belly turned mind," as Adorno puts it, in keeping with Hegel's own digestive imagery.[11] As we shall also see, this moment of recollection has also been interpreted as "opposed" to the moment of relinquishment, or kenosis. This chapter, however, will interpret them in their speculative identity. The recollection of spirit *is* its kenosis, and its kenosis *is* its recollection. The "recollection and Golgotha of absolute spirit" (*die Erinnerung und die Schädelstätte des absoluten Geistes*)[12] that end the *Phenomenology* refers on the one hand, to Calvary, the site of Christ's crucifixion, and therefore the transition from externality, materiality, and corporality to spirituality and ideality; but on the other hand, it refers to the *Schädelstätte*, in Luther's German, "the place of the skull," which reaffirms the so-called infinite judgment that *"the being of spirit is a bone"* (*PhG* §343).[13] It refers as much, therefore, to kenosis and relinquishing—of spirit externalizing itself once again—as it does to recollection and inwardization, affirming both as essential moments in the movement of the dialectic.[14] As Hegel writes in the preface to the *Phenomenology*: "The force of spirit is only as great as its expression [*Äußerung*], and its depth goes only as deep as it trusts itself to disperse itself and to lose itself in its explication of itself" (*PhG* §10).[15] The depth of spirit's inwardizing-recollection depends entirely on its simultaneous resolve to externalize and re-present what it finds there.

This chapter, then (and, from another angle, the following chapter too), concerns the transition between these two moments or "aspects" of spirit's "coming-to-be": from nature to history, from free contingency to conferred necessity, from passivity to activity, from irony to recollection-and-relinquishment. If "ironic" describes, first, spirit's passive experience of its unfurling nature, in all its contingency, contradiction, and surprise; this chapter will argue that it is what Hegel calls "recollection," which names the retrospective activity of conferring significance and meaning onto this experience—an activity of representing the past as a means of relinquishing or moving beyond it. These are also the two sides of speculative reading. Coming-to-be qua nature and coming-to-be qua history are analogous to the necessary misreading of the proposition and the subsequent rereading of the proposition which makes it speculative. This is the transition between reading passively, "looking on," to reading actively; from being a detached critical observer, taking note, to being a thinker and cocreator of what is read, suddenly forced to be engaged and critically intimate—one who recollects the spirit of what is read from its letter.

It will also, finally, be demonstrated that central to this activity of recollection is the activity of representation (*Vorstellung*) as epitomized by the image (*das Bild*). The image, for Hegel, is both that which spirit recollects and spirit's concrete expression—its kenosis. To grasp this is to grasp the role of representation in relation to the thought of the concept, which is not finally abandoned with absolute knowing, but recollected in the activity of recollection itself. For Hegel, a recollection is always, to some extent, artificial—a simplification, an exaggeration, a caricature, an "exemplum." It is this recollective process of representation which is also this representational process of recollection—critical, simplifying, and even vulgarizing—which stakes and realizes the irony of the true, from which further ironic truths can develop.

The *Phenomenology* as a Gallery of Images

In the same paragraph quoted from above, Hegel writes: "This coming-to-be exhibits a languid movement and succession of spirits, a gallery of images [*eine Galerie von Bildern*]" (*PhG* §808).[16] What does it mean for Hegel to describe this aspect of the *Phenomenology* (coming-to-be via self-mediation—responsive, relational, reconstructive; recollective—which drives and is spirit's history) as "exhibit[ing]" a "gallery of images"? For the reader that has made it to this final paragraph, "a gallery of images" will seem like an appropriate metaphor. The *Phenomenology of Spirit* is a work uniquely replete with images.

Along the "path of despair" (§78), the reader encountered a variety of strange characters and scenes. Early on in their journey they passed a party of drunks, calling themselves "the true." Each celebrant was their own individual, but all were united by their intoxication. In their bacchanalian revel, each passed out, unconscious, into the quiet repose of the whole (§47). The reader then came across a skeleton, each part helpfully labeled, but lacking the requisite flesh, blood, and breath to be alive, and therefore known (§51). A little later they were met with an image of "a *topsy-turvy* world" (verkehrte *Welt*) (§§157–60),[17] where sweet was sour, black was white, north was south, and crimes were moral goods; a world which challenged the authority of "the tranquil kingdom of laws" (*das ruhige Reich der Gesetze*) (§§149, 157) that is our home.[18] The world was posited by an evil genius, mad with the inflated sense of her own understanding. If, she asked, there is a distinction between appearance and reality, between the sensible and supersensible worlds, what if the two are total opposites? The only thing that is certain is the distinction itself (§§157–58). Soon they encountered a master and a servant in a struggle of life and death, each staking their lives to prove their worth to themselves—and to each other (§187). In this fight, the whole being of the servant was seized with dread. Everything solid and stable for him shook to its foundations. Death became his new master (§194). To conquer his fear, he worked. He formed with his own hands a *thing*, fashioning his own nothingness into a positive being, realizing himself in an external object, and thus as his own individual with his own mind (§§195–96). He was, therefore, victorious. However, his newfound freedom brought him no joy. He was soon found seeking comfort in various forms of sophistry—in scientism (§§198–201), in nihilistic resignation (§§202–5), and then in the opinions and authority of experts. He sought it in spirituality, transcendence—in the "shapeless roar of the pealing of bells" or "all-suffusing vapor" (§217); and then merely in the animal routines of eating and shitting (§225)—but to no avail. In the end the man with the unhappy consciousness went to a priest. He surrendered everything—his decisions, his freedom, his "blame" (*Schuld*) (§§226-28)[19]—and, while his actions and his being remained to him a sham, his enjoyment a sorrow, he found some solace in the intimation of a union with God, albeit through the intercession of a mediator (§230). Further along the path of despair, observing reason, the reader came across a physiognomist (to be punched in the face), and then a phrenologist (whose skull needed to be smashed) (§339). They were then presented with a penis (too busy pissing [*pissen*] to procreate) (§346).[20] They met a vain, facetious "wit" or "*Geist*" (a sardonic pun on Hegel's master term) (§520)[21] with a taste for the surreal, who wouldn't stop talking. A one-man variety show, his zaniness was that of an eclectic musician, Rameau's nephew, singing now in Italian, now in French, first bass, then falsetto, "alternately raging and then being placated, imperious and then derisive" (§521). He disdained, disoriented, and derisively laughed at all he saw, eventually even himself (§524). Then, on finding universal freedom to be terror, the work and deed of which is a meaningless death, a final erasure of a self which was already nothing, an "unfulfilled empty dot" (*unerfüllte Punkt*),[22] they saw an image of a severed head of cabbage and a mouthful of water, swallowed (§590). Next, they came across a beautiful soul: an aesthete and a Romantic; so sensitive, so conscientious, so moral. Terrified of the dangerous world and its corrupting influence, terrified of being polluted by contact with the mundane and the profane, he fled, first from actuality and then from himself, in a desperate attempt to preserve the purity of his heart. He yearned for *something*, but he knew not what. Nothing pleased him. He collapsed under the weight of his own innocence. It paralyzed and consumed him. The last image of this pitiful figure showed him as nothing but a shapeless vapor, dissolved into thin air, vanished (§658). Then, they met a self-appointed critic and judge, detached and ruthless in his condemnations of the confessions of the wicked (§665). The confessor confessed: "*I am he.*" But this confession was not reciprocated by the judge, conceited in his assumed position of guiltless authority, confident in his superiority over those he discredited. This hard-hearted judge clutched to his pride, refusing to give himself up to mutuality and reciprocity, to the recognition of his own implication in the spiritual substance of what is, for fear of the guilt that it might entail (§§666-67). But in doing so he revealed himself to be just another beautiful soul, frightened of being polluted by the messiness of collective existence. And, like all such beautiful souls, his "innocence" consumed him; he shut himself away, renouncing any and all connection with an other, and thus denied himself any existence at all. As a judge of all except himself, he became a nobody, "disordered to the point of madness," and wasted away in a fit of consumption (§668). They then met a prophet, a poet. He reflected to the people the truth of who they were—we are. A product of the world and yet its unacknowledged legislator, and endowed by the muse, Mnemosyne, with the gift of memory (*Erinnerung*), he recalled the essence of the past for the spiritual enrichment of the present. A mere vessel, an organ of truth, he lost himself in his universal song (§729).[23] But the unhappy consciousness soon returned, to announce that God was dead (§752). Trust in the eternal laws then faded away. The statues became mere stones, corpses from which their living souls had flown, just as hymns through repetition became empty words. The tables of the gods were stripped of their food and drink; games and festivals ceased to bring joy and unity; the works of the muse, Mnemosyne, were rendered impotent. However, a young girl took these relics of the past and gathered them up. She represented them as pieces of beautiful fruit, broken off from a tree, and gifted them to the reader. (The fruit, we learn, does not exist. Nor does the tree that bore it. Nor the earth upon which the tree grew. They are, in a sense, "inorganic.") The reader took the fruit, and wiped a drop of rain (or was it a speck of dust?) from its skin. In the gleam of the girl's "self-conscious eye" (*in den Strahl des selstbewußten Auges*), the reader saw the trees, the air, the light—all of the conditions which nourished this fruit, and allowed it to grow—as an *inwardized-recollection* [Er-Innerung] (§753).[24]

Even if the conceptual intricacies and precise order of these stages of spirit encountered and sublated in its coming-to-be are forgotten in the haze of retrospection, the shapes themselves are preserved, recollected in these and other images. "Shape," or *Gestalt*: the word itself implies an external form or outline, a *Grundriß*, fashioned not found; an aesthetic shorthand or mnemonic index for the "wealth of its substance" (§808).

The Fate of Representation

In some ways this mode of literary-philosophical presentation may seem in keeping with the range of Romantic, early post-Kantian thinkers who promoted the aesthetic as the means and end of absolute knowledge. From Fichte to Schelling, Schiller, the Schlegels, Novalis, and the early Hegel himself, the promise of a unified system of philosophy would be fulfilled through a radicalization of Kant's aesthetic theory: his theorization of the simultaneous distinction and inseparability between concept and intuition, a priori knowledge and aesthetic intelligibility. These philosophers held that, with his 1790 *Critique of Judgment*, Kant had demonstrated the possibility of a sensuously embodied absolute meaning, principally in art, beyond the constraints of concepts and conceptually mediated intelligibility; a kind of ultimate meaning which could render spirit sensuously, reflectively, and therefore totally intelligible to itself, thus disclosing the true nature of reality. This was a possibility which, as Robert Pippin notes, "was of such significance that for the early Schelling ... and the Schlegel brothers, this artistic attestation and comprehension of such unity was *more* significant than any philosophical articulation."[25] In the words of Schelling himself, in his 1800 *System of Transcendental Idealism*, "Philosophy attains, indeed, to the highest, but it brings to this summit, so to say, the fraction of a man. Art brings *the whole man*, as he is, to that point, namely to a knowledge of the highest, and this is what underlies the eternal difference and the marvel of art."[26]

This position is similar to that of the earlier 1796-97 so-called "Oldest System Programme of German Idealism" (the existing manuscript of which is in Hegel's handwriting but is thought to be written earlier—possibly by Hegel but more likely by Schelling, Hölderlin, or an unknown fourth author). This text heralds "the Idea which unites all, the Idea of *beauty*, the word taken in the higher platonic sense. I am now convinced that the highest act of reason, which embraces all Ideas, is an aesthetic act, and that *truth and goodness* are brothers *only in beauty* — The philosopher must possess just as much aesthetic power | as the poet [*Dichter*]."[27] Following on from (or perhaps extending and exaggerating) Kant's third critique, the author holds that beauty is that which will unite truth and goodness. Practical reason and theoretical reason may be resolved into a purposive whole by the judgment made in the indeterminacy of aesthetic reflection. The aesthetic, for the early Hegel, Schelling, et al. thus represented the promise or placeholder for the realization of freedom.

This is the position held in Hegel's essays on *Faith and Knowledge* and *Natural Law*, written in 1802-3, immediately prior to his work on the *Phenomenology of Spirit*. This time, however—and significantly, for our purposes—he makes reference to "the image" in general, rather than to aesthetics or fine art in particular: "For just as each part or aspect of philosophy is capable of being an independent science, so each such science is thus immediately an independent and perfect image [*ein selbständiges und vollendetes Bild*], and in the form of an image [*der Gestalt eines Bild*], can be accepted and expounded by an intuition which purely and happily keeps itself free from contamination by fixed concepts."[28] In stark contrast with the later Hegel we have come to know, here it is the concept, or at least the spuriously fixed concept, which contaminates the purity of the image, and not vice versa. The image is also presented here as the vehicle and means of mediation by which a thing can be known in its totality—what he later calls "the totality of the widespread image."[29] As Malabou notes, this conception of the image is developed less from a radicalization of Kant's third critique as presenting a unification of truth and goodness in the beautiful and more from a reinterpretation of Kant's first critique as managed by an economy of visibility.[30] These early essays (*Faith and Knowledge* in particular) reconceive the Kantian notion of the a priori synthesis—that is, the originary relation between subject and object, and the identity between concepts in their difference—as the pure image which reconciles thought and being, logic and ontology. Following Fichte in reading for the spirit of Kant against his letter (a reading which will be elaborated in more detail in the following chapter), Hegel rereads the epistemological claims made in the first critique as an "ontological theory in disguise."[31] The a priori synthesis, for Hegel, is of ontological and not only epistemological import, to the extent that it forces us to understand reality as an undifferentiated whole that only becomes separated into subject and object once it imposes a conceptual schema upon itself. And it is an image (as opposed to a concept, for example) as it comes from the transcendental *imagination*, that which "provides us with pure determinations of time and space, that is, pure 'images' given before any empirical phenomena."[32] Pure images thus "form a spatial and temporal scene for the synthesis that goes beyond the analytic closure of the concept without transgressing experience."[33] In this sense, for Hegel, the a priori synthesis qua image is "nothing but the speculative form of God."[34]

To what extent does this or any other idea of the image remain of "absolute" importance for the Hegel of the *Phenomenology* and beyond? Returning to the beginning of this final chapter on absolute knowing, with the reader having passed through the carnivalesque range of characters and images recollected above, Hegel himself arrives to inform the reader, us, that we have reached the exit. The journey is over and now, no longer needing figurative representations or examples to learn from, he tells us, we are ready for what lies beyond—namely, the pure thought of the concept, or philosophy as such. "The *content* of the representational thinking [*des Vorstellens*] is absolute spirit, and the sole remaining issue is that of sublating this mere form" (*PhG* §788).[35] This echoes a number of points throughout the *Phenomenology* (which we will return to), but which is, again, epitomized in microcosm by Hegel's speculative proposition. As developed in the previous chapter, the assumption of formal logic in the reading of a proposition, for the Hegel of the *Phenomenology*, spuriously asserts both a fixed subject—be it grammatical or the subject qua "self"—and an abstract identity, in which "the name as a name,... denotes the pure subject, the empty, conceptless 'one.'" It is, therefore, a form of re-presentation, and as such, Hegel continues, it also falls for the trap of the "sensuously intuited or represented self" (*PhG* §66). In contrast, the speculative proposition—or, rather, the speculative *reading* of a proposition—as Hegel develops it, avoids or sublates the errors of this ratiocinative form by demonstrating that sensuous immediacy is always already mediated, that the subject is unfixed and dynamic, and that true identity is always an identity of identity and nonidentity.

This account suggests neither, as before, a conception of the beautiful image as the means of unification between truth and goodness, or theoretical and practical reason; nor a conception of the pure image as the originary a priori synthesis, as the means of identification between the subject and its predicates in their difference. Instead, the image and all other such picture-thoughts are here deemed apparently expendable, true in their content but false in their form. It may at first appear that Hegel's earlier notion of the originary "pure image" does not succumb to this later critique of representation. Does the "purity" of the a priori synthetic image not mean that it is free of the contingencies of the inessential and the sensuous? On the contrary, the pure image does not elude the economy of representation but in a sense epitomizes it as an abstract representation of a representation. The pure image is a representation abstracted from all particular and sensuous content while remaining wedded to the logic of the senses—it is a sensuousness without sense. It is still, therefore, a decidedly aesthetic absolute.

When one looks over Hegel's work following the *Phenomenology*, this apparent shift—from valorizing representation to dismissing it—seems decisive. Indeed, one might go as far to call it an epistemological break. From the Jena *Phenomenology of Spirit* onward, throughout his Heidelberg *Encyclopedia Outlines* and his Berlin lectures, to the final edition of the *Science of Logic*, he argues that, while *Vorstellung*—translated variously as "picture-thinking," "representation," or, in more colloquial usage, "idea"[36]—may share the same content as philosophy, this content is obscured by its contingent, arbitrary, and sensuous form. *Vorstellung* is *illustrative* of thought and is therefore not pure thought itself. As such, so the story goes, it is inadequate for *Wissen* proper. As Hegel seems to suggest above, one of the most important preparations to undertake before engaging in real philosophy (that is, one assumes, the thought of the *Science of Logic*) is *Vorstellung*'s overcoming. While before the aesthetic was held to be that which would mend all broken middles, here it is presented as a dangerous obfuscation.

The clearest formulation of this kind of argument comes at the beginning of the 1817 *Encyclopedia Logic*: "Given that the determinacies of feeling, intuition, desire, volition, etc., insofar as we are *conscious* of them, are usually called *representations*, it can be said quite generally that philosophy replaces representations with *thoughts* and *categories*, but more specifically with *concepts*. Representations may generally be regarded as *metaphors* of thoughts and concepts. By merely having representations, however, we are not yet familiar with the meaning they have for thinking, i.e. we are not familiar with *their* thoughts and concepts."[37] The two main kinds of *Vorstellung* must, however, be distinguished. One is the more prosaic thought of *Verstand*, or the understanding—the kind of commonsense thinking with which we relate to the empirical world in an individual and immediate (and therefore spurious) sense, the thinking of ordinary, everyday, moment-to-moment consciousness whose purview is facts (verified or refuted by reference to external objects, such as sticks, thinking back to Brandom's example)—and therefore not truth. This *Verstand-Vorstellung* constitutes one of Hegel's prime targets throughout and especially in the first part of the *Phenomenology*. In contrast, *Vorstellung* raised to its highest level, as it appears at the end of the *Phenomenology*, the sublation of which is "the sole remaining issue," the last step necessary for absolute knowing, refers more specifically to the kind of thinking in which we represent thoughts and concepts as normative fictions (for instance, in art, law, ethics, and especially, for Hegel, religion). It is the kind of thinking apparently reserved for when we have not yet reached the lofty heights of absolute knowing, and are as such unable to think with "pure thoughts," but are nevertheless in some kind of communion with the true. "*Thinking* has not been inactive at all in what is religious, right, and ethical," he writes, "its [i.e., thought's] activity and its products are *present* and *contained* therein."[38] To repeat from above: the content of *Vorstellung* is absolute spirit but the form must be sublated.

This position is also found in both the *Science of Logic* and in the *Encyclopedia Philosophy of Mind*:

> Nature and spirit are in general different modes of exhibiting *its* [the absolute idea's] *existence*, art and religion its different modes of apprehending itself and giving itself appropriate existence. Philosophy has the same content and the same purpose as art and religion, but it is the highest mode of apprehending the absolute idea, because its mode, that of the concept, is the highest.[39]

> This knowledge [science, philosophy] is thus the thinkingly cognized *concept* of art and religion, in which the diversity in the content is cognized as necessary, and this necessity is cognized as free.... The whole question turns entirely on the difference of the forms of speculative thinking from the forms of representation and of the reflective intellect.[40]

"If *Verstand* brings with it the errors of empiricism," as Fredric Jameson puts it, "picture-thinking on the other hand is already an experience of truth, albeit a distorted and preconceptual one. Reason must transcend and transform the errors of *Verstand*, but it must hermeneutically recover the truths of *Vorstellung*, even though the latter have also been formed into images in accordance with the logic of the senses and of externality."⁴¹ Thoughts are re-presented in *Vorstellung*, in order for their truthful content to be more easily, initially approached; and then reason, when capable, must extract this truth content from its inessential form in order for it to be truly known. This is one possible explanation, according to Hegel, for why the speculative philosophy of the *Logic* is at times so difficult to grasp—it assumes not only some preexisting knowledge but the absolute knowledge of its reader, and it therefore lacks the convenient yet ultimately obfuscating presence of representation. As the above passage from the *Encyclopedia Logic* continues:

> One aspect of what is called *the unintelligibility* of philosophy relates to this. In part, the difficulty consists in a certain inability, which is really merely a *lack of training*, to think abstractly, i.e. to hold on to pure thoughts and to move among them. In our ordinary consciousness, thoughts are clothed in and combined with familiar sensuous and spiritual material, and when we think things over, reflect, or reason about them, we intermingle our feelings, intuitions, and representations with thoughts....— The other aspect of the unintelligibility of philosophy is due to the impatience of wanting to have before oneself in the form of a representation what exists in our consciousness in the form of a thought and a concept.⁴²

Hegel, again, appears to offer something of a preemptory apologia for the obscurity and difficult nature of his writing.

This more particular relationship between representation and images, on the one hand, and religion, art, and literature, on the other, are perhaps most straightforwardly stated in his lectures on the philosophy of religion:

> In the first place, sensible forms or configurations belong to representation. We can distinguish them by the fact that we call them *images* [*Bilder*]. Those sensible forms for which the principal content or the principal mode of representation is taken from immediate intuition can in general be termed images. We are directly conscious that they are only images but that they have a significance distinct from that which the image as such primitively expresses—that the image is something symbolic or allegorical and that we have before us something twofold, first the immediate and then what is meant by it, its inner meaning. The latter is to be distinguished from the former, which is the external aspect. Thus there are many forms in religion about which we know that they are only metaphors. For example, if we say that God has begotten a son, we know quite well that this is only an image; representation provides us with "son" and "beget-

ter" from a familiar relationship, which, as we well know, is not meant in its immediacy, but is supposed to signify a different relationship, which is something like this one. This sensible relationship has right within itself something corresponding for the most part to what is properly meant with regard to God.

So there are many representations that derive from immediate sensible intuition as well as from inner intuition. Thus we soon know that talk of God's wrath is not to be taken in the literal sense, that it is merely an analogy, a simile, an image. The same holds for emotions of repentance, vengeance, and the like on God's part. Prometheus, who instructs human beings, and of Pandora's box—these, too, are images having a nonliteral meaning. Thus we hear of a tree of the knowledge [*Erkenntnis*] of good and evil. When the story arrives at the eating of the fruit, it begins to become dubious whether this tree should be taken as something historical, as a properly historical tree, and the eating as historical, too; for all talk of a tree of knowledge is so contrary [to ordinary experience] that it very soon leads to the insight that this is not a matter of any sensible fruit, and that the tree is not to be taken literally.[43]

Each of these instances, from across a broad stretch of Hegel's oeuvre, where he discusses the relationship between thought and its representation (be it felt, intuited, figurative, metaphorical, analogical, etc.), seem to suggest, in turn, an unequivocal and fairly conventional position regarding the relationship between the apparent dichotomy of philosophy and literature. While literary representation (whether in the literary arts per se, or more specifically in the transcribing or writing of thought) may possess a certain truth content, its form is nonetheless inessential, fictional, and constructed; constrained to the spurious logic of externality and the senses—the aesthetic. Hence: "Philosophy does nothing but transform our representations into concepts."[44]

Er-Innerung

To return to the *Phenomenology*, then, at last, we might think upon reaching its end, we are about to achieve what we were promised from the outset—that is, thinking which is liberated from its childish dependency upon illustrations, metaphors, and representations in order to think the truth: The ancient quarrel between philosophy and literature is about to be resolved, with philosophy victorious and literature redundant.

However, what we actually get with the chapter on absolute knowing is something far more complicated and, if read closely, greatly destabilizes the above account of the role of picture-thinking in relation to the thought of the concept. Despite expectations, what we are presented with is not pure thought or a final synthesis, devoid and purified of the contingencies of figurative language and imagery, but yet more images. (Is not "the gallery of images" itself an image?) The chapter on absolute knowing presents nothing immediately new, no final or revelatory insight, but a summary or catalog (a form which Hegel had apparently denounced in the preface with the images of the annotated skeleton and the "rows of sealed and labelled boxes in a grocer's stall" [§51]) of that which came before, followed by a final, rhetorical flourish, replete with images, and even some poetry:

> The *aim*, absolute knowing, or spirit knowing itself as spirit, has its path in the recollection of spirits [*die Erinnerung der Geister*] as they are in themselves and are as they achieve the organization of their realm. Their preservation according to their free-standing existence appearing in the form of contingency is history, but according to their conceptually grasped organization, it is the *science of phenomenal knowing*. Both together are conceptually grasped history [*begriffne Geschichte*]; they form the recollection and the Golgotha of absolute spirit [*bilden die Erinnerung und die Schädelstätte des absoluten Geistes*], the actuality, the truth, the certainty of its throne, without which it would be lifeless and alone; only —
>
> Out of the chalice of this realm of spirits
> Foams forth to him his infinity.
> [*aus dem Kelche dieses Geisterreiches
> schäumt ihm seine Unendlichkeit.*] (§808)[45]

Why is this? Why more images? How can we account for both Hegel's claim to have sublated *Vorstellung* and his simultaneous usage of it? As Comay puts it, does the ending of the *Phenomenology* "contradict or confirm his own infamous pronouncement of the supersession of the 'poetry of *Vorstellung*' by the 'prose of *Denken*'? Is this the triumphant absorption of the aesthetic or a testimony to its persistence: display of a trophy or confession of defeat?"[46]

It has become commonplace to criticize or else make excuses for this final chapter—for its brevity, its obscurity, its reckless pace, and its apparent inconsistencies such as these. Jameson, on the one hand, calls it "a most sketchy and disappointing anticlimactic conclusion for so intricate a work."[47] It is perhaps emblematic of what Derrida identifies as Hegel's propensity to "[rush] toward the economy of a reconciliation that causes the wrong itself to be simply forgotten or annihilated."[48] A succession of *dei ex machina* are brought onstage before the final curtain call to tie up any loose ends. Hyppolite, on the other hand, while acknowledging some flaws, is more sympathetic, and makes excuses for the simultaneous obscurity and briskness of Hegel's conclusion, mentioning "the difficulty of the subject matter, Hegel's varied intentions, [and] probably also a hasty composition which is sufficiently explained by the circumstances of the book's publication"[49]—these circumstances, as Pinkard describes them, ranging from bankruptcy, to an accidental pregnancy, to war.[50] By his own admission, Hegel hastily wrote the book's final pages on the eve of the battle of Jena. In the same letter to Niethammer that contains Hegel's famous soaring description of seeing Napoleon "riding out of the city on reconnaissance" ("it is indeed a wonderful sensation," he writes, "to see such an individual, who, concentrated here at a single point, astride a horse, reaches out over the world and masters it"), Hegel also complains of his desperate money problems, and also his struggle to get the manuscript of the *Phenomenology* finished and safely delivered on time: "How dearly I wish you had arranged for cash payment to be made for merely part of the sum, and that you had not made the final deadline so strict! . . . God will, I hope, deliver my scribblings to you within the deadline. As soon as you learn how some money can be sent to me, please dispatch it most urgently. Before long I will have absolute need of it."[51] Caught up in the excitement of the historical moment, overwhelmed by personal hardship, and maybe seduced by the soaring rhetoric of his own prose, perhaps he simply forgot about "the sole remaining issue" with which he had introduced the chapter: "that of sublating this mere form [i.e., *Vorstellung*]." Perhaps that final sublation slipped his mind. Or perhaps, a more generous reader might suggest, absolute knowing is not to be found in the *Phenomenology* at all. Perhaps the *Phenomenology* is all-*Vorstellung* and it is only in the *Logic* where we can find "pure thought," the prose of *Denken*. As Speight has noted: "The *PhG* is, with good reason, often thought to mark within Hegel's life a sort of Prospero's farewell to the employment of literary and imaginative arts";[52] a final indulgence in picture-thinking before renouncing it forever—*rough magic abjured, and charms all o'erthrown.*[53]

A similar contradiction is apparent in an earlier section, with Hegel's foremost critique of *Vorstellung* in the *Phenomenology of Spirit*, which ends with the aforementioned image of the penis (too busy pissing . . .): The more thinking occupies itself with representations, Hegel writes,

> the more tawdry is the appearance of this content, which is either solely for consciousness, or is solely expressed naively by consciousness. — The *depth* from which spirit pushes out from its inwardness but which it only manages to drive to the level of *representational consciousness* and then

abandons it there — and the *ignorance* [*Unwissenheit*] of this consciousness about what it says — are the same kind of connection of higher and lower which, in the case of the living being, nature itself naively express in the combination of the organ of its highest fulfillment, the organ of generation, with the organ of pissing [*Organs des Pissens*]. — The infinite judgment as infinite would be the completion of self-comprehending life, whereas the consciousness of the infinite judgment which remains within representational thought conducts itself like pissing. (*PhG* §346)[54]

The truth which is grasped solely at the level of representation, Hegel argues, is like an "organ of generation"—a penis—which can only piss. Typically, "*Organs des Pissens*" is translated as "organ of urination."[55] As Verene has noted, however, this translation erases Hegel's wordplay: while representational consciousness masquerades as knowledge, as *Wissen*—as seminal and generative—what it amounts to is mere *Pissen* by comparison.[56] The stark contradiction of this passage, however, is that just at the moment where Hegel appears to bitterly denounce thought which remains stuck at the level of representation, as a perverse coincidence of the high and the low, corrupting and cheapening the absolute spirit which is its content, he is at the same time representing this juxtaposition with the image of a penis. As Mladen Dolar has noted, "this parting shot is really the limit to flabbergast the interpreters. Most of them cautiously decided to pass over it in silence."[57]

Verene is the only critic to offer a substantial study of Hegel's use of images in the *Phenomenology of Spirit* and of what this might mean for our understanding Hegel's philosophy more generally. On discussing the ending of the *Phenomenology*, Verene begins by rehearsing the commonly held view, as above, that "the much-awaited, final and direct explanation of absolute knowing,... seems rather slight and abstract—an anticlimax."[58] He goes on to argue, however, that the ending of the *Phenomenology* in fact evinces the absorption of the aesthetic and the poetic into the thought of the speculative by way of a dialectical reversal. This concluding passage, he writes, is Hegel's "final irony"—his last trick. Once again, the dialectic has led us to accept one thing, one final certainty—"that religion is not absolute knowing because it delivers the content of absolute spirit in the form of picture-thinking"—and once again he then rudely, comically undermines that position: he "uses this very form to conclude absolute knowing and the *Phenomenology* itself."[59] The ironic experience of discovering one's own misreading, thus necessitating a rereading, as represented in microcosm by the speculative proposition (as developed in the previous chapter), extends to the *Phenomenology*'s final moment. In Verene's words:

> The *Phenomenology* ends with an image—Calvary, the throne, the cup foaming forth.... Calvary is an image of an end that is also a beginning. It is an image of suffering and triumph through suffering. It is a master image of opposites—finitude and infinitude and the circle of beginning and end.
>
> By concluding the *Phenomenology* in this way Hegel reminds us that the image is still with us. The *Begriff* still has a connection with the *Bild*.[60]

This connection between the *Begriff* and the *Bild*, as Verene argues throughout his study, and as I intimated at the opening of this chapter, is one of recollection (*Erinnerung*). In short: Thinking gains its access to the concept by recollecting (both internalizing and recalling) the past as an image. The image is the form in which the developed concept is "stored," and, once recalled, from which further concepts are developed. It is not the concept but the concept's support: Philosophy or logic does not think in images but must be constantly referring back to or recollecting its internalized past *as* an image in order to subsist and develop. Absolute knowing, therefore, consists not in superseding *Vorstellung* once and for all, but in realizing, or recollecting, its essential function in the act of recollection itself.

From the outset, Verene modestly provides a caveat for his argument: "The contrast I make between *Bild* and *Begriff* is not Hegel's. Hegel does not employ *Bild* in the *Phenomenology* as a special term."[61] For Verene, the introduction of the image-concept dialectic is something of a creative misreading, or perhaps a *de re* reading in the Brandomian sense where Verene provides the context of the interpretation. But perhaps Verene does not take his own argument seriously enough. While Hegel's references to *das Bild* in the *Phenomenology* are relatively scant, it can be demonstrated that they are made with both precise intention and conceptual specificity. What Verene has intuited in the *Phenomenology*—the recollective function of the image for the thought of the concept—is in fact vindicated by Hegel's later systematic articulation of "representation" in the third volume of his *Encyclopedia Outline*, a section which is subdivided into "recollection" (*Erinnerung*), "imagination" (*Einbildungskraft*), and "memory" (*Gedächtnis*). This section has become particularly famous because of the importance given by Derrida and de Man to the latter subsection.[62] For Hegel, memory is the faculty of the mind that produces signs—that is, signifiers which re-present yet exist in arbitrary relation to a semantic content. For Derrida and de Man, Hegel shows how this productive, mechanical memory is speculatively identical to thinking itself. Consequently, for Derrida in particular, this subsection proves central for his understanding of Hegel as "the first thinker of writing."[63]

What has received less attention, however, at least from literary theorists, is the significance of Hegel's discussion in this section of the relationships between representation, recollection, and imagination. "Representation [*Vorstellung*]," Hegel writes, "is the recollected [*erinnerte*] intuition and, as such, is the mean between intelligence's immediate finding-itself-determined and intelligence in its freedom, thinking"[64]—where "intuition" stands for the immediate, sensory cognition of an object which exists externally to intelligence. "The path of intelligence in representations," he continues, "is to make the immediacy inward."[65] That which is immediate, in order to be mediated—that is, to be thought—must first be interiorized and become thinking's own. This is what Hegel calls "recollection" (*Erinnerung*), the process by which a content "is not only intuited as it just *is*, but at the same time *recollected*, posited as *mine*. Determined in this way, the content is what we call an *image* [Bild]."[66] As such, what was before an intuited immediacy, irreducibly particular, and a mere moment of sensory experience, becomes "immortal" and universal: "I lift the content out of the *particularity* of space and time, the particularity to which the content, in its immediacy, is bound"; and, in doing so, I can now "represent [it] to myself wherever I am, even what is remotest from me in external space and external time."[67] While "what is represented gains this immortality only at the cost of the *clarity* and the *freshness* of the immediate individuality, the all round determinacy, of what is intuited"—that is, although "the intuition is obscured and blurred, when it becomes an image"—it is in turn only by sacrificing the immediacy, freshness, clarity, and complexity of the intuition that it becomes available to thought.[68] To reformulate the epigraph to this chapter from Proust: For Hegel, thinking cannot be awakened except through an image, and the simplicity of this recollected image, which consists in the suppression, pure and simple, of the real, is a "decided improvement." While that which is "*recollected* within intelligence" is "no longer existing"—is not preserved externally in the world by merit of being recollected—"the image" of it is "*preserved unconsciously.*"[69] Intelligence is thus conceived by Hegel as a "nocturnal pit in which is stored a world of infinitely many images and representations"—a "gallery of images," we might say. This "nocturnal pit" of images, Hegel writes, is "the universal requirement to conceive the concept as concrete."[70]

This invocation of the "nocturnal pit" of images gets to the crux of the difference between Hegel's and Aristotle's accounts of the relationship between thinking and representation, in spite of Hegel being deeply inspired by Aristotle's claim in *De Anima* that even pure thinking (*noein*) must depend upon an element of *phantasia*, or imagination.[71] As Jennifer Ann Bates notes, while images for Aristotle are produced by the *outward* activity of sensation (en-)*lightening* the world (suggested by the etymological link between "*phaos*" [light] and "*phantasia*" [imagination]), images for Hegel are produced equally by the *inward* activity of internalizing the world into "*darkness*"—the unconscious "nocturnal pit."⁷² Hegel illustrates (pun intended) this darkness most graphically in his 1805–6 Jena lectures, delivered shortly before the 1807 publication of the *Phenomenology*: "This [is] the Night, the interior of [human] nature, existing here— *pure Self*—[and] in phantasmagoric representations it is night everywhere: here a bloody head suddenly shoots up and there another white shape, only to disappear as suddenly."⁷³

To return to the *Philosophy of Mind*, Hegel then gives a remark which recollects a famous image from his past work, as if to give a performative illustration of this role of image recollection in relation to the concept. He writes: We conceive the recollected image containing in possibility the thought of the concept "as we conceive e.g. the seed as *affirmatively* containing, in *virtual* possibility, all the *determinacies* that come into *existence* only in the development of the tree."⁷⁴ This recalls the moment from the preface to the *Phenomenology* when Hegel illustrates the idea of the true as a process with the image of a tree: "When we wish to see an oak with its massive trunk and spreading branches and foliage, we are not content to be shown an acorn instead. So too, Science, the crown of a world of Spirit, is not complete in its beginnings" (*PhG* §12). To further develop this metaphor, we might then think of recollected-internalized images as seeds that we carry around with us, ready to plant and cultivate. While philosophy should not be "content" with such images, or mistake such picture-thoughts for concepts, they are nonetheless essential for the growth of such concepts. In turn, just as seeds are not destroyed or abandoned by the growth of the tree, but preserved therein, producing yet more seeds for the development of yet more trees, so these images are recollected and internalized by the development of the concept, which produces in turn more images for the production of more concepts. As Hegel continues, "The seed comes out of the existing determinacies and *returns* to its simplicity, to the existence of being-in-itself again, only in something else, in the seed of the fruit." Intelligence is thus conceived as "the free *existence* of the *being-in-itself* that recollects itself into itself in its development," and "this *in-itself* is the first form of universality that presents itself in representation."⁷⁵ The recollected image founds the universal.

It is surprising that Verene only mentions in passing this systematic articulation of representation, recollection, and the image in his study, dismissing Hegel's presentation of recollection here as merely "a particular moment of intelligence in his account of the psychology of the theoretical mind."⁷⁶ With its discussion of feeling, attention, and intention, this account is perhaps closer to what would become known in the twentieth century as phenomenology, than it is to the phenomenology of Hegel's science of the experience of consciousness. In this section, Hegel is trying to describe the ways in which consciousness and thinking might be developed from the intuitive experience of phenomena from a first-person point of view. However, by generalizing these terms as elaborated in the *Encyclopedia* to the development of absolute knowing—that is, by applying the meanings of these terms "representation," "recollection," and "image" as they are found in the *Encyclopedia* to where they appear in the *Phenomenology*, we find that, pace Verene, Hegel *does* employ *Bild* and *Erinnerung* in the *Phenomenology* as special terms.

Erinnerung exists as a latent concept throughout the body of the *Phenomenology*, but is named just four times, in passing, before the final chapter (§§13, 303, 753, 766). It appears just as many times in the final paragraph alone (§808), its significance developing on each occasion. Hegel announces it to be the organizing principle of the entire preceding narrative.

First: immediately after invoking the "gallery of images" exhibited by spirit's history, Hegel writes: "While its consummation consists in spirit's completely *knowing* what *it is*, in spirit *knowing* its substance, this knowing is its *taking-the-inward-turn* [Insichgehen] in which spirit forsakes its existence and gives its shape over to recollection. In taking-the-inward-turn, spirit is absorbed into the night of its self-consciousness."[77] This moment represents the recognition of spirit's coming-to-be in terms of its "nature"—its *immediate* coming-to-be—as described at the beginning of this chapter. Recollection is introduced here as the initial response of spirit when it stops to look back along the path traveled. In knowing "its substance" to be nothing more than this, and absolute spirit as nothing but the sum of these past mistakes, with agency lost and self forsaken, it gives itself up to introspection and interiority. This inadequate form of recollection—*Insichgehen*, literally a "going-into-oneself"—is thus melancholic, the activity of a beautiful soul. The "night of its self-consciousness" in which spirit then finds itself should be considered strictly analogous to the "nocturnal pit" from the *Encyclopedia*, "in which is stored a world of infinitely many images and representations."

"But," as Hegel continues, "its vanished existence is preserved in that night, and this sublated existence—the existence which was prior but is now newborn from knowing—is the new existence, a new world, and a new shape of spirit.... That *inwardizing re-collection* [Er-Innerung] has preserved that experience; it is what is inner, and it is in fact the higher form of substance."[78] Here, recollection is not, as above, the helpless backward glance; the realization that history happened behind our back and that there's nothing that we can do to change it. It is instead the realization that the recollection of this past, the preserved experience, is something to be learned from. Melancholia turns to mourning. The seed that is recollected in the tree is not finally destroyed but preserved and productive of further seeds and further trees. The preserved past experience produces a "new existence, a new world, a new shape of spirit." This echoes an earlier mention of recollection from the preface: "While the initial appearance of a new world is just the whole enshrouded in its *simplicity*, or its universal ground, still, on the other hand, the wealth of its bygone existence is in recollection still current for consciousness" (*PhG* §13). On first reading, this may seem to profess simply that every novelty preserves within itself the moments of its own history. However, read alongside the account of recollection in the *Encyclopedia Outline*, we can see that, in a speculative sense, "the initial appearance of a new world," "the whole enshrouded in its *simplicity*," *is* this very recollection; the recollected image is at once the seed to be planted from which further thought is developed. The recollection of spirit's past as an image is both a condition and the very existence of its future.

The third and fourth iterations of *Erinnerung* in this paragraph, already quoted, affirm then that it is this power, the power of recollection, that is the path to absolute knowing. Recollection is not just the interiorization of and learning from the past but the act of re-presenting it before us, with and against which thinking can define and refine itself. To repeat:

> The *aim*, absolute knowing, or spirit knowing itself as spirit, has its path in the recollection of spirits as they are in themselves *and* are as they achieve the organization of their realm. Their preservation according to their freestanding existence appearing in the form of contingency is history, but according to their conceptually grasped organization, it is the *science of phenomenal knowing*. Both together are conceptually grasped history; they form the recollection and the Golgotha of absolute spirit [*bilden die Erinnerung und die Schädelstätte des absoluten Geistes*], the actuality, the truth…

Recollection is thus both "preservation" and "organization," both the interiorization and re-presentation of the shapes of spirit as a gallery of images. The *Phenomenology*'s final conjunction of *die Erinnerung und die Schädelstätte* is not an opposition, but an apposition—a speculative identity.

What does it mean to claim this? It means that speculative thinking does not abandon picture-thinking once and for all but finds the function of picture-thinking in relation to the thought of the concept in the activity of recollection. This complicates the commonplace account of the relationship between the *Phenomenology* and the *Logic*; an account which, it must be said, is propagated by Hegel himself: that the *Phenomenology* is the "ladder" to the *Logic* (*PhG* §26), a ladder which, once climbed, to paraphrase Wittgenstein, must be thrown away;[79] that it is a necessary presupposition or introduction to science—necessary if only because, by cataloging and demonstrating all the failed paths to the absolute, it ends by announcing its own superfluity. In truth, neither the sublation of *Vorstellung* into *Denken* nor the succession of the *Phenomenology* by the *Logic* signal the superfluity of picture-thinking nor the total victory and exclusivity of "pure" thought; the former are constantly recollected by the latter by the means of the former, and the latter are forced to repeatedly confront the fact that the former are still implicated. This is a similar point to one made by Comay and Ruda: "In moving from the *Phenomenology* to the *Logic* Hegel does not simply violate the Kantian prohibition: we do not simply step away from appearance to reality, from the phenomena to things in themselves. We rather learn that our propensity to illusion does not derive simply from the deficiencies of natural consciousness but is inscribed in the act of thinking—and therefore in being—as such."[80] What consists in absolute knowing is not finally going beyond illusion (beyond despair, error, *Vorstellung*, or the *Phenomenology*) but in recollecting the necessity of illusion in and as the activity of recollection itself. What these moments suggest is that thinking must choose representation where it wanted purity (appearance where it wanted reality, snakes where it wanted a ladder, pissing when it wanted sex) since by starting with the latter it remains stuck at the starting block and only gets the former; while it is only by going through the former that the latter opens up.

Some Examples

HISTORY

Erinnerung (of, and in the form of *Bildern*) is thus the basis of *Bildung*; it conditions and drives the progress at every stage, even with absolute knowing. This tryptic of *Bildung, Erinnerung,* and *Bild* can be demonstrated with regard to historical consciousness and experience with reference to the passage in the preface where Hegel describes the recollection of the past, which he identifies with the "the history of the cultural formation of the world" (*Bildung der Welt*) as being "sketched in silhouette" (*im Schattenrisse*) (*PhG* §28).[81] Recollected past events are "shapes which spirit has already laid aside," he writes, "fragments of knowing," which have also, at once, become "acquired possession[s]"; they are viewed in an oblique and simplified form, their concrete reality and particularity lost, rendered as an image, a sketched silhouette against which, and with which we define ourselves. Despite being "laid aside," passed over, sublated, they nevertheless "constitute the substance of the individual, or, his inorganic nature"—that is, his history.

Comay beautifully exposits this passage:

> History can be encountered only as spectral, monochromatic, shrouded in shadow—a series of frozen snapshots, fleetingly apprehended (were it not for this acceleration, we would perpetually have to repeat the past in real time), belatedly absorbed. The past presents itself as at once an ephemeral trace to be deciphered and a stony burden that must be metabolized as food for thought (the only safely edible fruit is the inedible or inorganic one)—both shadow and stone. History makes its appearance in the border zone between light and darkness—a shape made visible as a blind spot or absence of illumination. The silhouette is also an image of dismemberment: we engage with history only obliquely and in abbreviation—a series of disembodied facies, viewed in profile, inaccessible to direct frontal encounter.... Silhouettes are both mnemonics and provocations: they are what we ultimately remember of the past, an assortment of textbook summaries, episodic flashback, and coarse reductions; and their lack of subtlety is also what challenges us to revisit this past.[82]

This can be elaborated, again, with reference to Hegel's discussion of the passage from intuition to thought via recollective-representations and images in the *Encyclopedia Outline*, in which he gives a candid judgment of the requisite skills of a good historian. We might expect that a historian should occupy themselves primarily with the wealth of historical nuance and detail. Not so, argues Hegel. The true skill lies in the historian's recollection of the past from their *intuition* of its detail (in the strictly technical senses of these words developed above). "A talented historian," Hegel writes, "has before him in vivid intuition the *whole* of the conditions and events he is to describe; by contrast, one who possesses no talent for the portrayal of history confines himself to individual details and overlooks the substantial."[83] As we shall see in the following chapter, this is the difference between the speculative thinker who rescues the spirit from the letter, and the "letter-bound man" who obsesses over trivialities and pedantries at the expense of the whole.

THE *PHENOMENOLOGY*

This requirement is not just limited to history, Hegel argues. On the contrary, it is "rightly insisted that in all branches of knowledge, and *especially in philosophy* too, one should speak from intuition of the subject-matter."[84] The importance of recollection and images should also be insisted on, therefore, for the experience of reading the *Phenomenology of Spirit*. One can say with some confidence, albeit anecdotally, that what is initially, discursively recollected of the *Phenomenology* in either casual or classroom discussion is not the minutiae of its particular arguments or positions but its gallery of images: the master and the slave, the unhappy consciousness, the beautiful soul, the night in which all cows are black, the chopped head of cabbage and the mouthful of water, the hard-hearted judge, Golgotha, the foaming chalice.

Many of these images function as specific, albeit veiled historical or literary allusions. The famous "night in which, as one says, all cows are black" satirizes the featureless, indifferent identity of the absolute in Schelling's *Naturphilosophie* (*PhG* §16). Others are multireferential, contested, or else, in the words of Drew Milne, "sufficiently general and particular that [they] can generate confident but very different allusions in the eyes of [their] beholders."[85] The master and the slave, for example, refer to French colonizers and Haitian revolutionaries, feudal lords and serfs, God and man, man and wife;[86] the beautiful soul, meanwhile, refers to Shaftesbury, Wieland, Jacobi, Goethe, Novalis, Schlegel, and Jesus.[87] However, while the philological identification of these allusions and their historical contextualization may indeed be enlightening, what is of primary importance is not the empirical or historical referent of these images, but the fact of their being images, for it as images that they are recollected.

This point has been elucidated recently by Žižek, who argues that in order "to properly grasp the dialectical relationship between a concept and its examples, a third term has to be introduced, that of *exemplum*."[88] While Shaftesbury, Novalis, or Schlegel may be examples of those who are subject to Hegel's critique of the purity-obsessed moralist, or else while French colonizers and Haitian revolutionaries, or feudal lords and serfs, may work as empirical case studies (or may even have been inspirations) for Hegel's account of the development of self-consciousness through an asymmetrical struggle for recognition, because of the complex wealth of historical detail that permeate each of these examples, they never properly fit the purity and simplicity of the conceptual thought. This is why an *exemplum* is needed, defined by Žižek as a "fictional singularity which directly gives body to the concept in its purity"[89]—or, as I have shown, what Hegel calls an image. Žižek elaborates this with reference to Hannah Arendt's thesis of the "banality of evil" illustrated by the *exemplum* of Adolf Eichmann.[90] Although the reality—that is, the *example*—of Eichmann does not fit Arendt's thesis (as Žižek notes, "far from a non-thinking bureaucrat just following orders, he was a fanatical anti-Semite fully aware of what he was doing"), this does not undermine it.[91] The truth of a concept is developed from the recollected image, however fictional it may be, and not the empirical external facts.

WORDS

This importance of representation and recollection in the reading of the *Phenomenology* may even be seen at the level of the word: The negative, reflection, withdrawal, emptying out, recoiling, grasping (*begreifen*), advancing and returning, recollecting, even spirit itself, are also initially recollected in their representational, figurative form. After all, as Hegel explicitly states: "Every spiritual content and all relationships generally … are representations; spirit itself is a representation."[92] These concepts are all, at least initially, with their written representation, metaphorical images. As Hegel says in his lectures on aesthetics: "In the first place, every language already contains a mass of metaphors.… *Fassen, begreifen,* and many words, to speak generally, which relate to knowing, have in respect of their literal meaning a purely sensuous content."[93] Even *Aufhebung,* before being grasped conceptually, is first represented in the mind in metaphorically spatial, material terms: to lift up, to rise to the next level, to transcend; to preserve, to suspend; to destroy.

Of course, this is not to say that the gallery of images is all that remains of the *Phenomenology*, with the wealth of its conceptual substance replaced by cartoonish outlines. The master-slave, the beautiful soul, the negative, *begreifen,* spirit, etc. are neither reducible to nor exhausted as images; their images are not the horizon of their being thought. It must be emphasized that Hegel's fundamental concerns remain with *der Begriff* and not *das Bild*. What it does mean, however, is that these *Grundriße* are the initial forms of that which is thought, from and against which the conceptual detail can be elaborated, without which the concept would cease to exist; and that this passage from *das Bild* to *der Begriff* is not one of simple, linear, progressive abstraction but one of constant recollection. Hegel's philosophy is, therefore, no "white mythology," as Derrida describes metaphysics—that which "has erased within itself the fabulous scene that has produced it, the scene that nevertheless remains active and stirring, inscribed in white ink, an invisible design covered over in palimpsest": metaphor, figuration, employed but disavowed.[94] On the contrary, Hegel is fully cognizant of the imaginary origin, or rather the origin in the image, of the concept, not erased, but recollected.

* * *

If, then, "the image" for the young, Romantic Hegel was the beautiful link between truth and goodness; and if the image for the Hegel of the essays on *Faith and Knowledge* and on *Natural Law* was the Kantian synthetic a priori judgment representing the identity of identity and difference; then the image of the *Phenomenology* is the recollected and represented history of spirit as a simplified *shape*, a mnemonic shorthand for a wealth of conceptual detail, with and against which the present spirit can define itself, in order to move beyond itself. It is therefore in the activity of recollection that representation or picture-thinking finds its function in relation to the thought of the concept.

Marx's Imagery: Difficult to Swallow

Perhaps this account of dialectical style, for which conceptual thinking draws upon the powers of representation and figuration for the purposes of recollection, can account for the lurid style of another great dialectician: Karl Marx.

The literary character, poetic energy, and graphic imagery of Marx's work have always proved contentious. While a reading of Louis Althusser would prompt the idea that the style of Marx's *Capital*, for instance, is (at best) inessential ornamentation or (at worst) a deathly distraction from what is essentially "a system of basic scientific concepts" requiring "systematic rigour" to be read properly;[95] a reading of Keston Sutherland would suggest that Marx's style is absolutely essential, as that which explicates and intensifies "the unbearableness and infinite indignity of life under capital."[96] As I have argued elsewhere, I agree with Sutherland on this question.[97] But what Jameson alone (as far as I can tell) has identified, albeit without mentioning its Hegelian provenance, is that Marx's imagery, like Hegel's, always functions as the shorthand end-product of a process of recollection. A "modulation into the figurative," he writes, is "always the sign that Marx's text has risen to a certain consciousness of itself, has reached a height from which for a moment it can look out across the totality of its object and of the system as a whole: the long-term memory of its argument as a whole, rather than the short-term work of its decipherment of detail and of the dynamic of capitalism's internal machinery."[98] This critical style of boiling down and rendering the complexity and specificity of his argument into a reduced simplified form which recollects that which came before is exemplified by and perhaps even analogous to his account of the process of commodification itself, whereby human labor is reduced to "a mere *Gallerte* of undifferentiated labour"[99]—*Gallerte* being not the palatable-because-abstractly-conceptual "congelation" of the official translations but, as Sutherland identifies, the disgusting image of "a 'semi-solid, tremulous' comestible mass, inconvertible back into the 'meat, bone [and] connective tissue' of the various animals used indifferently to produce it."[100] The image of *Gallerte* is intended, as Sutherland argues, "not simply to educate his readers but also to *disgust* them."[101] It is an aesthetic, graphic shorthand which recollects all the previous depersonalized, difficult conceptual detail and argumentation concerning the commodity form and re-presents it as something at once simplified and far harder to swallow. With Marx's *Gallerte*, the Hegelian idea of the image as something which is *er-innert*—recollected and internalized, *consumed*—takes on a gruesome satirical twist.

Grey in Grey; Remembering and Repeating

One of Hegel's most memorable images of all, from the preface to his *Philosophy of Right*, encapsulates this very process, this essential activity of recollection, for thought, via representation: "When philosophy paints its grey in grey, a shape of life has grown old, and it cannot be rejuvenated, but only recognized, by the grey in grey of philosophy; the owl of Minerva begins its flight only with the onset of dusk."[102] As T. M. Knox notes, this metaphor of philosophy's "grey in grey" is an ironic reference to Goethe's *Faust*, in which Mephistopheles rejects the dull abstractions of philosophy in favor of the colorful immediacy and freshness of life: "Grey, dear friend, is all theory, / And green life's golden tree."[103] Philosophy, in contrast to (what Mephistopheles conceives of as) "life," "always comes too late."[104] It cannot, therefore, instruct or advise; it can only recollect, and can only understand after the fact. In recollecting, however, it drives spirit forward. That philosophy paints, not only in grey, but "grey in grey" emphasizes that re-collecting is a form of repetition. Philosophy can offer no pure novelty, no greenery in and of itself; it can only recollect or repeat, literally re-call, that which already is, or rather was. "Grey in grey warns against philosophy's pride of *Sollen* [ought]," Rose writes, "against any proscription or prescription, any imposition of ideals, imaginary communities or 'progressive narrations.' Instead, the 'idealizations' of philosophy would acknowledge and recognize actuality and not force or fantasize it."[105] Philosophy should not, and indeed cannot, provide political activists and militants with an answer to Lenin's famous question: What is to be done? What "is," re-cognized as the identity of identity and nonidentity is what is absolute—not what "ought" to be. It is only after what was coming-to-be has come to be that philosophy can think it; only then can the owl of Minerva begin its flight.

This may seem awfully conservative; an apologia for the status quo and a capitulation to what exists. Indeed, this is the grounds upon which some Marxist and then poststructuralist thinkers have criticized Hegel. Ernst Bloch, for instance, criticizes this notion of recollection as repetition or recapitulation, designating it as that which ensures the closed "magic circle" of Hegel's system, and hence that which precludes its thinking of novelty.

Bloch draws a connection between *Erinnerung* and Plato's concept of *anamnesis*, developed in his *Meno* and *Phaedo* dialogues: the idea that the acquisition and development of knowledge is not one of learning something new but of remembering—the difference being that while for Plato all knowledge is innate and resides in the soul, and to learn is to recollect this knowledge that one has always already had, for Hegel, the *Erinnerung* which drives the *Bildung* of spirit is always a recollection of spirit's historical experience.[106] Bloch writes:

> The Hegelian process of the result, therefore, is within the circle of anamnesis as within a magic circle. Everything here is full of New: however, in every final moment, especially at the end of the circle in general, the newest (in Hegel's gigantic breaking philosophy, and in spite of it) must have always already been the oldest, with its prearranged, preordained, complete beginning. This prevents even the system of development from remaining a system open to development: it is subdued to the First, although the latter is not developed and not consumed, after which it starts. The *restituto in integrum* brings back the *expeditio in novum* with the rope of *epistrophé*.[107]

For Bloch, "everything" in Hegel "is full of New," but because everything new is necessarily recollected from the past, it has always already "grown old." The *Bildung* is plotted from the first so has no *Bildung* of its own. *Erinnerung* as *epistrophé*—repetition and return—thus ensures the restitution of a hypostasized law of the same. Bloch returns to this criticism in the first volume of *The Principle of Hope* (1954), in which, with reference to the same passage from the preface to the *Philosophy of Right*, he complains that "the closed-circuit thinker Hegel, the antiquarium of what is unalterably already existing,... prevailed over the dialectical process-thinker Hegel with his crypto-practice."[108] It is not coincidental that Bloch's critique here appears within the context of a discussion of Marx's "Theses on Feuerbach" (1845); Hegel's recollection only interprets the world, when the point, however, is to change it.[109] Bloch's critique also parallels Heidegger's complaint, referenced in the introduction, that, as a thinker of the past, Hegel has no adequate concept of futurity. As Hegel "speaks about having been but never about the future," he limits his philosophy to a kind of perpetual irrelevance and anachronism.[110]

Derrida and Hamacher have similar worries. For Derrida, Hegel's *Erinnerung* is a symptom of his "irrepressible philosophical desire to summarize-interiorize-dialecticize-master-*relever* the metaphorical division between the origin and itself."[111] For Hamacher, it is "the cultic recollection" by which Hegel the megalomaniac asserts his "mastery,"[112] and lays claim to the "absolute interiorization"[113] of the past; *parousia* and *pleroma*. For both, it is the movement of idealization by which all disparity is swallowed into harmony, all difference into homogenous identity, and all beginnings into their ends—resisted only by the irreducible exteriority and alterity of the letter. Despite his admiration for Hegel as "the first thinker of writing" and "the thinker of irreducible difference," Derrida views the moment of recollection as the eschatological moment of spurious and violent totalization, where the trace of difference (and therefore of writing) is erased. It is, once again, the moment where Hegel "rushes toward the economy of a reconciliation." This is why, Derrida writes, "all that Hegel thought within this horizon, *all, that is, except eschatology*, may be reread as a meditation on writing."[114]

However, and contra Derrida and Hamacher, this *Erinnerung* for Hegel is not simply a final inwardization. It is not an act of voracious consumption without remainder. Nor is it a moment of eschatological or apocalyptic fulfillment. Derrida writes in passing, in a footnote, that *Erinnerung* and *Entäußerung* [recollection and relinquishment], and *Inwendig* and *Auswendig* [inside and outside], are oppositions.[115] Despite the parenthetical nature of this comment, it reveals the key to his prejudice. For Hegel, *Entäußerung* is not opposed to *Erinnerung*, and *Auswendig* not opposed to *Inwendig*. Instead, each is the ironic truth of the other. Each pairing does not form a dichotomy but a dialectic. Just as consumption is followed by excretion, inwardizing-recollection is followed by a relinquishing or kenosis; each depends on the other. This is why each of Hegel's major works finish not with a final interiorization of all remaining objects, with the absolute subject licking the plate clean, but with a dramatic "emptying out"—with the idea, or spirit, relinquished (*entäußerte*) into time: The *Phenomenology* ends with "spirit relinquished into time"—its "kenosis" and self-externalization (*PhG* §808); the *Logic* ends with the idea "*freely discharg*[*ing*] itself"; and the *Encyclopedia Logic* ends with "the absolute *freedom* of the idea" which consists in nothing but a decision. It "*resolves* [entschließt] *to release* freely *from itself* the moment of its particularity."[116]

The specificity of the German word *Entäußerung* is instructive here. While the stem *Äußerung* refers to an expression or utterance, the *Ent-* prefix signifies and enacts both a return and an immanent negation. An *Entäußerung* is thus an utterance which, in spite of being a first utterance, is at once a repetition of that utterance, and a repetition which undoes itself. And this is why an *Entäußerung* is not opposed to an *Erinnerung* but represents its speculative or ironic truth. When spirit recollects and internalizes itself it at once re-presents and externalizes itself in a new shape, and in doing so it "*resolves to release* freely *from itself* the moment of its particularity"—to repeat from the *Encyclopedia Outline*—as the condition of its continuation. *Entäußerung* names the moment when an *Erinnerung* stakes itself and goes to the end to discover its ironic truth—or, to use Hegel's imagery from earlier, it is the moment when spirit plants the seed that it has (re-)collected in order to grow a tree. Again, it is not coincidental that this is the word that Luther used to translate Christ's *kenosis*. As the expression of the concept in its particularity, which is both its undoing and yet the condition of its life, *Entäußerung* finds its ultimate exemplum in God's relinquishing of himself through his incarnation and death as the condition of the life of his (holy) spirit.

Derrida and Hamacher are therefore correct but in a wrong way: particularity and externality *are* that which prevent the system from enacting some final messianic or eschatological mending of all broken middles, but they are also that which render the system open to the future, free, dynamic, moving, alive, "without which it would be lifeless and alone" (*PhG* §808). Spirit's self-relinquishing is the moment of revolutionary resolve (*Entschluß*) where it externalizes itself, stakes itself, and goes to the end to discover again its own ironic truth. This is also correlative to the moment of speculative reading when, after discovering the nonidentity inhering in the identity asserted, the reader resolves not to suspend this difference but to follow it to its end, to rerealize and reassert the truth of the proposition beyond the fetters of the abstract self-identification implied by its propositional form—to realize the spirit of the letter.

This is why, Rose writes (and perhaps with Bloch's kind of Marxian critiques of Hegel in mind, according to which recollecting the world precludes the possibility of changing it), that Hegel's philosophy which paints grey in grey does "not [render philosophy] *ex post facto* justification, even less *a priori* rejuvenation, but reconfiguration, oppositional yet vital — *something understood*."[117] Rose does not explicate by what medium this reconfiguration occurs. I have argued in this chapter that it is re-presentation. Hegel writes that "*die Philosophie ihr Grau in Grau malt*."[118] The verb *malen* here (meaning "to paint," but also "to draw," or "to picture") is yet another artistic image (after the "sketched silhouette" and the "gallery of images") which emphasizes the artificiality of Hegel's *Erinnerung*—its status as an image. It is the "painting" of what is recollected which is the medium of philosophy's "oppositional reconfiguration" with and against which thinking defines and refines itself. The owl's flight signals, then, not only the comprehension of the past but its retroactive representation, which at once sets the conditions for the opening up of the future. As Hegel stresses, spirit does not recollect the shape of life which has grown old in order to renew it: "It cannot be rejuvenated ... by the grey in grey of philosophy." On the contrary, it is only by representing its own past to itself that spirit can risk completing the work of mourning for itself—completing the work of understanding.

Suspicion or Trust?

A surprising comparison that can be made here is with the art of caricature. "In caricature," Hegel says in his lectures on aesthetics, "the specific character is exaggerated and is, as it were, a superfluity of the characteristic." At first, just as a metaphor or allegory initially appears as a distraction of style on the way to thought, the exaggerated nature of the caricature seems excrescent to the truth of its subject. "But," as he goes on, "the superfluity is no longer what is strictly required for the characteristic, but a troublesome repetition whereby the 'characteristic' itself may be made unnatural."[119] The effect of caricature is that it recollects its subject both hyperbolically and superfluously, but in doing so it retroactively renders the truth itself as hyperbolic: "unnatural." From this, perhaps we can begin to account for Hegel's polemical criticisms of Schlegel and Novalis, which, as noted in the previous chapter, are often noted for their lack of both nuance and textual justification. Past *shapes* of spirit, and hence the recollection of past philosophies, for Hegel, are just that: not faithful reconstructions but caricatures; broad shapes and provocative outlines. In painting its grey in grey, philosophy's recollection "troublesomely repeats" what appears to be "natural," but it is only in doing so that it can perform its "oppositional yet vital" "reconfiguration" of actuality, and in doing so move beyond it.

As Comay expounds upon Hegel's phenomenological method: "Hegel illuminates the pathological within the normal. Exaggeration reveals uncomfortable features of experience that would otherwise be invisible."[120] Perhaps this is one reason why Adorno aphorizes in *Minima Moralia* that "in psycho-analysis nothing is true except the exaggerations."[121] What are the dreams, delusions, and neuroses of the analysand if not the recollected-internalized (*er-innerten*), exaggerated images of their repressed past life, "preserved unconsciously" in "the nocturnal pit" of the unconscious mind, to be then brought to speech and externalized (*entäußert*), in order to get over them? Again, an *Ent-Äußerung* is an "utterance" which moves beyond itself only by returning itself, just as the process of analysis, for Freud, is a process of *Durcharbeiten* via *Erinnern* and *Wiederholen*—of "working through" by recollecting and repeating.[122]

In one sense, this resonates with Malabou's insight that Hegel is a philosopher of simplification. In spite of what is perhaps the most common prejudice about his writing—that it is unrelentingly and perhaps unnecessarily difficult—Malabou claims that everything in Hegel's thought tends toward radical simplification and abbreviation. Dialectical simplification, Malabou argues, is the means by which spirit both accounts for its own history and moves beyond it; that is (although Malabou does not use this terminology), it is the means by which spirit repeatedly recollects and relinquishes itself. Every sublation or *Aufhebung* can thus "be interpreted as a labour of speculative mourning"[123]—as a work of both systematic and selective memory which works through its own past and gives it specific determination and meaning; which reduces the multiplicity and complexity of a past stage of spirit to a singular, distinctive characteristic: what Hegel calls its shape, or *Gestalt*. It is for this reason, according to Malabou, that *der Grundriß*—that is, the précis, abridgment, plan, sketch, or outline—is paradoxically "the best and most appropriate format for a work of philosophy."[124] This is why "Hegel's *Encyclopedia*" is actually an *Enzyklopädie der philosophischen Wissenschaften im Grundrisse*—an *Encyclopedia of the Philosophical Sciences in Basic Outline*—an important point which is often overlooked due to the conventional shorthand (i.e., "Hegel's *Encyclopedia*"). As Hegel himself writes in the preface to the first edition, the philosophical genre of "an outline" offers "a new reworking of philosophy according to a method that will someday be recognized … as the only true method, identical with the content."[125] Hegel's *Encyclopedia Outline* is an abridgment or summary of an encyclopedia for which there is no ur-text.

Where my account differs from Malabou, however, is that she argues that the work of simplification for Hegel is always one of abstraction, whereby a thing is stripped of its sensuous form and reduced to its purely logical content: "Simplification takes the *sensuous configuration* of existence and reduces it. It shapes the figure (*Gestalt*) into an abbreviated form-determination (*Formbestimmung*), which is made of logical essentiality."[126] In the *Phenomenology*, however, as demonstrated, one finds a different version of simplification whereby that which is thought through or passed over, sublated, is then recollected, internalized, and re-presented as a series of picture-thoughts—a "gallery of images"—a new shape from which further thoughts can develop. This is why, in the *Phenomenology*, the shapes of spirit are not merely abstracted into a purely logical schema but presented as a series of caricatured dramatis personae: the master and the slave, the unhappy consciousness, the beautiful soul, the hard-hearted judge, and so on.

My account of recollection differs more starkly, however, from Brandom's. For Brandom, Hegel's "*Erinnerung* rationally reconstructs the experiential past into an expressive genealogy of a Whiggish history."[127] For such a history, "each step is necessary, not in the prospective sense that things could not have happened otherwise … but in the retrospective"—

and, perhaps, rather banal—"sense that if they had *not* happened, some aspect of what the story claims was all along implicit would not have become explicit."[128] He argues that "retrospective reconstrual and retroactive recontexting"—that is, recollection—"is reason's march through history."[129] Developing from Brandom's own terminology, this could be described as a *de re* historiography. Rather than understanding the past on its own terms, *de dicto*, Hegelian recollection reconstructs the past both in light of the present—conceived apparently a priori as the highest rational achievement yet—and as the present's condition of possibility. Crucially, then, recollection for Brandom's Hegel is always reparative; it is always a labor of forgiveness. In his own words: "When recognition takes the magnanimous form of recollection, it is forgiveness, the attitude that institutes normativity as fully self-conscious of *trust*."[130] The errors of history—defined by Brandom as our failed individual and institutional attempts to develop determinately conceptual norms and semantic relations—are redeemed and forgiven by an act of recollection which locates in each of them a moment of rational truth which helped us on the way to where we are now. The rational kernel is "recollected" from the irrational husk. This is the "spirit of trust" of Brandom's title: Hegel, for Brandom, entrusts "the next generation to do for its time what he has done for his: to take on the forgiving recollective labor of explication that makes a rational history."[131] This, Brandom argues, is the labor of the *Phenomenology*: to make "the case that nothing is for nothing, that all things happen for the best."[132]

If Hegel's *Phenomenology* did make this case, it would not take a reader of Adorno to realize its total inadequacy when tasked with accounting for or recollecting the horrors of the twentieth century (from the Holocaust to the failures of state socialism), or the still unfolding horrors of the twenty-first (from the destruction of Gaza to the destruction of the planet)—not to mention the horrors of slavery, torture, discrimination, and genocide which persist throughout human history.[133] It is not surprising, then, that Brandom does not make substantial reference to one historical event in the eight hundred pages of his book. Perhaps anticipating such a riposte, however, he concedes euphemistically that there may be "strains" in any "recollective undertaking": elements "that can*not* be smoothly, successfully, or convincingly given a satisfactory norm-responsive explanation. Indeed. But," he continues, "we must now ask: Whose fault is it that the doing, or some aspect of it, is unforgivable—the doer or the forgiver? Is the failure that of the bad agent or of the bad recollector? Is whose fault it is a matter of how things anyway just are? Or is it at least partly reflective of the recollector's failure to come up with a more norm-responsive narrative?"[134] We should therefore, Brandom argues, "acknowledge at least equal responsibility on the part of the unsuccessful forgiver."[135] To use a particularly "strenuous" example, does this mean that, for Brandom, the only reason we cannot forgive Hitler is because we are yet to develop a "satisfactory norm-responsive explanation" for his positive role in world history, and that we are at least equally responsible for the horrors committed in his name for our inability to reconcile them with a Whiggish history of unending progress?

Forgiving recollection as Brandom conceives of it is not "the meaning of working through the past" (to use Adorno's phrase),[136] but (to use Brandom's own words against him) mere "semantics with an edifying intent."[137] (He must have forgotten Hegel's caution in the preface: "Philosophy must beware of the wish to be edifying" [*PhG* §9].) The source of Brandom's error is that, like Derrida (albeit with a favorable emphasis), he views the moment of *Erinnerung* as the eschatological "rush toward the economy of a reconciliation that causes the wrong itself to be simply forgotten or annihilated"; and as opposed to the moment of *Entäußerung* that posits that which is recollected in a new shape, not so it can be accommodated or stomached, but precisely in order for it to begin to be moved beyond. What is at stake is, for an example, the question whether we forgivingly recollect and commemorate Edward Colston as a generous philanthropist and benefactor, whose engagement with the slave trade was an unfortunate excess; or else whether we recollect him as a monstrous personification of capital, responsible for the theft, abuse, and extinction of thousands of Black lives.[138] By overlooking the re-presentative and relinquishing *telos* of recollection, then, Brandom also overlooks that recollection is both radically uncertain, and radically committed. It *may* be redemptive and forgiving, realizing the unintended truth or spirit of the past in the present through an act of fidelity (as Hegel realized the spirit of Luther, as I will argue in the following chapter); but it may also be radically damning, critical, and unfaithful (as we saw with Hegel's acerbic reaction to the Jena Romantics). Recollection, then, is always the name for reinterpretation, for rereading—for a rereading which is a site of commitment and heated contestation, and thus of continually renewed meaning.

If there is a "spirit of trust" at all in Hegel, it refers to the trust required to follow the internal movement of the dialectic to its apogee, to realize its ironic truth, to discover what happens when we resolve to bring abstraction to concretion, and immediacy to mediation. It is not, though, the vulgar "Leibnizian optimism" that trusts that "all things happen for the best."[139] On the contrary, the dialectic demands our trust in spite of the fact that, if we can anticipate anything at all—with whatever we posit, or take to be the case, or do—we are bound to learn through an ever-painful experience that we meant something other than we meant to mean, an experience which compels us to go back and repeat (*PhG* §63). The spirit will exceed the letter. Recollection is, then, the critical moment where we return to spirit's coming-to-be and represent it as a gallery of images—each image singular, exemplary, reductive, hyperbolic; possibly forgiving, possibly passionately hateful—from which we can risk thought and action, and relinquish ourselves once again.

The Spirit and the Letter [CHAPTER THREE]
Or A Series of Letters concerning
the Spirit and the Letter within
Hegel's Philosophy

It should already be clear that Hegel has an obstinate commitment to the spirit over the letter. Even apart from spirit or *Geist* in the technically Hegelian sense of the word, he always has an eye for the overall spirit or ethos of something against the specificity of its particular details. As demonstrated in the previous chapter, speculative thinking's activity of recollection, for Hegel, is reductive to the point of caricature and often presents little if any interest in nuance or fidelity to any supposed original meaning or intention. It does not confine itself to specifics but has before it the vivid intuition of the whole.[1] Historical phenomena and past stages of spirit are rendered not in their wealth of empirical minutiae but "sketched in silhouette" (*PhG* §28); Hegel's historiographical shapes of spirit do not represent past epochs merely "as they were"—that is, "to the letter"—but in broad and provocative outline. This does not suggest a willful interpretative laziness or violence but instead epitomizes Hegel's phenomenological "methodless method," which consists merely in following the path of any position to its disavowed extremes; in illuminating "the pathological in the normal";[2] in distinguishing the ironic truth or "spirit" of something from the false integrity of its "letter." It represents a firmly held conviction in the triviality, pedantry, and tyranny of literalization. Hegel is thus a firm adherent to St. Paul's dictum: "The letter kills, but the Spirit gives life"; or "*der Buchstabe tötet, aber der Geist macht lebendig,*" in Luther's German.[3]

John Smith refers to this idea of "the spirit and the letter" with reference to Hegel's philosophy throughout his book on the influence of classical rhetoric on Hegel's notion of philosophical representation but only as a pun—exploiting the fact that the idiom "the spirit and the letter" includes a key word from Hegel's philosophical vocabulary (that is, of course, "spirit").[4] Smith does not, then, refer to the ubiquity of the phrase "the spirit and the letter" in the discourse of nineteenth-century German philosophy (especially in the works of Fichte), as well as in biblical hermeneutics, nor to its origins in Pauline Christianity, nor to Hegel's explicit invocations of this phrase throughout his lectures and correspondence. Frederick Beiser, Terry Pinkard, and Paul Franks all refer in their surveys of German Idealism to Reinhold and Fichte's distinction between what they both called the spirit and the letter of Kant's philosophy, but what remains to be emphasized in particular is how it was through this motif that philosophers from Kant to Hegel articulated both their own methods of interpretation, cultural and political critique, and their own self-understanding.[5]

To take perhaps the most obvious example of such an invocation, in the introduction to his 1827 lectures on the philosophy of religion, Hegel attacks all interpretations of the Bible which begin from their own presuppositions. Such "argumentative thinking," he argues, "makes some assumption or other, and proceeds according to the relationships of the understanding [employed in the kind] of reflection that we have developed within us through our education, without any criticism of these relationships."[6] Hegel continues: The problem with such a hermeneutics is that it "involves assumptions, which themselves can be called in question." As such it operates "according to caprice and chance" and not according to necessity—that is, it does not operate according to the necessity of the immanent movement of the dialectic.[7] Such a capricious and subjective hermeneutics nonetheless frequently makes spurious claims to necessity when it comes to the Bible, on the merit that that which it interprets is supposedly infallible. In Hegel's words, "the argumentative theology of the Christian church pretends nevertheless to possess a firm footing, asserting, 'For us the firm footing is the Bible, it is the words of the Bible.'" It is here that Hegel invokes St Paul's maxim from 2 Corinthians 3:6:

> But against this one can quote the essential sense of the text, "the letter kills [*der Buchstabe tötet*]," etc. One does not take the words [of the Bible] as they stand, because what is understood by the biblical "words" is not words or letters as such but the spirit with which they are grasped. For we know historically that quite opposite dogmas have been derived from these words, that the most contrasting viewpoints have been elicited from the letter of the text because the spirit did not grasp it. In these instances appeal was to the letter, but the genuine ground is the spirit.[8]

The present chapter will elaborate this dialectic between the spirit and the letter as it is developed throughout Hegel's work. It is a dialectic which he frequently and anxiously returns to, sometimes explicitly, sometimes more obliquely. In what follows I offer first a chronological account of the dialectic's development across Hegel's work, drawing from both major works and letters (*Briefe*), from the period of his early theological writings to that of the *Science of Logic*, as well as from Kant and Fichte. I will then argue that Hegel inherited and developed his mature conception of the spirit and the letter from the theology and biblical hermeneutics of Martin Luther, an inheritance and development which, in turn, is emblematic of this relationship between the spirit and its letter—that is, Hegel realized the spirit of Luther.

Letters against Letter-Bound Thinking

In an early letter to Schelling from April 16, 1795, Hegel draws a connection between biblical literalism and political despotism: "Religion and politics have joined hands in the *same* underhanded game. The former has taught what despotism willed: contempt for the human race, its incapacity for any good whatsoever, its incapacity to be something on its own." In this letter, Hegel argues that the German church has betrayed its Lutheran roots with a dogmatic insistence upon the letter of the Bible against its higher spiritual meaning and the authority of the church against the autonomy of the believers. This religious prescriptivism, whereby the faithful are instructed on the meaning of scripture, rather than being granted with the freedom to interpret it for themselves, has resulted in turn in a supposedly secularized culture of political submissiveness and critical apathy. However, Hegel continues: "With the spread of ideas as to how everything *ought* to be"—the emphasis is his—"the indolence that marks people set in their ways, who always take everything the way it is, will disappear." (*Mit Verbreitung der Ideen, wie Alles sein soll, wird die Indolenz der gesezten Leute, ewig alles zu nehmen, wie es ist, verschwinden*).[9] The word "ought" here is playfully ironic. "The spread of ideas as to how everything *ought* to be," for the young Hegel, consists in the spread of ideas that are freely and independently thought, without the imposition or mediation of an external authority—without the tyranny of any "ought" at all. The category of "how everything ought to be" has no presupposed content but consists only in that which is self-determined, self-actualized, and self-legitimated. It is that which has developed within itself according to necessity, its content being its own legitimation. Of course, while the *letter* of the Kantian "ought" does not entail such imposition or authority but, on the contrary, the theoretical and practical freedom of the rational agent—who is commanded only that one ought to be better simply because one can be[10]—Hegel, as we shall later see, is concerned with exorcising Kantianism's disavowed imperious *spirit*.

This argument regarding the letter and spirit of Christianity and their analogs in law and freedom finds a more developed articulation in Hegel's early theological essays. Indeed, the titles of his most famous writings from this period correspond to the two sides of this dialectical coin: "The Positivity of the Christian Religion" refers to the historical realization of Christianity grounded in the external authority of rules imposed by clergy (i.e., a Christianity of the letter); while "The Spirit of Christianity" refers to the religion's higher truth, grounded in love, and realized only by the free spirit of the community of believers. In the first of these essays, he identifies "the fundamental error at the bottom of a church's entire system"—namely, "that it ignores the rights pertaining to every faculty of the human mind, in particular to the chief of them, reason. Once the church's system ignores reason, it can be nothing save a system which despises man."[11] In building a church grounded upon external authority—that is, in the letter of the law, as opposed to the free spirit of human reason—it undermines the being of humanity itself; and this finds its political corollary in humanity's actual subjugation.

Hegel derives this term "positive" from the jargon of jurisprudence. While positive *law* describes the set of manmade laws in any given legal or political community (as opposed to natural law, which constitutes the inherent laws of God, reason, or nature, which underly any historically or locally particular legal construction), positive *religion* refers disparagingly to any doctrinal religion whose normative power depends merely on the fact of its being established. In both cases, "positivity" is that which relies on the dictates of authority and normativity, and not those of reason.

In both of these early theological writings, Hegel rehearses various tropes of Lutheran antisemitism by blaming this positive legalism on the insidious persistence of Christianity's Jewish prehistory—"the Jews" being a people "overwhelmed by statutory commands which pedantically prescribed a rule for every casual action of daily life," whereby "the holiest things, namely, the service of God and virtue, was ordered and compressed in dead formulas," with life reduced to "a monkish preoccupation with petty, mechanical, spiritless, and trivial usages." While "the letter which kills" is not explicitly mentioned here, Hegel finds everything in common between it and (his antisemitic conception of) Judaism: its legalism, its pedantry, its prescription, its defilement of the sacred, its sacralizing of the material. Both have a tendency toward the formulaic, the mechanistic, the trivial, and the dead.[12]

In turn, from religion and politics to philosophy, Hegel finds an analog of Judaism's letter-legalism in Kant. Hegel argues that the commandment to "'Love God above everything and thy neighbor as thyself' was quite wrongly regarded by Kant as a 'command requiring respect for a law which commands love.'"[13] In positing love as a duty commanded by law, a law requiring imposition and implying opposition, love loses any semblance of being love at all. In Kant's hands, love to the letter and of the letter becomes an unattainable ideal commanded by an unknowable superego that sadistically enjoys the subject's unremitting failure to meet its demands. While Kant appears to elevate ethics above any prescribed dogma, leaving the interpretation of the one categorical imperative to the autonomy of human reason, the unwitting truth of the Kantian "ought" constitutes in fact the coldest, most abstract, and unknowable terrorism—a manifestation of the law at its most severe, extirpated of all sensuousness, particularity, and desire.

Adorno and Horkheimer would follow this logic to its end to find the ironic truth of Kant in Sade.[14] Such readings epitomize Hegel's reading for the spirit against the letter. Once again, we can see that reading for the spirit against the letter does not necessarily suggest an interpretative violence or manipulation but rather a resistance against the arrogated authority of the letter itself. As Comay writes: "Hegel's critique of Kant is merciless and unremitting.... The accuracy of this reading is not the issue here: it's clumsy and can be mean-spirited, and is meant to appear so."[15]

* * *

In another letter to Schelling, written a few months later on the August 30, Hegel is even more explicit in his favor for the spirit over the letter, directly invoking this Pauline distinction:

> What I might write concerning your dissertation [*De Marcione*] would serve to bear witness to my joy over the free spirit of higher criticism which holds sway in it, a spirit uncorrupted—as I could only expect from you—by the venerability of names. It is a spirit which keeps the whole in view, and which does not sacralize words. And I would also compliment your perspicacity and learnedness. I have at once found confirmation in it of a suspicion I have harbored for a long time, namely, that it would perhaps have done more credit to us and mankind if some heresy, no matter which, damned by councils and creeds, had risen to become the public system of belief, instead of the orthodox system maintaining the upper hand.[16]

In this passage, "names" are singled out as epitomizing the violence of "the letter": irreducibly particular, synoptic, and arbitrary; given, but also alterable; they spuriously fix and determine their referent, and obstruct and corrupt any development and any vision of the bigger picture: of the spirit.[17] Orthodoxy and heresy, for Hegel, therefore, must swap places: that which is orthodox is in fact the most profound heresy, while that which is heretical to orthodoxy, to the accepted opinion of "councils and creeds," should be raised to "the public system of belief." Hegel's point is not that we need a new orthodoxy to replace the old one but rather that the only true orthodoxy (literally, "sound doctrine") is the one that resists stasis absolutely, distinguishes its spirit from its letter, and moves beyond itself. That which *remains* true to orthodoxy, cannot be true at all. This is the case with Hegel's philosophy, everywhere: in order to be what it is, spirit, the concept itself, must change.

It is not at all incidental, therefore, that the dissertation of Schelling's which Hegel praises so much, his 1795 *De Marcione Paullinarum epistolarum emendatore*, is a study of Marcion of Sinope's emendations of St. Paul's epistles—emendations which attempt to render the spirit of the epistles against their letter, and, even more crucially, epistles in which this spirit-letter distinction was first made.[18] This preoccupation with religious emendation persists throughout Schelling's work. For example, as he would go on to say in a later lecture on the study of theology:

> The earliest books on the history and doctrines of Christianity are merely a particular—and, moreover, imperfect—manifestation of it; its idea is not to be sought in these books whose value is to be measured by the extent to which they express this idea and are in consonance with it. Already for St. Paul, the proselytizer of the Gentiles, Christianity had become something different from what it was for its founder. We must not stop at any arbitrarily chosen point of time; we must have the whole of history and the world that has produced Christianity before our eyes.
>
> One of the operations of the modern pseudo-enlightenment—which, with respect to Christianity, might rather be called a dis-enlightenment—is the attempt to "restore" it, as the saying goes, to its "original" meaning, to its early simplicity, in which form it is sometimes referred to as "primitive" Christianity. One might have thought that Christian teachers would have been grateful to later ages for having extracted so much speculative matter from the meagre contents of the earliest religious books and for having drawn it up in a system. To be sure, it may be easier to talk about the scholastic chaos of the old dogmatism, to write popular treatises and to indulge in hairsplitting and playing with etymologies than to grasp the universal import of Christianity and its teachings.[19]

From its very inception, an essential component of Christianity is that it must move beyond itself; from Christ to Paul to Marcion (to Augustine to Luther to Hegel), the spirit of Christianity is always in a process of realization, necessarily becoming something other than itself in order to be truly what it is. The dogmatic fixity of the letter, of origins, of orthodoxy, of law, "kills"; the spirit, meanwhile, is always developing and moving forward, generating further truth from truth: it is the very life it gives.

Meanwhile—to return to the letter above—as Hegel immediately goes on to despair at Fichte's enjoyment of his own celebrity, he despairs even more at the pedantry and sophistry of his "letter-bound" readers: "Fichte grieves me. Beer glasses and swordplay of ancient student custom [*Landsväterdegen*] have withstood the power of his spirit. Perhaps he would have accomplished more had he left them to their coarseness and aimed merely at drawing to himself a small, quiet, select group. Yet his and Schiller's treatment at the hands of would-be philosophers [*seinwollenden Philosophen*] is still shameful. My God, what letter-bound men [*Buchstabenmenschen*], what slaves, still number among them!"[20] Fichte has been seduced by the archaic rituals and customs of university life, in spite of "the power of his spirit." But even worse, his spirit has been further depleted by so-called *Buchstabenmenschen*, those who have confined and bound themselves to the letter; supercilious pedants who nit-pick at the particular details and phraseology of Fichte's works and those he draws upon (namely Kant's critiques), who do so at the expense of grasping their overall truth, their spirit.

This particular invocation of the spirit-letter distinction is not only used with reference to Fichte but is itself Fichtean. From his 1794 lectures "Concerning the Difference between the Spirit and the Letter in Philosophy" onwards, the spirit and the letter became one of the governing dichotomies of Fichte's work. The following year he also wrote the ironically titled "Series of Letters concerning the Spirit and the Letter within Philosophy" (which he published in 1800). In particular, Fichte characterized his own philosophy, including his major 1794 *Wissenschaftslehre*, as a radicalization of Kant's, pushing the critiques to extremes not legible when reading to the letter but which nevertheless remain true to the Kantian spirit. In his own words: "He does Kant little *honour* who has not noticed in the whole contour and execution of his writing that he would impart to us not his *letter* but rather his *spirit*; and still less does he *thank* him."[21] For instance, while Kant argues that knowledge is epistemically limited to phenomenal objects of consciousness, and can make no claims about things in-themselves, Fichte claims that Kant unwittingly overcomes these limits when he posits a causal relation between things in-themselves and their appearances. Similarly, while Kant argues that God and freedom can be established via practical reason, as a necessary condition of moral agency, Fichte, consistent with this spirit, claims that the same can be said of reality itself. Positioning himself as the philosopher most true to the Kantian spirit, Fichte reserves his most polemical ire for those Kantian dogmatists who defend the critiques to the Kantian letter. Again, the most heretical Kantian is the most orthodox; the most orthodox Kantian, the most heretical. If the facts of consciousness and the faculties can ever be known to the letter, Fichte writes with bitter sarcasm, perhaps they "will finally be revealed by the anatomist's knife and pickled in alcohol, enabling our descendants to mail each other pieces of well-preserved understanding or half a dozen categories?"[22] Declining the dissected and pickled Kant on offer, Fichte was concerned with what could keep Kantianism actually alive and moving.[23]

Jacobi is the missing figure here, between Kant and Fichte, for first recognizing the ironic truth and unintended consequences of the Kantian philosophy—that is, its spirit against its letter. "The transcendental idealist must have the courage, therefore, to assert the strongest idealism that was ever professed, and not be afraid of the objection of speculative egoism, for it is impossible for him to pretend to stay within his system if he tries to repel from himself even just this last objection."[24] For Jacobi, Kant's transcendental idealism taken to its end necessitates a pure egoism: a total forgoing of the knowledge of any other minds or of external reality, which amounts to a denial of any thing in-itself. We can never know anything except our own minds. The key difference between Jacobi and Fichte is that Jacobi did not endorse this position but merely presented it as an epitome of the nonsensical places that unchecked speculation can take us, and, more precisely, the nonsensical core of Kant's critical philosophy. He distinguished the spirit from the letter, only to reject the both of them. For Jacobi, transcendental idealism represented the most "*absolute and unqualified ignorance*."[25] Fichte, meanwhile, fully assumed what he took to be the consequences of the Kantian event, not (as Jacobi argued) the radical solipsism of the empirical "I," but instead the self-positing of the absolute ego in the rational community.[26]

Indeed, Kant himself passionately resented this revisionism, publishing a polemical open letter to ex-friends such as Fichte and fellow Kantian heretic Jakob Sigismund Beck—a letter in which he insists that the *Critique of Pure Reason* says exactly what it means to, that he should know best because he wrote it, and that to look for a "spirit" of the work opposed to its "letter" is not only unnecessary, but betrayal:

> Since, finally, the reviewer [of Johann Gottlieb Buhle's *Entwurf der Transcendental-Philosophie*] maintains that the *Critique* is not to be taken *literally* with respect to what it teaches about sensibility and that, instead, anyone who wants to understand the *Critique* must first master the requisite (Beckian or Fichtean) *standpoint*, because the *Kantian* letter, just like the Aristotelian one, will kill the spirit, I therefore hereby declare that the

Critique is to be understood according to the letter and is to be considered merely from the standpoint of common understanding, insofar as it has been sufficiently cultivated to such abstract investigations.

There is an Italian proverb: "May God protect us only from our friends, we'll keep watch over our enemies ourselves." There are indeed well-meaning friends who are well disposed toward us but get everything reversed (clumsy) in the choice of the means that favour our ends; but there are also deceptive, cunning so-called friends who aim for our ruin and yet use the language of well-wishing (*aliud lingua promptum, aliud pectore inclusum genere* [who say one thing and have in their hearts another]). Before these so-called friends and their carefully laid traps one cannot be too well guarded.[27]

It is interesting to note that Kant's theorization of authorship and authority here is markedly different to the modesty he displays in the preface to the first edition of his *Critique of Pure Reason*, where he professes that "it is appropriate for an author only to present the grounds, but not to judge about their effect on his judges."[28] In this letter, by contrast, Kant seems eager to police his own reception.

To read such a letter as evidence of Fichte's error, however, is to miss the point. For Fichte, such bitter objections from Kant are not merely of little importance; in fact, and on the contrary, they represent the greatest triumph: the test of the truth of the Kantian spirit is that Kant himself should reject it. With his desperate "I therefore hereby declare," Kant positions himself as an exasperated parent lecturing a disobedient child, resorting to the infamous "Because I say so!"—a declaration of unquestionable authority which already bears the mark of its own impotence. In doing so, Kant not only defends but embodies the letter and, or of, the law. The mask of Kantianism slips, and laid bare is the disavowed tyranny of its categorical imperative, whose source of authority remains a mystery, unaddressed and unaddressable, a tautology of infinite regress: "I therefore hereby declare because I declare because I declare." But also laid bare is the letter's impotence in the face of its spirit, a spirit untethered from its point of origin. Kant's defense of his letter against his spirit only serves to embolden the spirit's resolve. His own Copernican revolution is thus no exception to the rule that, like Saturn, the revolution devours its children.

Fichte argues, therefore, that a freedom and spontaneity of interpretative, creative spirit is a prerequisite for the post-Kantian philosopher; they must demonstrate an aesthetic, even an artistic sensibility—a sensibility which is posited as spirit itself: "The philosopher has to possess an aesthetic sense, i.e. 'spirit,' (for without this he will not succeed in raising himself to the transcendental viewpoint). This does not mean that the philosopher must necessarily be a poet or a fine writer or an accomplished orator, but he must be animated by the same spirit that, when cultivated, serves to develop one aesthetically. Without this spirit one will never make any headway in philosophy, but will trouble oneself with the letters of the same without penetrating its inner (spirit)."[29] By discerning the distinction between the spirit and the letter within philosophy, Fichte thought, all prejudices and misunderstandings about the nature and function of philosophy may by overcome.[30] Crucially, he recognized that the spirit-letter distinction would have to be made with respect to his own philosophy—all future readers of Fichte would have to distinguish the spirit from his own letter, to render its universality from its particular form:

> Previously [he writes of his *Wissenschaftslehre*] I feared that, for better or for worse, I would have to bequeath my system to some future age which might be able to understand it, and that I would be forced to hand it down in the dead letters of that particular form in which it first present itself to me. But now I can embrace the solid hope of gaining agreement and advice even from my own contemporaries—the hope of seeing my system assume a universal form through the shared labour of many persons and the hope of bequeathing it as something living within the spirit and the manner of thinking of my age.[31]

This steadfastness against the temptations of the letter, whose inertia threatens to anesthetize thought, is the quality that Hegel most celebrates in Fichte, as he writes in his preface to the essay on the *Difference Between Schelling's and Fichte's Systems of Philosophy*: "The Kantian philosophy needed to have its spirit distinguished from its letter, and to have its purely speculative principle lifted out of the remainder that belonged to, or could be used for, the arguments of reflection. In the principle of the deduction of the categories Kant's philosophy is authentic idealism; and it is this principle that Fichte extracted in a purer, stricter form and called the spirit of Kantian philosophy."[32] For Hegel, Fichte's discernment of the core truths of Kant's philosophy from its letter—conceived as its textual presentation, the apparent authorial intentions, and its status as a fixed or positive doctrine—was the kick start needed to move German philosophy after Kant beyond itself. Indeed, as we saw in the previous chapter, Hegel himself undertook a similar enterprise of distinguishing the Kantian spirit from its letter in his essay on *Faith and Knowledge*, by explicating what Kant could not admit—namely, that the a priori synthesis is the pure image which expresses the identity and difference of the absolute, of ontology and theology. Therefore, while critics have noted Hegel's "self-serving interpretation" of Fichte,[33] and while there are important differences between Hegel's and Fichte's conceptions of the spirit-letter distinction and its import for philosophy, which I demonstrate below, it has been overlooked that Hegel has developed this method of interpretation, in part, from Fichte himself.

* * *

As an aside (although in keeping with the chronological account), it is interesting to note that in the later 1807 *Phenomenology*, Catholicism, as much as Judaism, occupies the place of the letter and literalism against the free spirit of revealed religion. This may seem counterintuitive given Catholicism's affirmation of mystery as a doctrine of faith, its use of symbolism and ritual, its basis in a developing and deepening sacred tradition, and its corresponding rejection of the doctrine of *sola scriptura* (the sole infallible authority of the Bible for faith and practice). It would be easy to present Protestantism, on the contrary, with its belief in the absolute material sufficiency and perspicuity of scripture, as a more obviously letter-bound form of Christianity. (I will return to this latter point in more detail with my discussion of Hegel's Lutheranism, below.) However, in his account of the unhappy consciousness, Hegel finds medieval Catholicism to be the most stupidly literal form of Christianity precisely because of this mystery, rituality, and tradition.

The unhappy consciousness, of which Catholicism is an instance, is the subject who is painfully and unhappily aware of the gulf that separates it as a finite individual from "the unchangeable" (i.e., God)—the unchangeable that, in its being-for-unhappy-consciousness "is only the *alien* essence passing sentence on it" (*PhG* §210). In contrast with spirit's preceding dramatis persona as the ataraxic skeptic, the happy relativist who finds a certain freedom in appearances, in "the multifarious shapes of life" (*PhG* §202), the unhappy consciousness cannot bear this uncertainty, and therefore commits to a blind devotion to this alien being. It seeks communion with this God, through prayers, rituals, and music, while at the same time professing its impossibility. "It only, so to speak, launches itself *in the direction* of thinking, and on that path it becomes *devotion [an das Denken hin und ist Andacht]*. As such, its thinking remains that of the shapeless roar of the pealing of bells, or that of a warm, all-suffusing vapor, or that of a musical thinking which does not amount to concepts, which themselves would be the sole, immanent, objective mode of thinking" (*PhG* §217).[34] As Stefania Achella has noted, Hegel's wordplay in the German serves to underscore the links between prayer, commemoration, devotion, and the failure to think. "The unhappy consciousness, as pure consciousness, tries to move toward thought, '*an* das Denken *hin*,' without however succeeding because, in its attitude of devotion (*Andacht*), it appeals to commemoration (*Andenken*)."[35] Consciousness believes (or acts *as if* it believes) it can reconnect with the lost, alien object of its worship by exciting the senses—but this, Hegel writes, is "only the struggle over an endeavor that must end in defeat" (*PhG* §217).

Paradoxically, this air of mystery and obscurity already betrays, for Hegel, a blind, desperate literalism. The Catholic's chasing after relics of the dead, canonization of the dead, and rote recitation of musical yet meaningless (at least to the reciter) syllables in Latin (the language of the dead), together demonstrate an "infinite *longing*" for the immediate sense-certainty promised but always denied by the literal (*PhG* §217). In the words of Comay: "The obsession with relics demonstrates the literalism of all melancholy; the thirst for tangible sensuous immediacy confirms the intractable remoteness of the object of desire."[36] While Hegel does not associate Catholicism, in this instance, with the legalism that he ascribes to Judaism, it represents what Rose might call an "aberrated mourning" for such a legalism,[37] fetishistically replacing the terminally lost object with whatever relics of "morbid remembrance" it can get its hands on.[38] It is a suspended, melancholic, and therefore insufficient *Erinnerung*. Thus, although a literalism without a letter, medieval Catholicism is not, for Hegel, any less literal-minded. On the contrary, through its desperate attempts to hide from itself the empty tomb by cluttering it with more and more *things*, it only succeeds in drawing attention to the structural emptiness that afflicts all letter-bound thinking. It yearns for "an object of immediate sense-certainty" and "for that reason, it thus turns out only to be the kind of thing that has vanished. For consciousness, what can thus be for it at the present time can only be the *grave* of its life" (*PhG* §217).[39]

* * *

In a later letter to Niethammer, on October 23, 1812, contemporaneous with the publication of the first part of the *Science of Logic*, Hegel repeats his position contra the letter, with more specific reference to textual criticism.

> Philology is becoming so erudite and is tending to mere word-learning. The Church Fathers, Luther, and the preachers of old quoted, interpreted, and manipulated the biblical texts with a freedom which, as regards historical scholarship, was for the most part devoid of scruples so long as they could thus read all the more instruction and edification into the texts. After the aesthetic quackery of *pleasingly to the point of charm* [*pulcre, quam venuste*] of which we still hear significant echoes, the scholarship of text crit-

icism and metrics is now the order of the day. I do not know if much of it has already gained ground with the personnel under your supervision. Yet the tendency no doubt awaits them, too, and in either case philosophy will go out rather empty handed.[40]

Like Socrates, Hegel is wary about how the fixing and rote mechanical learning of words instills a dulling of thought.[41] In the movement from frivolous and fanciful "aesthetic quackery" to dry and solemn "text criticism," one mistake has been replaced by another. Despite its earnest intentions for determining and cataloging the original meanings of texts and words, philology limits and constrains itself by obsessing over such trivial details. Just as this treatment perverted the spirit of Fichte's philosophy, so Hegel thinks it will pervert philosophy as a whole: "Philosophy will go out rather empty handed." He repeats himself in another letter on the same point a few years later still, to Ludwig Döderlein: "Philology has presently entangled itself in such an erudite cobweb-spinning and labor of barren industry—so fixing itself into [a concern with] means, externalities, and their unravelling—that its true content withdraws ever further from the unlucky souls who become ensnared by it."[42] Reading to the letter is both boring and tyrannical. Erudition, usually thought of as a requisite feature of good scholarship, is revealed to be, at best, tedious academicism, and at worst, obstinate dogmatism. Reading for the spirit, on the other hand, is how true meaning and liberation can be derived. It is concerned instead with the "true content" of a work, even if the positing of such a truth demands going beyond "the original," and beyond every succeeding interpretation. Indeed, Hegel explicitly admires the "freedom" with which Luther "quoted, interpreted, and manipulated" scripture.[43] I will return to this.

God Is Coal

To make reference to one final letter (*Briefe*), we can say that (1) the spirit and (2) the letter correspond to (1) the speculative and (2) the transcendental dialectic and the abstract, as schematically laid out in another letter to Niethammer on the topic of how to introduce school boys to philosophy.[44] (This rather formal communication was delivered together with the aforementioned, more personal letter, which makes reference to the interpretative practices of the "Church Fathers, and Luther.") This letter is significant because it highlights the transition from Hegel's early account of the spirit and the letter, by which the spirit is dialectical and self-actualizing but does not sit in any dialectical relation to its letter, to a dialectical consideration of this distinction itself, in which the spirit only arises from the contradictions within the letter, and in which the distinction between the spirit and the letter is one that is internal to the letter itself.

In teaching philosophy, one must start with abstractions, writes Hegel: "that which holds determinations fast and comes to know them in their fixed distinction."[45] This is an education of instruction via rote mechanical learning, of taxonomies, of reading from the textbook or off the blackboard. It represents the acquisition of knowledge at its most basic and least philosophical: mere formulas, factoids, and quotations to be memorized and recited. This corresponds to the letter at its most stupid. It is the letter of the letter: a fixed designation of an apparently fixed referent to be taken note of without further thought.

This finds its philosophical corollary in pre-Kantian dogmatism and its political corollary in the esoteric enforcement of dictatorial prescription and bureaucratic control. Kant, in the preface to the first edition of his *Critique of Pure Reason*, describes metaphysic's dogmatic slumber in terms of the political, but only metaphorically: "In the beginning, under the administration of the **dogmatists**, her [metaphysic's] rule was **despotic**."[46] Hegel, however, as we have seen throughout this chapter, perceived a literal correlation between the philosophical, religious, and political dogmatisms which "join hands in the same underhanded game."

"The dialectical," Hegel continues, "is the movement and confusion of such fixed determinateness; it is negative reason."[47] This second stage represents an intermediate education, where questioning and critical thinking are encouraged, where the apparently fixed and established knowledge which was learned prior is problematized. One must unlearn what has been learned by grasping the contingent and inherent limits of what has been internalized as a reified schema. As such: "The stage is more difficult than the abstract; and is at once the stage in which the young, eager for material content and sustenance, are least interested." Even the enthusiastic student, hungry for more knowledge, is resistant to having their existing knowledge made wrong.

This stage represents dialectical thinking in the strictly Kantian, transcendental sense. "The Kantian antinomies ... contain deep fundamentals of the antinomical [content] of reason," Hegel writes.[48] At this point, we may appear to be moving beyond the triviality and tyranny of the letter of the law. Indeed, the transcendental dialectic proceeds from the abstract precisely in order to guard against such metaphysical dogmatism. Even the very word "antinomy" is derived from the Greek "*anti-nomos*," "against the law." For Hegel, however, in their stasis, these anti-laws which reveal and mark the contradictions within the laws themselves, only serve to establish a new law of the law's contradiction—that is, they enshrine the law's limits in and as the law itself. As such, Hegel argues, although "the Kantian antinomies ... contain deep fundamentals of the antinomical [content] of reason," these fundamentals "lie concealed and are recognized in the antinomies so to speak unthinkingly and insufficiently in their truth.... The antinomies really constitute all too poor a dialectic. Nothing beyond tortuous antitheses." As Adorno and Horkheimer would go on to observe, Kant's critical philosophy, in accordance with its own principles, repeatedly condemns itself as dogmatic.⁴⁹ This is almost spelled out, albeit fondly, by Kant himself. The transcendental dialectic, he writes,

> limits all our speculative claims merely to the field of possible experience, not by stale mockery at attempts that have so often failed, or by pious sighing over the limits of our reason, but by means of a complete determination of reason's boundaries according to secure principles, which with the greatest reliability fastens its *nihil ulterius* on those Pillars of Hercules that nature has erected, so that the voyage of our reason may proceed only as far as the continuous coastline of experience reaches, a coastline that we cannot leave without venturing out into a shoreless ocean, which, among always deceptive prospects, forces us in the end to abandon as hopeless all our troublesome and tedious efforts.⁵⁰

Once again: confined, rigid, unanswering, and unanswerable. The antinomical and prohibitive letter is inscribed: *nihil ulterius*, go no further, keep off the grass, and don't ask questions!

This stage finds its political corollary in bourgeois resignation. In the words of Lukács, transcendental critique is, with its legislation of unsurpassable limits, "always, if not always consciously, an apologia for the existing order of things or at least the proof of their immutability" as "eternal laws of nature."⁵¹ Adorno, too, argues that it is Kant's antinomies of reason, keeping us in check, which make his philosophy "a theodicy of bourgeois life"—one which expresses "that refusal to make any significant statement on the crucial questions, and instead to set up house in the finite world and explore it in every direction, as Goethe phrased it."⁵² In the words of Alain Badiou, finally:

> Everything in him [Kant] exasperates me, above all his legalism—always asking *Quid juris?* or "Haven't you crossed the limit?"... The critical machinery he set up has enduringly poisoned philosophy, while giving great succour to the Academy, which loves nothing more than to rap the knuckles of the overambitious—something for which the injunction "You do not have the right!" is a constant boon. Kant is the inventor of the disastrous theme of our "finitude." The solemn and sanctimonious declaration that we can have no knowledge of this or that always foreshadows

some obscure devotion to the Master of the unknowable, the God of the religions or his placeholders: Being, Meaning, Life ... They render impracticable all of Plato's shining promises—this was the task of the obsessive from Könisberg, our first *professor*.[53]

Each of these eviscerating critiques of Kant owes a debt to Hegel. To repeat: For Hegel, the fundamentals of the antinomical content of reason "are recognized in the antinomies so to speak unthinkingly and insufficiently in their truth"—and this is because Kant presupposes in advance that the antinomies of reason constitute threats to the very employment of reason, and so must be avoided. In order to avoid such threats, Kant assumes, reason must know and respect its limits and stick within them. This is emblematic, for Hegel, of Kant's "tenderness for worldly things." For Kant, "It is not supposed to be the worldly essence that bears the blemish of contradiction, but it is supposed to fall to thinking reason *alone*."[54] In short, Kant refuses to entertain the possibility that antinomies are not just on the side of cognition or reason, but in "everything real.... In Kantian idealism, insofar as it concerns what belongs to reason, the deficiency is blamed on the thoughts, such that they are held to be insufficient."[55] The antinomies of reason are thus recognized in Kant's antinomies insufficiently for the antinomies are recognized as antinomies as such—that is, to the letter, or else as that which fixes the letter in its place. This apparently paradoxical thought, antinomical in its own right, demonstrates the need for one final step.

"The third form is the truly speculative form, i.e., knowledge of what is opposed in its very oneness, more precisely the knowledge that the opposites are in truth one. Only this speculative stage is truly philosophical. It is naturally the most difficult; it is the truth."[56] The move between the (transcendental) dialectic and the speculative is nothing more than a parallax shift of perspective.[57] The antinomical content of reason, rather than being conceived of as mere limit, is instead conceived as productive of reason as such. For Hegel, "the antinomy occurs not only in the four specific objects taken from cosmology [as identified by Kant] but instead in *all* objects of all genera, in *all* representations, concepts, and ideas"[58]—and this absolute antinomical content of reason does not limit reason, confining it to the picket-fenced coastline of experience, but drives it beyond itself into uncharted territories. To slightly alter Rose's formulation, with Kant's move from dogmatic metaphysics to transcendental idealism, hubris becomes humility; with Hegel's move from the transcendental to the absolute, humility becomes motile configuration.[59] What Kant conceives of as the external limit of reason, marked by the thing in-itself, the thing beyond reason which cannot be grasped, is transposed by Hegel into the defining character of reason itself: an antinomy which is no longer a contradiction between two irreconcilable positively existing objects which are external to one another (be they reason and the in-itself, truth and error, the absolute and cognition, and so on), but a minimal contradiction which divides the one object from itself—that which is "opposed in its very oneness." In short, while the transcendental dialectic recognizes and guards against the errors that truth is irrevocably prone to (but, as such, lays them down in law), the speculative dialectic begins by asking a different question: Should we not be concerned that the fear of error is already the error itself? (*PhG* §74).

Hegel continues to complicate matters by explicating that the speculative "is itself present in twofold form"—specifically, "1. in its common form, where it is brought closer to representation, imagination, and the heart, as for example when one speaks of the universal self-moving life of nature molding itself in endless forms.... Law, self-consciousness, the practical in general already contain in and for themselves the principles or beginnings of the speculative." The speculative in this first "common form" represents the content of the absolute at the level of picture-thinking (*Vorstellung*): that which is a self-generating and self-moving unity, propelled by its own immanent contradictions, but without being elevated to or thought at the level of the concept. Hegel lists "law, self-consciousness, [and] the practical in general," extending to art, religion, history, and culture. In each of these, the speculative is at work but not yet fully thought; merely brought "before representation."

Hegel continues: "And of spirit and the spiritual there is, moreover, in truth not even a single nonspeculative word that can be said; for spirit is unity with itself in otherness. As a rule when one uses the words 'soul,' 'spirit,' or 'God' one is speaking all the same only of stones and coals."[60] And "not even a single nonspeculative word that can be said." As such, Hegel implies not a hard distinction between the letter and the spirit but rather a speculative identity and nonidentity between them: "Spirit is unity with itself in otherness"—or, in this case, "spirit is unity with itself in the letter." The proposition which follows is even more surprising, and may appear to contradict the first. One might expect Hegel to illustrate this by saying that even the lowliest words can communicate the most profound spiritual truths. But Hegel proposes, to the contrary, that when one uses what appear to be the most lofty and spiritual words—"'soul," "spirit," or "God"— "one is speaking all the same only of stones and coals." A crucial misunderstanding needs to be avoided here. Hegel does not mean that when one speaks of "God" one is speaking equally of "coal" due to some irreducible tendency of words to vulgarize their objects. After all, language itself is speculative: it is adequate to grasp and express the true. As Hegel writes in the *Logic*, on the speculative nature of language: "It can delight thought to come across such words, and to discover in naive form, already in the lexicon as one word of opposite meanings, that union of opposites which is the result of speculation but to the understanding is nonsensical. Philosophy, therefore, stands in no need of special terminology."[61]

This is how we can reconcile these two apparently paratactic statements: that (1) not even a single nonspeculative word can be said, and (2) when one speaks of God one is speaking of coal (or else, when one speaks of the soul one is speaking of a stone). For Hegel, God *is* coal (the soul *is* a stone). What can this mean? It is a proposition that can only be grasped by first going through the insufficiencies of abstraction and the transcendental dialectic. At the level of abstract thinking, the word "God" seems perfectly suitable for its referent: a simple identity is assumed between the world and the words used to describe it. At the level of (transcendentally) dialectical thinking, meanwhile, this suitability is problematized: The word "God" is just an arbitrary signifier, a dead letter which spuriously fixes its referent, totally insufficient for representing the divine majesty of the creator. And yet words are all we have. God-in-himself thus remains an unknowable mystery beyond phenomena, while the word "God" is damned to be a "tortuous antithesis"—an idolatrous re-presentation of God as external dead matter. One might expect here that the speculative stage will be introduced to finally overcome this difference and to reconcile this antithesis. But in an ironic twist, the speculative does not magically bring to life what is dead, but instead finds life in this death itself—that is, the antinomy is not reconciled, but viewed in its productive capacity. At the level of speculative thinking, then, the word "God" represents divinity as inert, dead matter, but in doing so reveals that (speculatively) this is precisely what God is: unity with himself in otherness. This is manifested at its most extreme, for Hegel, with the incarnation of Christ: the eternal divine realized in history, locally, as a mortal human who eats, shits, cries, doubts, hurts, and dies. The speculative proposition that "God is coal" or that "the soul is a stone" echoes, therefore, the so-called infinite judgment found in the *Phenomenology of Spirit*, that "*spirit is a bone*"—"the proposition which lies in the concept of reason" as such, the judgment "that the self is a thing—the judgment which sublates itself" (§§343-44). In each case, the radical proposition delivers an ironic punchline: the infinity of spirit is only to be found by first going through the apparently spiritless, external materiality of the letter. While Hegel insists upon the irreducible antinomies of the letter, wedded as it is to abstract and insufficiently dialectical thinking, he at the same time demonstrates that it is only by perceiving these antinomies in their positive and productive light that spiritual truth is realized. The word "God" is always already speculative, but it is only by perceiving it as such that we are moved from the thought of representation to the thought of the concept.

This defines the second form of the speculative:

> 2. What is philosophical in the form of the concept is exclusively what has been grasped conceptually, the speculative proceeding out of the dialectic. This can be only scantily present in the gymnasium. It will generally be apprehended only by a few, and to some extent one cannot even really know whether it is apprehended by them. To learn to think speculatively, which is specified in the directive as the chief purpose of preparatory philosophical instruction, is thus surely to be seen as the necessary goal. Preparation for it is first abstract thinking and then dialectical thinking, and beyond that consists in attaining representations of speculative content. Because gymnasium instruction is essentially preparatory, it can consist chiefly in working into such dimensions of philosophizing.

The speculative proceeds out of the abstract and the dialectic; the spirit proceeds out of the letter. It is this which differentiates Hegel's inheritance of Paul's spirit-letter distinction from Fichte's. While Fichte conceives of the two as simply and definitely opposed, Hegel conceives of the two as speculatively opposed in their unity, with spirit only finding itself in the otherness of its letter. This corresponds to Hegel's speculative identification of the truth as both subject and substance—opposite, but one. For Fichte, the spirit is always creative ex nihilo, and always stands over and against the vulgar empiricism of the letter. It is "what is otherwise called *productive imagination*." Unlike "*reproductive imagination*," which "repeats something which was already present within empirical consciousness," the productive imagination of spirit "does not repeat anything"; it is "completely creative—and it creates something from nothing."[62] As such, Fichte presents spirit as totally antinomian; totally opposed to any letter, law, or fixed schema. As he writes in a letter to Schiller: "spirit obtains its rules from within itself. It needs no law"; and this extends to philosophy, which "is not at all a matter of the letter; it is pure spirit."[63]

Fichte's Romantic conception of spirit—colorful, immediate, and novel—is ultimately anathema to Hegel's—that which paints grey in grey. For Hegel, the spirit creates nothing from nothing, it only recollects that which came before, and is as such only in its unity with its opposite—that is, the letter. However, this bright hue of Fichte's spirit betrays an artificiality. While it claims to surpass the antinomies of Kant's transcendental dialectic, it only succeeds in burying them. Fichte raises the question of the letter only to dismiss it all too quickly in favor of a spirit whose authority remains a mystery, a mere "aesthetic sense" which dictates on a whim. For Hegel, on the other hand, there is no hard distinction to be drawn between the letter and the spirit; and while, following Paul, he maintains that the letter kills while the spirit gives life, he does so with the added, ironic qualification that it is only by being killed by the former that the spirit can bring us, and itself, to life.

Hegel and Luther

The earlier comments from Hegel, cataloged above, may have appeared to represent to the extreme a caricature of the radical idealist, disregarding empirical reality, proclaiming it to be irrelevant in the face of philosophical truth. It is a position which may seem especially pernicious and irresponsible in our own so-called post-truth era. However, in light of this later letter on the passage from the abstract to the dialectical to the speculative, we can see that this is not what Hegel's spirit-letter distinction amounts to. It is only through an initial naive and self-defeating commitment to the letter—a "mind-numbing literalism" to repeat from Comay and Ruda—that the ironic spiritual truth opens up.

Hegel's above references to biblical hermeneutics, Luther, and St. Paul, are not incidental. In fact, I will contend that it is only by recovering this dialectic between the spirit and its letter as derived, not only from Fichte, but also from Hegel's engagement with Lutheran theology (and, in particular, from Luther's seminal interpretations of Paul's epistles), that we can adequately understand them. While the young Hegel does at times assume a somewhat vulgar Lutheranism, dogmatically rejecting the letter (of the law) in favor of the spirit (of love and freedom), the Hegel of the *Phenomenology* and after, through a more nuanced engagement with (and ultimate sublation of) Luther, develops a more complex and dialectical understanding of this distinction.

The question of the relation between the spirit and the letter is, for Hegel, a broad one. It pertains to truth and reality, to civil society and the state, to speculation and reflection, to reason and metaphysics, to life and death, to subject and substance, to the community of believers and the crucified Christ. It pertains to ethics and law; to the juridical opposition between free subjects and subjected beings. However, in what follows, I will be occupied primarily with the dialectic of spirit and letter as a question of reading and writing, as a question of how the "meaning" of a work, discovered by reading, relates to its textual presentation—that is, I will read "the letter," "literally." Importantly, this is not to exclude the other valences of the spirit-letter dialectic listed above (truth and reality, ethics and law, etc.). The Pauline antithesis which posits that the letter kills while the spirit gives life was never only a question of hermeneutics. However, it will be demonstrated that an elaboration of this hermeneutics will in turn provide a heuristic through which these other dialectics might become legible; not least because it is only by understanding how the spirit of Hegel's philosophy self-consciously relates to its textual presentation that we can know how to begin to read it at all.

Hegel's dialectic of the spirit and its letter does not amount to a simple hierarchization of the former over the latter nor the opting for one at the total expense of the other. More particularly, he does not merely posit the spiritual truth of a text as determined by the whim of its reader. Instead, he demonstrates that it is only by tarrying with the impossible demand of the letter of the word, which strips its reader of all arrogance and self-righteousness, not only as debasement, but as a condition of grasping the true, that the spirit might be realized.

* * *

As already stated, the missing figure in this passage from Kant and Fichte to Hegel is one from three hundred years prior: Martin Luther. It is with Luther too, that the question of the spirit and the letter as a question both of law and of writing and hermeneutics comes into focus, by which we can read "the letter" as both "the letter of the law" and "the letter" as such.

Throughout this thesis, I have suggested a radically atheistic conception of Hegel's Christianity. The content of both the biblical narrative (including the birth, death, and resurrection of Christ) and the Christian doctrine (including the Trinity, the immortality of the soul, sin, and redemption) are for Hegel symbolic. The revealed religion of Christianity is speculative and true in its conceptual content, but it assumes the fictional form of *Vorstellung*. Throughout his lectures, Hegel dismisses religiosity that remains preoccupied with the narrative and doctrinal elements of Christianity as unthinkingly dogmatic. He notes, however, that "in recent theology very few of the dogmas of the earlier system of ecclesiastical confessions have survived or at least retained the importance previously attributed to them ... faith in the Trinity for example, or the miracles in the Old and New Testaments, etc."[64] While previously, philosophy has been burdened with the job of challenging such superstitions, theology's declining interest in such positive doctrines means "philosophy can operate without restraint in regard to them."[65] Crucially, of course, this does not mean that

Christianity for Hegel can be dismissed wholesale, nor that it is just one of many possible religious illustrations of the absolute. Instead, while the positive doctrine of Christianity is dismissed as incidental, Christianity is still cast as the uniquely necessary representational structure proximate to and even generative of Hegel's own conception of the dialectic.

Hegel is concerned not with whether Christian doctrine is historically or empirically factual—for example, whether the miracles in the Bible actually happened, whether the Trinity is a foundational doctrine or a later addition, or even whether the historical figure of Christ was actually God incarnate who died for our sins. He is concerned instead with the sense in which it is spiritually true. For example, regarding the Trinity, while Hegel concedes that it "may have entered Christian doctrine from the Alexandrian school, or from the Neoplatonists"—that is, that it may not be an element of Christianity's "original" meaning—he emphasizes: "It is still primarily immaterial where that doctrine came from. The question is solely whether it is true in and for itself."[66] What can this mean? Surely it is fundamental to the "truth" of Christianity that Christ's incarnation and death "actually happened." For Hegel, it is not so clear that this is the case. Spiritual truth appeals not to the facts of the past in isolation, but takes history or spirit as a whole, and considers the continuing presence of the past and its legacies. To inquire into the truth of Christ's incarnation and sacrifice, then, is to ask about their self-subsistent present actuality. In this sense, then, they are absolutely true, representing not an exception or deviation in history but epitomizing history's essential logic, "the recollection and the Golgotha of absolute spirit, the actuality, the truth, the certainty of its throne" (*PhG* §808), spirit's kenotic self-sacrifice which is the condition of its continuation. "'To sacrifice' means to sublate the natural," Hegel says. "'Christ has died for all.' This is not a single act but the eternal divine history."[67] Christ's incarnation and sacrifice should not be quibbled over as a matter of mere factual verification, as a singular historical event, for this overlooks its status as the realization of the historical truth that the absolute is not an immutable being (i.e., a transcendent God, or else, perhaps, a fixed letter) but always a being coming-to-be (spirit) dependent on both historical reflection (or recollection, *Erinnerung*) and intervention (or relinquishment, *Entäußerung*).

Despite his atheism, or even perhaps because of it, Hegel cannot be understood without reference to his Christianity. Graham Ward—albeit from an orthodox Christian perspective—gives this argument an explicitly biographical spin, arguing with reference to Hegel's early theological essays that he "could only become a professional philosopher when he had found the place from which he could speak philosophically, and that place has much to do with developing a philosophical theology on the basis of a Logos Christology."⁶⁸ In short, Hegel's logic finds its basis, both biographically and structurally, in strictly theological reflections upon the incarnation, mediation, and reconciliation as found in the Christ narrative. As John Milbank identifies, it has tended to be Schleiermacher who is identified as the turning point in the development of modern theology—but only insofar as it was Schleiermacher who first defined theology as having a discrete domain and method, distinct from those of modern philosophy (just as he undialectically defined the letter against the spirit).⁶⁹ For Hegel, on the other hand, the two can never be so neatly divorced: "Philosophy is only explicating *itself* when it explicates religion, and when it explicates itself it is explicating religion. For the *thinking* spirit is what penetrates this object, the truth; it is thinking that enjoys the truth and purifies the subjective consciousness. Thus religion and philosophy coincide in one."⁷⁰

It is at this point, however, that a qualification needs to be added: Hegel's Christianity and Hegel's Christ are explicitly Lutheran in character. Hegel trained to become a Lutheran pastor before turning to philosophy, and continued to proudly refer to himself as a Lutheran. Indeed, far from being a departure, Hegel's philosophical activities only served to bolster his Lutheran theology. For instance, after making incendiary remarks about the Catholic Eucharist in a lecture, remarks which caused him to be reported by a group of priests to the Ministry of Religious and Educational Affairs, Hegel defended himself without deference, only by stating simply that "I have ... explained and expressed Luther's teaching as true, and as recognised by philosophy as true."⁷¹ Similarly, in a letter to the theologian August Tholuck (this time criticizing his colleague's "facile" account of the early church's development of the doctrine of the Trinity as a spurious imposition of certain Platonic and Aristotelean ideas upon indeterminate passages of scripture), and with yet another proclamation of the spirit over the banality of the letter, Hegel writes:

> Does not the sublime Christian knowledge of God as Triune merit respect of a wholly different order than comes from ascribing it merely to such an externally historical course? In your entire publication I have not been able to feel or find any trace of a native understanding of this doctrine. *I am a Lutheran, and through philosophy have been at once completely confirmed in Lutheranism.* I do not allow myself to be put off such a basic doctrine by externally historical modes of explanation. There is a higher spirit in it than merely that of such human tradition. I detest seeing such things explained in the same manner as perhaps the descent and dissemination of silk, culture, cherries, smallpox, and the like.⁷²

To repeat from above, it is "primarily immaterial where that doctrine came from. The question is solely whether it is true in and for itself." The history of Christianity, for Hegel—and indeed history itself—is not some reconstruction of past events as a narrative of empirical facts, likened here to the spiritless abstractions of political economy or epidemiology but is instead a living, motile configuration, whereby the present's particular recollection of its past is what constitutes the present as such. "I am a Lutheran, and through philosophy have been completely confirmed in Lutheranism": Hegel makes this proclamation first as a sign of his unwavering Lutheranism in the face of trivializing and pedantic opposition but also as a suggestion that he finds the resources and justification for such a criticism in Lutheranism itself. Hegel's Lutheranism, therefore, while staunch, is not one to the letter; it does not express any fidelity to Lutheranism as a fixed doctrine, bound to the historically particular facts of the German Reformation and Luther's life. "There is a higher spirit in it than that of such human tradition." It is instead a Lutheranism of the spirit, one which is concerned with the truth of Luther's revolution in Hegel's own time.

Hegel explicitly equates this truth—that is, the spirit of Lutheranism—with his own philosophical system. Indeed, in his "Address on the Tercentenary of the Submission of the Augsburg Confession"—the Augsburg Confession being the document written by Luther and others which was presented to the Holy Roman Emperor on June 25, 1530, to formally declare their dissenting articles of faith—Hegel declares his own work as inaugurating the "second reformation." While asserting that "the things which our Luther set in motion were truly new," he also claims that Luther was "deaf" to the spiritual truth of, and what would truly follow from, his own novelty: "He left to others the immortal glory of defeating that tyranny which had usurped control of religion;... he was unable to perceive that God had *risen up*, and that it was *his* [i.e., Luther's] *trumpet* which now proclaimed the wondrous sound of Christian freedom."[73] The Christ event for Hegel refers, therefore, not only to the historical happenings in first-century Judea and its biblical representations but also to the Protestant (Lutheran) Reformation, and even his own philosophical system; and the transitions between each of these may be described as transformative attempts of the spirit of Christianity to distinguish itself from its letter. Again, this spirit is not some concealed ultimate meaning, distinct from and shining through its letter. It is instead nothing but this repetitive process of freeing itself from such fixed determinations and returning to itself—with the further qualification that what is returned to is produced only by this very process of return. To use some words from the *Logic*: The spirit of Christianity "*comes to be* only by being *left behind*...."

For the presupposition of the turning back into itself—that from which essence *arises*, essence *being* only as this coming back—is only in the turning back itself."[74]

* * *

The history of interpretations of Paul's spirit-letter distinction—that "the letter [*gramma*] kills, but the Spirit [*pneuma*] gives life"—presents a history of biblical interpretation itself. From Paul, to Origen, Gregory of Nyssa, Augustine of Hippo, Aquinas, Nicholas of Lyra, Luther, and Schleiermacher, each appeals to this antithesis to justify their methods of reading scripture.[75] Origen (and other Alexandrian followers), for instance, interpreted "the letter" as the literal, surface meaning of scripture; "the spirit" as the deeper, true meaning; and the relation between the two as one of allegory. Logical contradictions apparent on a literal reading of the text only betray the necessity for a different mode of reading by which these contradictions might be resolved. Apparent inaccuracies and discontinuities could be overcome by demonstrating how their allegorical meanings were consistent with the whole. This contrasts with the Antioch school of interpretation, which held that the truth of scripture was literal, not allegorical, and could be discerned through philological and historical investigation. Therefore, they interpreted the letter-spirit distinction not in terms of hermeneutics, of literal and spiritual meanings, but in terms of the law, along the lines of the Old and New Testaments. Augustine can be seen to represent a synthesis of the two, assuming Origen's allegorization as a given, but emphasizing the Antioch school's antinomianism:

> For the Scripture phrase, "the Letter killeth but the Spirit giveth life," is not only to be understood to mean that any figurative expression, whose natural meaning is absurd, is not to be taken literally, but that we should feed our souls by spiritual understanding, considering the inner meaning which it represents;... [they] are not only to be understood that way, but also, and indeed chiefly, as it is spoken most plainly in another place, "I should not have known evil desire unless the law had said thou shalt not covet."... The letter of the law, which teaches that we must not sin, kills, if the life-giving Spirit is not present.[76]

In contrast to the life-giving spirit of the New Testament, both the legalism and the supposed literal meaning of the Old Testament was, for Augustine (and many other medieval exegetes), mere "letter." Both its historical particularity and its sadistic prohibitions (prohibitions which inaugurate their own transgression), mean it can only ever constitute an obstacle to salvation—unless, that is, it is understood spiritually in the light of the New.

Luther's letter-spirit distinction, meanwhile, maps onto his theology of law and gospel. Although inspired by Augustine, this theology does not present a simple opposition between the Old and New Testaments. Instead, "law" refers to all demands made by God upon humanity (from the Ten Commandments to the Sermon on the Mount), while "gospel" refers to the Good News that God freely justifies humanity "*allein durch den Glauben*" (by faith *alone*)[77]—despite their inevitable failure to keep to such demands. This doctrine of *sola fide* is the central tenet of the Lutheran Reformation. No amount of good works will save someone from damnation, only accepting God's grace through faith.

A common misconception is that Luther thus proclaimed the law irrelevant, abolished by Christ's sacrifice. Indeed, this is the position of many Lutherans, such as when the early Hegel in "The Spirit of Christianity" describes Jesus's Sermon on the Mount in Matthew 5–7 as the "extinction of duty and law in love."[78] With Jesus, he writes, the law is made "superfluous."[79] This misconception is epitomized most colorfully by Nietzsche's psychological readings of Luther and Paul as analogous figures, both of whose interminable despair at their repeated sinning is spuriously overcome by a dismissal of the law itself: "The law was the cross to which he felt himself nailed: how he hated it! how he had to drag it along! how he sought about for a means of *destroying* it—and no longer to fulfil it!" But then, "a liberating idea": "henceforth history revolves around him! For from now on he is the teacher of the *destruction of the law*!"[80] According to Nietzsche, Pauline-Lutheran atonement consists in the abolition of guilt via the annihilation of that which causes guilt, namely, the law. This antinomianism is also the theme of Badiou's reading of Paul, in which faith and works, grace and law, spirit and flesh, life and death, and universality and particularity, are sorted undialectically into "good" and "bad" camps. "The law," he writes, "is what gives life to desire. But in doing so, it constrains the subject so that he wants to follow only the path of death."[81] The problem with sin for Badiou's Paul, then, is not that it breaks the law, but that it does not break *with* the law.

This, however, is not Luther's position. That the letter kills does not mean, for Luther, that it should be rejected in favor of an edifying spirit which guarantees salvation regardless of one's obedience to God's commands. On the contrary: "These then are the two works of God, praised many times in Scripture: he kills and gives life, he wounds and heals, he destroys and helps, he condemns and saves, he humbles and elevates, he disgraces and honors…. He does these works through these two offices, the first through the letter, the second through the Spirit. The letter does not allow anyone to stand before his wrath. The Spirit does not allow anyone to perish before his grace."[82] Only when one has been killed by the letter, spiritually crushed by the revelation of one's impotence in the face of it, can the grace of the spirit bring one to life. What has received less attention is how the distinctions between the letter and the spirit and law and gospel are, for Luther, always a matter of hermeneutics.[83] This is because the letter, for Luther, is never something imposed by an external ecclesiastical authority but rather something which is read and spiritualized by the believer. The letters (*Buchstaben*) of the Bible represent the external manifestation of God's Word, the absolute authority, which bring life and grace only by being read.

Luther's most extensive treatment of 2 Corinthians 3:6, in which the above quotation appears, is in a 1521 treatise against the German theologian Hieronymus Emser, brilliantly and sarcastically entitled *Answer to the Hyperchristian, Hyperspiritual, and Hyperlearned Book by Goat Emser in Leipzig—Including Some Thoughts Regarding His Companion, the Fool Murner*. While Emser follows Origen and the tradition of medieval exegesis of understanding the relationship between the spirit and the letter as one of allegory, where the allegorical meaning reveals the spiritual truth of scripture against its more literal sense, Luther radically broke with this mode of interpretation. Throughout his ministry, he railed against the allegorization of the Bible as a means for twisting the text to fit the interpreter's presuppositions or motives: "Allegories are empty speculations, and as it were the scum of Holy Scripture"; "Allegory is a sort of beautiful harlot, who proves herself specially seductive to idle men"; "Allegories are awkward, absurd, invented, obsolete, loose rags."[84]

The interpretation of the spirit and the letter as pertaining to allegory, then, shows "clearly that Origen, Jerome, Dionysius, and some others have erred and failed"; and Emser, drawing on this tradition, thus "builds upon sand."[85] For Luther, by contrast, the spirit and the letter, as a question of both law and hermeneutics, pertains to the authority of scripture, not allegorization. While Emser's hermeneutics (and the entire post-Origen tradition of allegorization) places scripture at the interpretative discretion of the reader, Luther presents the "letter" as that which exercises its authority over the believer by stripping them of their arrogance, revealing their impotence, and thus by pointing them to their need for Christ. Only once that has happened can the spirit do what the mere letters of the text cannot—namely, to give the believer grace and the spiritual enablement to live righteously and read speculatively. "It is impossible," he writes, "for someone who does not first hear the law and let himself be killed by the letter, to hear the gospel and let the grace of the Spirit bring him to life. Grace is only given to those who long for it. Life is a help only to those who are dead, grace only to sin, the Spirit only to the letter. No one can have the one without the other."[86] The impossible demand of the letter does indeed kill, but this death is the necessary condition for true life.

We can now clearly perceive Hegel's Lutheranism in this famous passage from the preface to the *Phenomenology*: "The life of spirit is not a life that is fearing death and austerely saving itself from ruin; rather, it bears death calmly, and in death, it sustains itself. Spirit only wins its truth by finding its feet in absolute disruption" (*PhG* §32). Similarly, this finds its hermeneutical corollary in Hegel's development of the speculative reading of the proposition, theorized in the first chapter of this book, in which the linear transition between subject and predicate, though suggested by the statement and its propositional form, encounters resistance. Hegel's reader is repeatedly confronted with the impossibility of following him to the letter, but it is only by doing so, and by being forced to reread it differently, that the speculative (i.e., spiritual) meaning is realized. In terms of the 1812 letter above, it is only by first tarrying with the impossible claim that "God is a coal" that its radical truth can be realized. Alan M. Olson writes of Hegel's Christology: "While the Incarnation is the concrete, representational symbol of the overcoming, it is Spirit that makes it actual and Spirit alone that makes it intelligible in the spiritual community."[87] Similarly, while the letter is the concrete representation of Hegel's philosophy, its corpus, it is its recollection via reading that makes it intelligible, actual, and *alive*—that makes it spirit. Mere philological or textual criticism, reading to the letter and only the letter, leaves the dead letter dead. In the words of Luther: "It remains letter, and does not yield more than that."[88] This does not mean, however, that one should ignore the letter for some presupposed overall conception, the general "spirit"—rather one should go through the hardness, the impossible demand of the letter, as it is here that the real spirit opens up.

This spirit which arises from the impossible demand of the letter represents a strange kind of freedom—not the typical Aristotelian conception of freedom as choice or capacity but on the contrary a conception of freedom as necessity, as fate. As it pertains to reading, the impossible demand of the letter does not give us the freedom to interpret the text arbitrarily but instead presents us with the freedom of speculative reading, which consists only in absolute submission to the irony of the dialectic. As Ruda puts it, apropos Luther: "The one who is truly free does not identify freedom with a given capacity, but instead experiences the despair that there is nothing we *can* do."[89] This is the "despair"—the *path* of despair—which is also the freedom that comes from following the dialectic to its apogee, to realize its devastating ironic truth which cannot *but* be accepted. What this devastating ironic truth is, for us, here, now, will be spelled out at this book's conclusion.

Karl Barth describes Luther's desire to communicate the true meaning of scripture by contrasting the literalist "historical reconstruction of the text" with Luther's "genuine understanding and interpretation," the "creative energy which Luther exercised with intuitive certainty in his exegesis." Luther's scriptural exegeses and acts of translation have immanent fidelity to scripture precisely because they go through and then beyond them. They break down "the walls which separate the sixteenth century from the first" so that when Paul spoke, "the man of the sixteenth century hears." Luther translates the Bible, and in doing so re-collects it. "The conversation between the original record and the reader"—and, perhaps, "the letter" and "the spirit"—"moves around the subject matter, until a distinction between today and yesterday becomes impossible."[90] This is the brilliance that Hegel praises too. "Luther made the Bible speak German," he writes in a letter, "the greatest gift that can be made to a people. For a people remains barbarian and does not view what is excellent within the range of its acquaintance as its own true property so long as it does not come to know it in its own language."[91] As long as a religion remains in a foreign language of antiquity, presented as rules and regulations by an external, hierarchical, ecclesiastical authority, or else wedded to some "original" meaning, it remains alien; it remains positive religion or else mere historical curiosity. In both cases: mere letter. Thus Luther: in translating the Bible, we "mustn't consult the Latin text about how to speak German, as these donkeys do, but we must consult the mother at home, children in the street, and the ordinary man in the marketplace, watch them mouth their words, and translate accordingly."[92] Hegel remarks in another lecture: "The Bible has [the] form of positivity, yet according to one of its own sayings, 'The letter kills, but the Spirit gives life.'" It is a question, then, Hegel continues, "as to which spirit we bring in, which spirit gives life to the positive." Not merely the spirit of the individual reader, in which case spiritual truth is either dictated as positive doctrine by the author, or reduced à la Fichte to human autonomy or genius. Instead, we must bring in the spirit as such: the motile and living truth of history which manifests itself in the consummation of its development.

This brilliance of Luther is also one Hegel aspires to. "I may say of my endeavor," he continues in the above letter, "that I wish to try to teach philosophy to speak German."[93] Again, "German" should not be read here as an expression of nationalism, but rather, like Luther, as a desire to make philosophy speak in its own particular historical moment, or spirit. To echo Hegel's concluding words in the *Encyclopedia Logic*, this marks "the absolute *freedom* of the idea," the point at which it "*resolves* [entschließt] *to release* freely *from itself* the moment of its particularity."[94] In this way, Hegel's entire philosophical system can be conceived as a recollection, a rereading, even a translation of the history and totality of philosophy itself for his own time. Hegel proclaims in the *Philosophy of Right*: "Philosophy,... is *its own time comprehended in thoughts*."[95] In light of what has been argued in this chapter, we can make a similarly formulated proposition: Philosophy is its own history recollected for its own time. In order to have immanent fidelity to Hegel's intention, we are required to make philosophy speak our own language, for our own time. We must tarry with the letter of Hegel's philosophy in order to realize its living spirit today.

Hegel Reading [PART TWO]

Après la Lettre [CHAPTER FOUR]
Hegel in a Postcritical Era

To recognize the rose in the cross of the present is to preserve subjective freedom in the realm of the substantial.

HEGEL

Hegel Contra Sociology

After three chapters of reading Hegel, it is now time to read *with* Hegel; it is time to paint grey on grey, and recollect a shape of life that has grown old.

"This essay is an attempt to retrieve Hegelian speculative experience for social theory."[1] So begins *Hegel Contra Sociology* (1981) by Gillian Rose. Despite being one of the most important and original contributions to the tradition of critical theory since the heyday of the Frankfurt School, this work's significance has not yet been fully realized. This neglect can largely be attributed to the density of the presentation of its argument. It is hard to disagree with Peter Osborne's early assessment of the book: *Hegel Contra Sociology* is "unashamedly, and sadly, an extremely difficult book."[2] And yet, in spite of this difficulty, it is one of the aims of this final concluding chapter to demonstrate that *Hegel Contra Sociology* both anticipates and provides essential insight into ongoing debates about the limits of critique in literary studies. By recovering and developing Rose's argument, it makes the case that it is only by turning to Hegel's critique of Kant's conception of critique—and in particular Kant's institution of the hard distinctions between subject and object, between preconditions and conditioned, and between any critical method and that which it seeks to apprehend—that we might move beyond the antinomies of literary theory and its instrumental-critical mode. It also argues that this might, in turn, open up the possibility for a recollection of critical thinking and reading in the moment of their crisis. This grey on grey brings together the work undertaken in the previous chapters to more directly address a way in which the spirit of Hegel might be realized in literary theory today—in which the ironic truth of Hegel might be recollected.

Rose's argument in *Hegel Contra Sociology* is that social theory, from

Durkheim to Weber, through Simmel, Adorno, Lukács, Althusser, and Habermas, unwittingly rests upon an identifiably neo-Kantian framework, and has thus failed to take account of Hegel's critique and surpassing of Kant's transcendental idealism. In particular, she argues that it is only by realizing the sociopolitical significance of Hegel's idea of "speculative experience" that we might be up to the task of comprehending, criticizing, and therefore transforming the social and political relations that determine us; that we might develop a critical theory (or a "critical Marxism"[3] as Rose calls it) that is worthy of its name.

Sociology aims to reveal the conditions of possibility of any given social phenomena with the assumption that the latter lack the inclination or self-reflective capacity to account for such preconditions. Such an activity of sociological reason is called (with an adaptation of a term used by Kant) "quasi-transcendental"—*quasi*-transcendental because, while it considers its object in light of what it presupposes (like Kant's transcendental idealism), this presupposition—that is, society—is posited as external to the mind. In Rose's words, while the quasi-transcendental "is an *a priori*, that is, not empirical, for it is the basis of the possibility of experience," as a "sociological" a priori, it "is, *ex hypothesi*, external to the mind, and hence appears to acquire the status of a natural object or cause."[4] While many of these sociologies "reject Kantian critical philosophy in fundamental respects," and while some are even "motivated by the desire to break out of the constrictions of the neo-Kantian paradigm,"[5] Rose demonstrates how nevertheless they unwittingly remain within it.

In particular, Rose picks out the work of the philosopher Rudolf Hermann Lotze (1817–81), arguing that in spite of being "now unknown,"[6] his reformulation of some of Kant's ideas provided the intellectual basis for the subsequent development of social theory. Lotze's innovation lies in "his strict separation of the logical question of validity from the epistemological question of cognition"—his separation of the question of how we can ascertain the logical validity of our knowledge of an object from the more empirical questions of experience, representation, and appearance—which he supplements with the third question of human significance and meaning, or what he calls "value."[7] In his own words: "All our analysis of the course of the world ends in leading our thought back to a consciousness of necessarily valid truths, our perceptions to the intuition of immediately given facts of reality, [and] our conscience to the recognition of an absolute standard of all determinations of value."[8] Rose argues that this distinction between values and validity in particular, recasting the Kantian dichotomy between cognition and its object, influenced the subsequent development of post-Kantian philosophy: "On the basis of Lotze's thought, critical, transcendental philosophy became transformed into the neo-Kantian paradigm of *Geltung* and *Werte*, validity and values"[9]—a paradigm in the form of a transcendental logic or methodology to be unquestioningly assumed in advance as distinct from the object to be apprehended. This is the case, Rose argues, even for apparently diametrically opposed "schools" of neo-Kantianism: "The Marburg School gave the question of validity priority over the question of values; the Heidelberg School gave the question of values priority over the question of validity. But in both cases the transformation of Kant's critical method into a logic of validity (*Geltungslogik*), a general method, excluded any enquiry into empirical reality. Objectification became the correlate of pure logic."[10] In turn, this influenced the subsequent development of social theory: "The development of the idea of a scientific sociology was inseparable from the transformation of transcendental logic into *Geltungslogik*, the paradigm of validity and values."[11] Again, this is in spite of the differences between rival social theories. On the one hand, "Durkheim," to take one paradigmatic example, "granted the question of validity priority over the question of values, and made validity into the sociological foundation of values."[12] He argued that "society" is the quasi-transcendental sociological a priori of experience, and therefore the ultimate criterion of its validity. "Society" is that which allows us to make sense of our experiences, identities, and cultural practices (our values) but only within the criteria of validity that society imposes. The question of the genesis and formation of that "society" is therefore beyond investigation. Society must just be accepted as a given. "Weber," on the other, "granted the question of values priority over the question of validity and made values into the sociological foundation of validity"—that is, contra Durkheim, Weber argued that it is values which confer and ground validity.[13] Even scientific knowledge, for Weber, is ultimately reducible to a historically and culturally specific value. In his own words, as quoted by Rose, "Even the knowledge of the most certain of our theoretical sciences ... is a product of culture." Unlike the Durkheimian approach, Weberian sociology does attempt to give a sense of the origin of these values, identifying this origin as an "ideal-type" (for example, the self-discipline, frugality, asceticism, and duty of the Protestant work ethic) which then has an unpredictable concrete realization and development as it comes into conflict with reality (such as the sixteenth-century Protestant work ethic's transformation into the industriousness and instrumental rationality of the nineteenth- and twentieth-century capitalist). However, this sense of origin and development still remains obscure, attributed to an initial irrational decision and a subsequent irrational development.

To put it simply, within the realm of sociological reason, to prioritize validity is to examine how society conditions us—it is to examine the objective (e.g., societal) determination of our experience and knowledge; while to prioritize value is to examine how our values might (wittingly or not) condition or mediate our society—it is to explore the "subjective" mediation of that objectivity. And yet, in spite of these apparently diametrically opposed approaches, each remain within the neo-Kantian paradigm insofar as each posit this dichotomous relationship between validity and values.

In this sense, Rose argues—and following Hegel's critique of Kant—neither can grasp the precise relationship between these spheres; the "status of the relation between the sociological precondition and the conditioned becomes ... ambiguous in all sociological quasitranscendental arguments."[14] Objective determinations may be gestured toward, and subjective mediations may be investigated, but they cannot be grasped in their unity—that is, objective determinations cannot be grasped in terms of the subjective mediations through which they are experienced, represented, misrecognized, reproduced, and transformed. While such a sociology may be capable of "provid[ing] an exposition of the abstract experience we are already living as immediate experience"[15]—of explicating the reified logic of social relations *as reified*—it is unable to account for the ways in which these social relations are experienced. As "pure" theory, it is rendered radically politically impotent: "In the name of a neutral method which seeks solely to justify knowledge, transcendental philosophy justifies infinite ignorance not finite knowledge."[16]

For example, most Marxist sociologies, according to Rose, fail to adequately critique capitalism because they fail to grasp it phenomenologically in terms of the subjectivity that capitalism both determines and is mediated by. For such sociologies, "subjects are merely 'bearers' of economic functions, such as, 'capitalist' and 'worker,' and the remainder of human personality is *directly* reduced to this defining function."[17] In the name of a critique of capitalism, of ascertaining and describing its logic and limits, human subjectivity and its possibilities are reduced to these abstract categories. By assuming an abstract rather than a speculative identity between objective determinations and subjective mediations—"base" and "superstructure" in Marxian jargon—and by positing that consciousness and its activities (such as religion and art) can only serve to legitimize prevailing social relations, these Marxisms render any effective critique impossible.

It is important to emphasize that neither Hegel nor Rose are under any illusions that the critic can simply step out of such quasi-transcendental frames. Nor are they recommending a wholesale rejection of the theory and practice of critique. What Hegel does think, though, is that despite their apparent inescapability, the relation between ourselves and such determining constraints might be comprehended through a radically immanent and phenomenological mode of critique, in which objective social determinations and their subjective mediations (or validities and values) are taken, not as a dichotomy, but as one. This is the key, Rose argues, to Hegel's speculative proposition: "In general religion and the foundation of the state is [sic] one and the same thing; they are identical in and for themselves."[18] Objective determinations (such as the state) and their subjective mediations (such as religion) must be exposited and comprehended in their identity—but only in order to recursively experience and discover the nonidentity which that initial abstract identity obscures. Objective determinations and their subjective mediations *are* identical but speculatively; they are opposed in their unity.

> This different kind of [speculative] identity cannot be pre-judged, that is, it cannot be justified in a transcendental sense, and it cannot be stated in a proposition of the kind to be eschewed. This different kind of identity must be understood as a result to be achieved.
>
> From this perspective the "subject" is not fixed, nor the predicates accidental: they acquire their meaning in a series of relations to each other. Only when the lack of identity between subject and predicate has been experienced, can their identity be grasped.[19]

This is emblematic of the intrinsic irony of speculative experience, as developed in the first chapter of this book in particular. The speculative identity and lack of identity between subject and predicate, between state and religion, between objective determinations and their subjective mediations, can only be recognized by first being misrecognized. We "[learn] from experience that it means something other than what it took itself to have meant, and this correction of its opinion compels knowing to come back to the proposition and now to grasp it in some other way" (*PhG* §63). To experience this different kind of identity is to transgress the limit between the implicitly Kantian dichotomy of our knowledge, action, and experience, and their conditions of possibility. Put differently: it is to keep alive the possibility of what our social and political determination deems impossible. It is only through this ironic, speculative experience of how substance is *mis*represented as subject—that is, without reducing them to an abstract identity—that what Marx calls the "coarsely sensuous objectivity" of life might be kept alive despite the dominion of capital's universal powers of abstraction.[20] This is what it means, to use another Hegelian phrase, to recognize the rose in the cross of the present: to preserve subjective freedom in the realm of the substantial.[21]

As Fredric Jameson reminds us, therefore, Hegel's phenomenology is an innovation first in form not content.²² Rather than presupposing any hard distinction between the subject engaged in critique and the social reality that it seeks to criticize, Hegelian phenomenology is a form of metacritical activity which immanently presents preconditions and their subjective mediations through a process of naive and unassuming self-reflection, in which the critique of phenomena and the discovery of their quasi-transcendental determinations are inseparable. Such a phenomenology, as the name might suggest, is explicitly experiential. Due to the immanence of its presentation, the reading consciousness of a phenomenology progressively discovers that it is always already implicated in, determined by, and misapprehensive of what it seeks to grasp. Not only does the reader find themselves to be reading a kind of bildungsroman (although, as suggested in the first chapter, this designation cannot be made so comfortably), they also find that they are its protagonist. However, by "demonstrat[ing] the domination of abstraction," it therefore "urges *us* to transform ethical life by re-cognizing the law of its determination."²³ That is, Hegel's critique does not merely critique knowledge by expositing its conditions of possibility; it makes possible an experience of the ascendency of that which we are determined by, an experience without which it cannot be overthrown. Perhaps, then, *Hegel Contra Sociology* is "unashamedly, and sadly, an extremely difficult book" not only in the generic sense that its argument is complex and its style abstruse but in the more radical sense that it provides us with the means by which we might experience the inimicality of social and political reality to life.

It is this speculative experience that Rose seeks to retrieve for social theory and Marxism in *Hegel Contra Sociology*, her overlooked masterwork.

Hegel Contra Literary Theory

Following Rose, this chapter is an attempt—or at least the *Grundriß* of an attempt—to retrieve Hegelian speculative experience for literary theory. As stated in the introduction, the "foundation" or "birth" of what can be sweepingly referred to as "theory" has often and increasingly been presented in terms of Hegel and a host of conceptual abstractions that he is said to have prefigured for it. In the words of M. A. R. Habib: "It was Hegel who first offered a comprehensive critique of the notions of identity and essence; it was Hegel who showed that both subjectivity and objectivity are constructions; that we achieve humanity only through mutual recognition; and it was Hegel who pioneered the insights that the linguistic sign is 'arbitrary,' and that 'reason' is historical and social in its very nature."²⁴ In spite of its variety, in spite of its various "schools" as conventionally and pedagogically identified—from Marxism, to feminism, structuralism, poststructuralism, psychoanalysis, postcolonialism, posthumanism, queer theory, new historicism, and so on—and even when explicitly distanced from him, "theory" is said to rest upon Hegel. In what follows, however, I will argue that what is often referred to as "theory" rests, like sociology, upon an implicitly neo-Kantian, and therefore pre-Hegelian, paradigm. The very idea of a theoretical or critical reading *of* a text—that is, in the instrumental application of the former (theory) as a method, an arsenal of concepts, or a reified system of tropes to the latter (text), in order to get behind it to find its "true" meaning (or else the impossibility of such a thing)—presupposes a neo-Kantian, transcendental structure, because it assumes the text as a given and then seeks to reveal and examine its conditions of possibility. Yet, as Rose's *Hegel Contra Sociology* has shown, "Hegel's thought anticipates and criticizes the whole neo-Kantian endeavour, its methodologism and its moralism, and consists of a wholly different mode of ... analysis."[25]

As already intimated, apparently similar interventions have been made in recent years by practitioners of so-called postcritique, with their professed wariness toward all "hermeneutics of suspicion."[26] Indeed, the governing force of a text which a hermeneutics of suspicion seeks to disclose might be understood as a quasi-transcendental: class struggle, will to power, and sexual repression are for Marx, Nietzsche, and Freud (respectively) often taken to be the objective determinations which underly all hitherto existing social and subjective phenomena; they constitute the condition and horizon of all that can be thought and acted. Likewise, just as Hegelian speculative experience allows us to comprehend the relation between underlying objective determinations and subjective experience (or validity and values) without prioritizing either in advance, postcritique aims to address the analogous dichotomy of the two dominant readerly modes: that of the critic intent on burrowing beneath the text to examine its disavowed preconditions, and that of the lay reader immersed unthinkingly in the experience of reading. In the words of Rita Felski, postcritique's most famous practitioner, "postcritical reading" is that which "slices across the dichotomy of skeptical detachment versus naïve attachment"; between "the furrowed brow of the scholar deciphering an intractable subtext and the blissful mien of the subway rider devouring a bestseller."[27] However, while right to criticize the detached methodologism and moralism of much contemporary critique, I will argue that such postcritics offer a false solution to its aporias and antinomies. Neglecting to realize the import of Hegelian speculative experience, and his implied methodless method (*meta-hodos*, "following the path") they too often regress to an uncritical and an insufficiently naive mode of reading.

The unique character of a truly Hegelian literary theory would be a critical theory of literature which is at once a speculative experience of it, and one which might facilitate the speculative experience that literature itself can provide. Literary theory which remains stuck in a neo-Kantian, diagnostic mode, on the other hand, neglects to realize the critical work that literature might be capable of. This criticality does not necessarily stem from the politics of a work nor from some metacritical reflection upon its own conditions of possibility. Instead, the critical work of literature may be found in its ability to affirm the possibility of a subjective freedom of life against the finite limits of its social and political determination: to "preserve subjective freedom in the realm of the substantial." Such a literary hermeneutics cannot be reduced to one of suspicion but nor is it any less critical for it.

In this reading I will follow Rose's own (in a sense) postcritical assertion that to read Marx, Nietzsche, and Freud as *merely* masters of suspicion is to neglect to read them holistically. As she says in a late interview: "They're seen as radical debunkers, but that's only the first, sceptical stage.... Underlying that is a positive vision which they want to re-insinuate, and they do it cleverly, *through* scepticism."[28] Negative critique or skepticism, for Rose as for Hegel, must always give way to its positive moment. After realizing the wrongness of its knowledge and action, consciousness must take the risk of staking itself once again. This is what Hegel calls the "self-consummating skepticism" of the dialectic and of the path of despair (*PhG* §78).

Kant's dictum still stands: "The **critical** path alone is still open."[29] And yet, critique as we know it appears to have "grown old." What is required, then, is not the abandonment of critical thought, but its recollection—a recollection which is not a "rejuvenation," a restitution or resuscitation, but which nonetheless opens up the possibility of the new, of a different kind of critique. As Robyn Marasco notes, to understand Hegel as a critical thinker needs some qualification. Indeed, Hegel did not describe his own work as critique.[30] Like Marx after him who, with Engels, produced a vociferous "*Kritik der kritischen Kritik*,"[31] Hegel disdained critical philosophies in the Kantian sense—those concerned merely with accounting for knowledge by identifying its limits and conditions. For Hegel, this amounted merely to a justification and legitimation of existing knowledge, rather than an account of its formation (and deformation). It is the argument of this chapter, however, that in spite of this distancing from the idiom of critique, Hegel's own critique of critical critique marks not an abandonment of critique or a profession of critique's superfluity but instead yields a transformed critical path—namely, "the path of despair." It argues, then, that a critical literary theory after Hegel and Marx would not just expose the preconditions of a particular text or act of reading but might make the inhumanity of these preconditions explicit, and even our complicity in creating and sustaining them: a speculative experience of such objective determinations which would intensify the necessity of destroying them.

Theory after *Kritik*?

Literary theory is just as diverse, if not more so, than the social theory that Rose reassesses in *Hegel Contra Sociology*. Any attempt to talk about it as a whole risks neglecting the particularities of its historical manifestations and the vast differences between its major traditions. Can a common denominator be identified notwithstanding such differences? Rose shows that all dominant strands of sociology, in spite of their divergences, "rest upon an identical framework: 'the neo-Kantian paradigm.'"[32] Likewise, is it possible to show that literary theory derives from or rests upon a single paradigm?

To identify "critique" as such a paradigm may seem insufficient, in part because the word lacks agreed or stable definition. As Willi Goetschel notes with reference to philosophical critique (although it seems just as true of the critique of its literary counterpart), although critique "assumes the central function of legitimizing theoretical practice ... there appears to be no agreement on what critique might mean." This is not to suggest, though, that the definition is particularly contested either, as "the question of what it means is treated in a surprisingly casual way, given the fundamental role it plays in the context of theoretical self-explanation and legitimation."[33] Another reason for why "critique" might seem a vague answer to the question of a literary theoretical paradigm is that the word, at least within literary studies, is often taken to be synonymous with the very activity or practice of literary studies. What would literary theory do if not critique—however the word may be understood?

It is this latter point that has been picked up on by followers of a so-called postcritical turn who argue that literary theory has uncritically presupposed critique as the horizon of its activity at the expense of other modes of interpretation. These proposed "other modes" vary between surface,[34] distant,[35] and machine reading;[36] thin description;[37] reading with the grain;[38] reading as an act of acknowledgment;[39] actor-network theory (ANT);[40] and object-oriented,[41] implicative,[42] and computational[43] criticisms—to name just a few. In spite of their differences, what unites these new approaches in literary criticism is a wariness toward (if not a mere abandonment of) critical reading and theory. The "post-" in "postcritique," therefore, signals both a temporal designation and an evaluative—one could even say a critical—stance.

The name Rita Felski has become almost synonymous with this trend. This is not necessarily because her literary analysis is emblematic of the postcritical. Her applications of ANT and the work of the contemporary Frankfurt School to the analysis of literary texts greatly set her apart from the literary studies of Franco Moretti or Timothy Bewes, for example. Indeed, it is hard to say whether a positive thing called "postcritque" really even exists, for as John Guillory has contended, "it has failed to move beyond the phase of manifesto."[44] Felski's near-synonymity with postcritique is instead because her work *The Limits of Critique* (2015) represents the most polemical articulation of what is apparently wrong with the critical paradigm in literary studies—the "manifesto" in question. Its publication and the resulting controversy thus functioned to draw together these different approaches to literary studies under the banner of single critical term.

In this work, Felski notes that it is often taken for granted that the job of the literary theorist is "to draw out what a text fails—or willfully refuses—to see."[45] But why? she asks. "What sustains [the critic's] assurance that a text is withholding something of vital importance, that their task is to ferret out what lies concealed in its recesses and margins?"[46] Felski presents the origins of this style of critical thinking in terms of Paul Ricoeur's characterization of Marx's, Nietzsche's, and Freud's interpretations of Western culture as assuming a "hermeneutics of suspicion."[47] It is to this hermeneutics that Felski limits her definition of critique. What unites these "masters of suspicion," she writes, "is their conviction that radicalism is not just a matter of action or argument but also one of interpretation" and that the "task of the social critic is now to expose hidden truths and draw out unflattering and counterintuitive meanings that others fail to see."[48] Felski is at pains to insist that she does not reject critical-suspicious reading tout court. Indeed, the title of her work, "*The Limits of Critique*," is ironic insofar as "critique" since Kant has been understood as the identification and setting of limits. Instead, she takes issue with the way in which critique has become the uncritically presupposed paradigm in the humanities, and particularly literary studies—with "the relentless grip, in recent years, of what we could call an antinormative normativity: skepticism as dogma"[49]—and the ways in which such a hypercritical mode can distract from the more modest job of literary interpretation: "trying to figure out what something means and why it matters."[50]

Putting its contents to one side for the moment, there is at least a Hegelian tenor to the mode of postcritique's intervention. "My aim," Felski writes, "is not just to describe but to *redescribe* this style of thinking."[51] This is a Hegelian gesture insofar as philosophy for Hegel (as we saw in the second chapter of this book) is always retrospective; it always comes after the fact, once "a shape of life has grown old"—or "run out of steam" in the words of Bruno Latour.[52] That which falls under its gaze can only be recollected in its death throes. Only then does the owl of Minerva spread its wings—as Hegel's famous image has it.[53]

As mentioned, the postcritical redescription of critique often begins with the suspicious hermeneutics of Marx, Nietzsche, and Freud, as theorized by Paul Ricoeur. This link can also be found to be made in works by theorists such as Latour, Stephen Best and Sharon Marcus, and Heather Love.[54] Without contesting the specifics of this account, it is interesting to note how infrequently and vaguely postcritics recollect or redescribe the critical paradigm of literary theory with reference to Kant, especially given its implicitly Kantian character, and given that it was with Kant that critique was transformed into a theoretical method; or else, that theoretical method was transformed into critique. In the words of Willi Goetschel, it was only with Kant that critique "assumed an epistemological function and thereby achieved theoretical dignity."[55]

Drew Milne, in his anticipatory essay on "Criticism and/or Critique" highlights the Kantian heritage of critical theory and, by extension, of the critical reading of literary texts: "the modern coming together of criticism, critical reading and critique can be traced back to Kant, who made the term 'critique' and its practice central to modern thought." Indeed, as Milne notes, it was Kant who heralded "our age" as "the age of criticism" and who insisted that "to criticism everything must submit."[56] "The age of critique" is not now what it once was, with the dialectic of enlightenment which played out through the twentieth century revealing the inherent illusions, blindness, and tyranny of any claim to a totally disenchanted reason. However, what has persisted from Kantian critique to the critique of today is its self-reflexive form, which seeks to identify both the conditions of possibility of both the subject and the object of knowledge. In the words of Milne, Kant's revolution consists in a method for the delimitation of "the epistemological conditions by which the subject of knowledge, the knower, knows, the object, or the known. The critique of reason's conditions of possibility marks out Kant's conception of critique as a new philosophical reflexivity: the self-critique of enlightenment."[57] Almost all varieties of critical theory involve this methodological presupposition of Kantian critique. The key distinction is that while Kant's critique involves the identification of universal transcendental conditions, critical theory involves the identification of *quasi*-transcendental conditions. This is the same reason why, according to Rose, all sociologies inherit the antinomies of Kantian critique. The main difference is that the Kantian question of a priori conditions has become the post-Kantian question of a priori sociological conditions.

This shift also constitutes what might be called critique's "suspicious" turn. To take just one paradigmatic example, also drawn upon by Milne, Foucault argues that the function of critique after Kant is not only to legitimate theoretical practice, but to "transform the critique conducted in the form of necessary limitation into a practical critique that takes the form of a possible crossing-over [*franchissement*]"—a possible transgression. As such, he continues, "criticism is no longer going to be practiced in the search for formal structures with universal value but, rather, as a historical investigation into the events that have led us to constitute ourselves and to recognize ourselves as subjects of what we are doing, thinking, saying."[58] That is, while Kantian critique seeks to justify and legitimate knowledge claims by deducing their a priori conditions, critique after Kant seeks to "interrogate, unmask, expose, subvert, unravel, demystify, destabilize, take issue, and take umbrage" (to cite Felski's inventory)[59]—to investigate the disavowed contingency of our object so as to present and actuate the possibility of its transgression.

One might rejoin here that Kant's critical philosophy was defined by a suspicion toward the metaphysical assumptions that had been the dogma of previous philosophies, and that only then could it begin to justify true knowledge. More broadly, is suspicion not always a condition of ultimate justification? Every process of justification in the tribunal of reason must begin with the implicit acceptance that that which is on trial may *not* be justified. This is certainly the case. However, Kant's critique is ultimately a project of justification, and not suspicion, because it does not seek to interrogate the conditions (and therefore limits) of possibility so that they might be transgressed, but to insist upon their universal validity. In contrast with Hegel, to be a condition of possibility, for Kant, means to be unchangeable by time, thought, or action; an absolutely secure possession. As Deleuze puts it, in his account of Kant's critique: "Kant merely pushed a very old conception of critique to the limit, a conception which saw critique as a force which should be brought to bear on all claims to knowledge and truth, but not on knowledge and truth themselves; a force which should be brought to bear on all claims to morality, but not on morality itself. Thus total critique turns into the politics of compromise: even before the battle the spheres of influence have already been shared out."[60] It may be tempting to suggest that this move from justification to suspicion is analogous to the historical-philosophical move from Kant to Hegel. In a broad sense, this analogy works, and indicates the long shadow of Hegel's influence in critical and literary theory. As Sally Sedgwick has noted in her book *Hegel's Critique of Kant*, the two major respects in which Hegel's conception of critique differs from Kant's are: (1) that "critique as Hegel employs it does not result in the ultimate justification of the common, familiar assumptions with which our inquiries begin" but "instead undercuts them"; and (2) that "critique for Hegel deflates our claims to know ourselves at the start of our inquiry."[61] Put differently: "The assumptions we took to accurately capture the universal and necessary conditions of our science, turn out to be contingent. Critique, as Hegel exercises it, exposes the need to move beyond them."[62] By this account, while Kantian critique seeks to justify knowledge, Hegelian critique seeks to undermine it; while Kantian critique seeks to identify the universal transcendental horizon of knowledge, Hegelian critique seeks to reveal that what we took to be universal and necessary are in fact particular and contingent; while Kantian critique seeks to delimit a firm foundation from which to begin, Hegelian critique shows that we are always "beginning in the middle."[63] Hegel's critique of critique, therefore, at once explicates and actuates the ironic truth of critique as its own opposite. With Hegel, the humble setting of limits gives way to the radical transgression of those limits, while the justification of knowledge gives way to its complication. To take a more specific example, it may be tempting to interpret Hegel's speculative identification of philosophy with the history of philosophy—the idea that "philosophy ... *is its own time comprehended in thoughts*"[64]—as a movement beyond Kant's transcendental subject via a historicization of the transcendental subject, an insistence upon the historical contingency of the transcendental itself. This would in turn imply the historical contingency of all knowledge, including Kant's apparently universal transcendental deduction of the categories.

While all of this represents an accurate account of the differences between Kantian and Hegelian critique, and would indeed signal a move from justification to suspicion, it is nonetheless only a partial account. What is left neglected is the idea of Hegelian speculative experience and the phenomenological form that Hegelian critique takes. In this sense, modern critique after Kant, despite its insistence of the contingency and particularity of the transcendental, still remains in an implicitly Kantian mode. To return to Foucault, for example, although he insists that his mode of critique is "not transcendental—in the sense that it will not [à la Kant] seek to identify the universal structures of all knowledge [*connaissance*] or of all possible moral action"[65]—it is at least *quasi*-transcendental insofar as it seeks to account for the constitution of particular knowledges, discourses, and activities with reference to their historical conditions of possibility. Although it does not posit or accept "formal structures with universal value," it posits formal structures with particular value in advance of their discovery, or the experience of them. In turn, the experiences of the reader or critic are posited in advance as mere effects of the structure. As such, the critique implicit in Foucault's discourse analysis is neo-Kantian insofar as its exposition of the relation between objective determinations and their subjective mediations remains transcendental, as it offers no experience of their formation and deformation (that is, their *Bildung*), nor of their relation.[66]

Only Bruno Latour, among the postcritics, in his polemics against critique and self-reflexivity in the social sciences (which greatly influenced the current postcritical trend in literary studies[67]) makes reference to Kant's critiques as the original, critical sin. For example, in his essay "The Politics of Explanation: An Alternative" (1988), Latour criticizes the tendency of sociologists to offer social explanations for the natural sciences. Such social explanations of knowledge, he argues, are patently self-contradictory: "they make it impossible for their own explanations to be seriously believed by anyone. Their arguments in feeding back on themselves nullify their own claims."[68] If the sociologist aims to compromise the claims of the natural scientist by demonstrating that the latter is influenced by social factors, why can they not see that they too must fall victim to their own argument—that they too are influenced by social factors? With polemical flourish Latour claims that this can only lead sociologists into an infinite feedback loop of self-reference, leaving them "entangled in a sort of aporia similar to the famous 'all Cretans are liars,'" an aporia "from which they cannot escape except by indefinite navelgazing, dangerous solipsism, insanity and probably death."[69] It is in this essay that Latour attributes this reflexivity to a "hidden Kantianism": "They all think that objects, things-in-themselves, are somehow out of reach," and this enables the sociologist "only to expose reflexive claims, never to talk *about* something." Latour's rhetoric builds throughout this passage to explode with a mid-paragraph rallying cry: "Down with Kant! Down with the Critique! Let us go back to the world, still unknown and despised."[70] This point is reiterated in his later essay, "Why Has Critique Run out of Steam?" (2004), in which he criticizes the "mistake" of the humanities and social sciences "to believe that there was no efficient way to criticize matters of fact except by moving *away* from them and directing one's attention *towards* the conditions that made them possible." Again, this critical paradigm is attributed to scholars "remaining too faithful to the unfortunate solution inherited from the philosophy of Immanuel Kant."[71]

At first, Latour's argument may seem parallel to that of Rose's in *Hegel Contra Sociology*. Both criticize sociology's methodological attempts to expose the conditions of possibility of any social practice or theory; both argue that attempts to contextualize knowledge in this way preclude the possibility of any real knowledge at all; both criticize the methodological detachment of sociological critique; and both attribute these problems to an often unwitting inheritance of the philosophy of Kant. The crucial difference, however, once again, is Hegel: while Rose enjoins us to move beyond these antinomies of sociological reason by learning from Hegel's critique and surpassing of Kant, Latour enjoins us to regress from Kant to a precritical realism. While Rose calls for a radicalization of critique through a retrieval of Hegelian speculative experience, Latour calls for critique's abandonment. He writes: "If you sneer at this claim ['Down with Kant! Down with the Critique!'] and say 'this is going back to realism,' yes it is."[72] In short, for Latour, Kant's critique is only invoked as a misstep, or a dead end, from which we need to retrace our steps.

While Rose after Hegel calls not for the premature overcoming but the comprehension of the diremptions or dichotomies that have, since Kant, structured the critical method (and so provide a speculative experience of the corresponding diremptions which characterize social and political life), Felski after Latour quite unashamedly asks us simply to ignore or, to use her chosen metaphor, "circumvent" them. "The word 'circumvent' is intentionally chosen," she writes in *Hooked*. "The point is not to interrogate or deconstruct such oppositions"—these oppositions being the "surprisingly stubborn dichotomies" of critique: "art versus society, text versus context, sophisticated versus naive response"—"but to walk around them in order to arrive somewhere else." This is characteristic of a particular postcritical anti-intellectualism, a refusal to adequately and substantially "interrogate" the antinomies of critique—that is, a refusal to actually do the work—opting instead to merely judge these antinomies from the outside and "walk around them" and assume something different, when in actuality what is required to "arrive somewhere else"—to realize a genuinely postcritical method, perhaps—could only be achieved through the comprehension of the antinomies of critical reason.

The Limits of Recognition

I have criticized the so-called postcritical turn for its regression from an implicitly Kantian critique in literary theory to a precritical realism or subjectivism. Correspondingly, I have argued that in order to move beyond the antinomies of literary theory and its critical mode we must turn to Hegel's critique of critique, which in turn opens up the possibility for critique's recollection. However, here I want to discuss the most recent and ongoing work of Felski, whose postcritical engagement with the contemporary Frankfurt School approaches a kind of experiential and phenomenological literary theory which might be seen to be comparable to that which I am proposing—and, for that reason, needs to be all the more carefully distinguished from it. This seems especially necessary given the frequent straw manning of Felski as resistant to theory and critique tout court—straw manning that, it must be said, probably arose in response to her own straw manning of critique in her unfortunately generalizing and polemical *The Limits of Critique*. While Felski does not engage with Hegel directly, in this more recent work she does so vicariously through her engagement with, in particular, the contemporary Frankfurt School social philosopher Axel Honneth, whose work is motivated by a desire to move sociology beyond its Kantian paradigm and to insist upon the subjective mediation and experience of social relations—work which, most importantly, takes Hegel as its point of departure. However, again, with reference to Rose's *Hegel Contra Sociology*, I will demonstrate that Honneth (and by extension Felski), by neglecting the specificity of *speculative* experience and the particular phenomenological form of Hegel's critique, remain within this paradigm.

As already stated, Felski does not engage anywhere with Hegel directly, only once making an oblique reference in her book *Hooked: Art and Attachment* (2020) to Hegel as just another emblem of methodological critical detachment: "Whether one turns to Hegel or Foucault, it is only by distancing oneself from what exists that one can gain any kind of critical purchase on it."[73] This throwaway comment is especially ironic, given that, as we have seen throughout this book, Hegel's development of a phenomenological critique was founded on the sole presupposition that it is only by "setting aside every reflection" and "simply ... tak[ing] up *what is there before us*"[74]—as he puts it in the *Logic*—without any further presuppositions, that thinking might begin; and given that it was motivated by a resistance to any such critical detachment, any supposition of a distinction between the instrument and object of critique. In the same sentence, therefore, Felski indicts Hegel for critical detachment while unwittingly echoing his rejection of it. She immediately goes onto complain that "at a philosophical level,... detachment has been hailed as a precondition for any form of knowledge"[75]—without acknowledging that, for Hegel, the assumption of such critical detachment as a precondition for knowledge in fact precludes the possibility of any knowledge at all.

Nevertheless, and in spite of its avowedly postcritical stance, Felski's recent theoretical work draws from the post-Habermas era of Frankfurt School critical theory, some of which explicitly takes up Hegel and his critique of Kant. For instance, in two recent articles ("Good Vibrations" [2020], and "Recognizing Class" [2021]) and in her forthcoming monograph, *Remix: On Literature and Theory*, and the 2021 Clark Lectures upon which it is based, Felski seeks to address the neglect in literary scholarship of the contemporary Frankfurt School—figures such as Honneth, Nikolas Kompridis, Hartmut Rosa, Rahel Jaeggi, and Robin Celikates.[76] "While the Frankfurt School crops up frequently in literary studies," she writes, "it does so as an intellectual formation preserved in amber: Weimar Germany and its aftermath. The figures cited are Theodor Adorno, Walter Benjamin, sometimes Georg Lukács or Ernst Bloch"[77]—while the work of the later figures goes unnoticed. This neglect is attributed, in part, to the later Frankfurt School's own neglect of aesthetic questions: "Speaking from, and to, the fields of social and political theory, they rarely cite literature and never literary critics.... The highly attuned aesthetic sensibilities of Adorno or Benjamin have long since vanished; heavily 'sociologized' in its form as well as its content, German critical theory no longer registers on the radar of literary scholars."[78] As Amanda Anderson remarks, Habermas in particular has become associated in literature departments with "plodding style, an embarrassing optimism of intellect, and dangerous complicity with the Enlightenment"[79]—and those sociologists in his wake are therefore tarnished by association. Another reason why literary studies has not engaged with such thinkers is that their critical theory demonstrates little interest in many of the key concerns that occupy literature departments today—race, gender, sexuality, and the environment.[80] And yet, Felski argues, this work deserves the attention of literary scholars for its distinctive preoccupation with what she calls "experiential concepts"—phenomenological concepts which "stake a claim that's anchored in fine-grained attention to ethical, affective, and aesthetic life." Listing "acknowledgment," "affinity," "recognition," and "disclosure," she suggests that, opposed to "abstract" concepts, these experiential concepts prompt the reader to engage with and test them with reference to their own experience.[81]

Finally, this "return to the Frankfurt School," as Felski dubs this most recent phase of her work, is done to "acknowledge intellectual debts"[82]— that is, perhaps, to demonstrate that her postcritical work has a rigorous academic basis and is not, as some have argued, a celebration of the individual reader response at the expense of scholarly expertise.[83] She claims that this acknowledgment serves to bolster her own arguments concerning the limits of critique in literary studies, with the affinities between her position and theirs demonstrating that "such arguments are not just the provenance of unrepentant aesthetes and retrograde lovers of literature as hostile critics like to claim, they actually make up a major strand also in social and political thought."[84] In other words, it seems that with this most recent work, Felski is keen to push against the claims of her detractors that postcritical literary scholarship must by definition collapse into uncritical subjectivism or aestheticism.

In her article "Recognizing Class" (which was also presented as her second Clark Lecture, "On Recognition"), Felski seeks to bring Axel Honneth into a "common constellation"[85] with the autotheoretical memoir *Retour á Reims* (2009) (*Returning to Reims* [2013]) by the sociologist and queer theorist Didier Eribon. In *Returning to Reims*, Eribon reflects on his upbringing in working class France and his increasing distance from and embarrassment about these origins as he grew up—motivated largely by his homosexuality. In particular—and this is the focus of Felski's article—he grapples with the lived experience of social class. His memoir is driven by a conviction that this lived experience (this subjective mediation of objective determination, to use Rose's terminology) must be confronted in order to begin to grasp why, for example, his family who always voted for the Communist Party would end up supporting the National Front; or why the act of reciting a poem in English to his mother might provoke hostile resentment; or why he is still burdened by a sense of shame toward his working class roots. Despite the apparent particularity of these experiences, they function as indexes to broader discussions of trenchant and ongoing issues with contemporary sociological research and leftist politics and the entrenched chasms between academic thought and the working class. Above all, for our purposes, Felski lauds *Returning to Reims* for both arguing for and realizing a kind of sociology which resists the reduction or collapse of the complexities of lived experience into a reified schema, logic of categories, or social explanation.

Although Eribon makes no mention of the Frankfurt School—he even proclaims that "I detested Germany, and the German language. I found them repulsive"[86]—Felski locates in *Returning to Reims* certain affinities with Honneth. What is distinctive about Honneth, and what he has in common with Eribon, is an insistence that class relations cannot be dealt with as a "purely" economic or sociological issue. Focusing not only on social or political determinations, Honneth directs his gaze to the ways in which these determinations are subjectively experienced and mediated. A guiding question of his research is therefore: "How is it that the *experience* of disrespect is anchored in the *affective* life of human subjects in such a way that it can provide the motivational impetus for social resistance and conflict, indeed, for a struggle for recognition?"[87] In other words: class and class determinations, for Honneth, only have meaning and existence in relation to moral and affective intuitions such as pride, belonging, resentment, or shame; all of these subjective mediations take the form of a "struggle for recognition"; and only by taking this struggle into account can we understand the possibility of social resistance. Felski finds this in stark contrast to the concepts of recognition as found in "the two most frequently cited parables of literary theory—Jacques Lacan's account of the mirror stage and Louis Althusser's anecdote of being hailed on the street by a police officer." While with these theories, she argues, "recognition was downgraded to misrecognition or political subjection," she finds in Honneth's theory of recognition an antidote against both the "rational, autonomous individual of liberalism" and this critical "flattening of persons into effects of linguistic or ideological structures."[88]

Crucially, as this phrase "struggle for recognition" implies, Honneth's sociology is motivated by a Hegelian critique of sociology's hitherto existing Kantian paradigm. Indeed, in the chapter "From Kant to Hegel" in his book on the history of the concept of recognition, Honneth argues that "a deficit in the history of sociology is that it has failed to take proper account of Hegel's formative role for the emergence of this discipline in the nineteenth century."[89] And, at the conclusion of the book, he summarizes his argument—namely, that while "the Kantian-influenced tradition of German Idealism offers such a fundamental insight into the nature of social recognition ... only Hegel managed to free it from the transcendental realm and insert it into a social reality of a 'spirit' that has become objective in the shape of institutional forms, moral habits and the living humans who deal with both."[90] While Felski only makes a passing reference to the Hegelian tenor of Honneth's terminology (i.e., the "struggle for recognition"),[91] her subsequent reading of *Returning to Reims* is colored by Honneth's Hegelianism—his resistance to transcendental explanations of social phenomena and to the assumption of an abstract identity between objective determinations and their subjective mediations; and his corresponding insistence on the sociopolitical importance of the lived, affective experience of social categories.

Honneth develops his theory of recognition not, as one might expect, from Hegel's *Phenomenology of Spirit*—which includes the famous parable of the "life-and-death struggle" for recognition between the master and the slave (*PhG* §187)—but instead from his earlier *System of Ethical Life*.[92] It is in this text, Honneth argues, that the young Hegel began to develop a social philosophy of mutual recognition in which the "claim" of individuals "to the intersubjective recognition of their identity ... is built into social life from the very beginning as a moral tension, transcends the level of social progress institutionalized thus far, and so gradually leads—via the negative path of recurring stages of conflict—to a state of communicatively lived freedom."[93] In other words, it is the work in which Hegel began to develop a theory of society as grounded on the individual's demand for recognition of their identity from others. It is this demand for recognition, for both Honneth and his young Hegel, which is the motor of social and political progress. Starting as a "moral tension," the struggle for recognition transcends to progressively higher levels in which the recognition of difference is institutionalized, and particular identities, needs, and commitments are mutually respected, mediated, and policed. In the *Phenomenology*, by contrast, this "conceptual model of a 'struggle for recognition' had lost its central position within Hegel's theory,"[94] reduced to a particular stage of the development. It is this particularity that Honneth disputes in other theories of recognition. As Felski notes, while the defining role of recognition in social and political life has become a common theme of social theory in recent decades,[95] what makes Honneth distinctive is his insistence that the struggle for recognition is a fundamental, even existential feature of human nature: "Rather than being a recent trend that is tied to multiculturalism and recent social movements—as [Nancy] Fraser assumes—the desire for recognition is a basic human need, even as it takes on historically variant forms."[96] Honneth's work *The Struggle for Recognition: The Moral Grammar of Social Conflicts* (1992) can be understood as an attempt to revitalize this earlier project from Hegel's *System of Ethical Life*, in which (at least according to Honneth's reading) recognition is not a particular historical sociopolitical phenomenon but rather a fundamental, existential human need.

Although, as already stated, this theory is motivated by a desire to move beyond the Kantian antinomies of sociological reason via Hegel, it can be demonstrated that it nevertheless remains within this Kantian paradigm. It is a Kantian reading of Hegel because it takes a concept from Hegel—that is, recognition—and employs it as the precondition of its quasi-transcendental metacritical argument. To repeat Honneth's claim: "The intersubjective recognition of their identity ... is built into social life *from the very beginning*." As such, it neglects that which moved Hegel beyond transcendental philosophy—that is, the phenomenological form of his critique, and his idea of speculative experience, both of which depend upon the refusal of all methodological presuppositions, for which nothing can be "built in from the very beginning." This is the same criticism that Rose makes of Habermas and Althusser with reference to Marx. Habermas and Althusser, she argues, in spite of their differences, remain with a Kantian paradigm because they take a concept from Marx and elevate it to the status of a precondition, thus neglecting the phenomenological exposition of the preconditioned and conditioned in their speculative identity: "Thus Jürgen Habermas has 'taken' three kinds of action from Marx, and made them into the preconditions of three knowledge-constitutive interests"; similarly, "Althusser has used Marxist concepts as the precondition of his metacritical argument, 'structures,' 'apparatuses,' 'ideology.'"[97] Honneth claims that his critique "departs from the Kantian tradition in that it is concerned not solely with the moral autonomy of human beings but also with the conditions for their self-realization in general"[98]—that is, their struggles for recognition. However, this is precisely the reason that his metacritique remains *within* the Kantian tradition: because it takes social life as a given and then seeks to examine its conditions of possibility in the idea of a struggle for recognition.

Furthermore, although Honneth cites Rose's *Hegel Contra Sociology* in an endnote as having a "very strong interpretation of the concept of 'mutual recognition'" which he also claims to be "comparable" to his own,[99] their readings are in fact profoundly at odds.[100] In particular, Rose's argument concerning the *System of Ethical Life* is that this early text represents Hegel's "first 'phenomenology'"[101]—that is, his first experiment with an immanent, phenomenological, and speculative form of critique, in which objective determinations and their subjective mediations are exposited in both their identity and nonidentity. Contrary to Honneth's claim, far from positing recognition as the precondition of social life, Rose argues that Hegel's phenomenological critique in the *System of Ethical Life* reveals that recognition under bourgeois property relations is necessarily a misrecognition. Recognition occurs only "as an imperfect unification or as a *relation between the two*," as Hegel puts it; and therefore absolute ethical life—"the absolute oneness of ... individuals"—remains barred.[102] Just as the *Phenomenology* progressively recollects the necessary series of failed attempts to achieve absolute knowing, the *System of Ethical Life* presents a series of necessary but failed attempts to achieve ethical life or real recognition—from work, to family, commodity exchange, legal contracts, robbery, and war. But it is ultimately discovered that each of these, endemic to bourgeois property relations, presuppose a misrecognition.

This argument is made most clearly in the *System of Ethical Life* in the early section on "work." As Rose puts it:

> The simplest mediation is one in which the relation or lack of identity predominates ... in work. Work was accomplished by using a tool, and the product of labour belonged to the individual as his possession. By working, using a tool, or possessing the product, the individual sees himself, but in a formal way. He does not see the activity of others in his own activity, nor does he see other aspects of his own activity.
>
> By making the world, the tool, the product, his own, by appropriating them (*an-eignen*), the individual recognizes himself in a formal and partial sense. Appropriation, making someone or something into one's own ("an" means "into," "eignen" means "own"), is the simplest but formal way of re-cognizing oneself. It does not see what is excluded, the relation or nonidentity. Hence this recognition is a new form of mis-recognition and remains so as long as it occurs within bourgeois property relations.[103]

It is in alienated work that, in Hegel's words, the "unity" of the collective—"the activity of others in [the worker's] own activity"—"hovers over the single individual, [but] he does not emerge from it or abstract himself from it; it is in him but it is concealed in him; and it appears in this contradition, namely, that this inner light does not absolutely coincide or unite with the universal light hovering over him as something according to which he is driven on, as impulse or striving."[104] The critical implication which is made here—not by methodologically jumping the gun to examine the sociological preconditions but instead by phenomenologically expositing the immanent misrecognition of recognition itself—is that the possibility of real recognition will only be realized by a different system of property and work relations. The totality and unity of absolute ethical life "hovers" over the worker but he does not and cannot recognize it except through the formalized and therefore compromised medium of a property or work relation. As Rose explicates it, Hegel's phenomenological exposition reveals how the real recognition of absolute ethical life cannot be achieved under bourgeois property relations for "they make people into competing, isolated, 'moral,' individuals who can only relate externally to one another, and are thus subjected to a real lack of identity. Bourgeois private property presupposes real inequality, for the law which guarantees abstract, formal property rights presupposes concrete inequality (lack of identity)."[105] With this, Rose presents Hegel as anticipating Marx's theory of the fetish-character of the commodity, in which "the definite social relation between men ... assumes here, for them, the phantasmagoric form of a relation between things."[106] Under bourgeois property relations—that is, under capitalism—recognition between humans can only take the form of relations between things, in commodities, in alienated labor. Since recognition can only occur through this compromised medium of commodity exchange, real recognition remains an impossibility.

Honneth, however, is blind to this conclusion because he assumes recognition in advance of his critique as its quasi-transcendental precondition. In other words, Honneth is blind to the capital relation and commodity fetish that guarantee both that recognition is impossible, and that misrecognition is misrecognized as recognition; and this is because he assumes and idealizes recognition as a fundamental and inalienable feature of human sociability. As Felski puts it, albeit admiringly: "In contrast to Adorno—and his present-day avatars—Honneth steers clear of capitalism-as-body-snatcher scenarios; to portray one's fellow human beings as voided of agency and unwittingly controlled by social forces is to enact the very dehumanization one claims to diagnose. Rather, he shares with French sociologist Luc Boltanski the conviction that critical consciousness is ordinary, part of daily life rather than estranged from it. It is only via attention to everyday struggles over recognition—even if submerged or ambivalent—that scholars can adequately reckon with conditions of injustice."[107] Following Honneth, Felski thus instrumentalizes recognition as an originary ideal that, if recovered, would address the various failings of misrecognition and promote a more liberal, understanding world in which differences and grievances are adequately acknowledged and negotiated. But, by neglecting the misrecognition that resides behind every recognition within class society, legible only via a speculative critique, Felski neglects too that, as Rose puts it, it is totally "possible to mean well, to be caring and kind, loving one's neighbour as oneself, yet to be complicit in the corruption and violence of social institutions."[108] Meanwhile, the actual "[condition] of injustice" that precludes the possibility of such recognition is dismissed as a boogie-man, the talk of doomsayers and conspiracy (critical?) theorists. If there *seems* to be a truth, then, to Honneth's dismissal of his Frankfurt forebears—that "there is an atmosphere of the outdated and antiquated, of the irretrievably lost, which surrounds the grand historical and philosophical ideas of Critical Theory, ideas for which there no longer seems to be any kind of resonance within the experience of the accelerating present"[109]—this can only appear to be the case by focusing on "lived experience" at the expense of objective determinations, an exclusive focus which is as mistaken and as quasi-transcendental as the inverse.

Felski's employment of Honneth's concept of "recognition" in her reading therefore also results in a profound misrecognition of Eribon's incendiary depiction of class society. By focusing exclusively on the lived experience of class as presented in *Returning to Reims*, Felski concludes by indicting Marxism for its ideal of a classless society: "To what extent can one wholeheartedly will the extinction of one's own way of life, an existence that may be experienced as constrained and riven by deprivation, but also a source of felt belonging—of memory, identity, and personal history?"[110] For Felski, this line of questioning constitutes a fine-grained attention to the complexities of class—its ups and its downs. But this sentimentalism is radically conservative. Marx's point is not that working class identity should be abolished but that the very fact of this class-belonging precludes the possibility of real self-identification. For Marx, any imagined self-identification with one's class category under capitalism can only ever misrecognize one's real existence. To be "distort[ed]" into "a fragment of a man" and "degrade[d] ... to the level of an appendage of a machine" is not a "way of life."[111] The solution to the exploitation of the working class, therefore, is not in the provision and celebration of a genuine working class self-identity but in the demonstration that the reality of this exploitation precludes the possibility of any such thing. This is what Marx means when he writes that "in the fully-formed proletariat, the abstraction of all humanity ... is practically complete.... Man has lost himself in the proletariat."[112] It is on this point that Felski and Marx can, perhaps, agree: The category of the proletariat is a violent abstraction which reduces human subjectivity to its economic determinations, which steals humanity from itself. But while Felski wrongly identifies this as a feature of Marxist criticism, for Marx it is a feature of social and political reality itself. It is what he calls a *real* abstraction. Put differently, it is not that Marxist criticism reduces subjectivity to its economic determinations but that this is what capital itself does. The task of Marxist critique, then, is not only to disclose these determinations which flatten and erase human subjectivity but to keep alive and insist upon the life that they squander. This can only be done by providing what Rose, after Hegel, calls a speculative experience—that is, an experience of the contradiction between our economic determination and our subjective freedom; the contradiction between capital and life. Without this speculative experience, humanity remains "lost ... in the proletariat," and real life remains lost in life under capital.

Felski is also, therefore, misrepresentative of Eribon's own critique. Eribon does, indeed, criticize his own youthful Marxism as "little more than a way of idealizing the working class, of transforming it into a mythical entity compared to which the actual life of my parents seemed utterly reprehensible" and as "a vector for a kind of social disidentification."[113] However, this is a specific self-criticism of a purely academic and therefore impoverished Marxism. Marxism does not "idealize the working class." In Marx's words, "socialist writers" do not "regard the proletarians as *gods*." On the contrary, Marxism ascribes the proletariat with a "world-historic role" by demonstrating that their alienation can only be overcome by "abolishing the conditions of its life," an abolition which cannot take place "without abolishing all the inhuman conditions of life."[114] It is in fact Felski who risks idealizing the working class, for her insistence that their sense of "belonging" is reason enough to deny their emancipation. Taken to the extreme, such "attempts to organize the newly created proletarian masses without affecting the property structure which they strive to eliminate" constitute what Walter Benjamin calls fascism: "Fascism sees its salvation in giving these masses not their right, but instead a chance to express themselves."[115] Nowhere, by contrast, does Eribon suggest that class society should be preserved due to the attachments some might have to their imagined class identity. On the contrary, Eribon's account of the misrecognitions of and between class identities radically magnifies the horror of class relations and their inimicality to real recognition and hence the necessity of the destruction of the social order upon which they are based. "In fact," he writes, "there is little or nothing they can do when faced with the irresistible forces of the social order, forces that operate both in secret and in the light of day, and that impose themselves everywhere and on everyone."[116] It is the speculative experience of this determination and its hostility to life which is productive of the injunction to overthrow it. By retrieving this idea of speculative experience, by presenting the contradictory relation between capital and life, literary theory might realize a kind of critique which is neither detached, nor methodological, but which might keep alive the possibility of real life against the domination of real abstraction.

Jameson's Hegelianism?

If neo-Kantian critical literary theory is empty, postcritical literary theory is blind. The former, critically detached, seeks to excavate the text to examine its disavowed conditions of possibility at the expense of the text itself. The latter, though, presents meaning as reducible to an immediate, affective, and subjective experience. To return to Rose, both reproduce the neo-Kantian dichotomy of validity and value—the only substantial difference being which side is privileged.[117] It is only by retrieving Hegelian speculative experience for literary theory that this impasse might be broken. That is, it is only by practicing a literary criticism whereby the reader or critic comes to discover—through the irony, shock, and surprise of the dialectic—the contradictory relations between their sociopolitical determination and their subjective experience that the truth of the text might be realized, and that the critique of such determinations might be linked to their revolution.

Fredric Jameson's 1971 *Marxism and Form: Twentieth-Century Dialectical Theories of Literature* was the first work to explicitly call for such a literary criticism. Not only did it provide Anglophone literary critics with an introduction to the work of Frankfurt School critical theory and Hegelian Marxism more generally—from Adorno to Benjamin, Marcuse, Bloch, Lukács, and Sartre—it brought these different approaches together for the first time in order to intimate a future possible dialectical and phenomenological literary criticism.

Marxism and Form's final chapter, entitled "Towards Dialectical Criticism," begins by summarizing the "organizational dilemma" faced by any dialectical criticism: the dialectic's drive toward holism and totality.

> The peculiar difficulty of dialectical writing lies in its holistic, "totalizing" character: as though you could not say any one thing until you had first said everything; as though with each new idea you were bound to recapitulate the entire system. So it is that the attempt to do justice to the most random observation of Hegel ends up drawing the whole tangled, dripping mass of the Hegelian sequence of forms out into the light with it. So it is also that at some point or other books or essays on Marx dutifully end up as rehearsals of historical materialism as a whole. There is no content, for dialectical thought, but total content.[118]

Jameson would go onto repeat this point nearly forty years later in the introduction to *The Modernist Papers* with the comment that, "for good or ill, the dialectic requires you to say everything simultaneously whether you think you can or not."[119]

However, Jameson then goes on (in *Marxism and Form*) to offer by way of solution the innovation of Hegelian phenomenology:

> It is for this reason that phenomenology (like the other great contemporary philosophical systems not a discovery of new *content*, but an innovation in *form*) seems to have an answer to what would otherwise, for us, be an organizational dilemma. For phenomenology is precisely the attempt to tell not what a thought is, so much as what it feels like. It aims not at making statements about content (that being momentarily placed between parentheses), but at describing the mental operations which correspond to that content in all their temporal specificity. Its mode of proof, for the reader, consists not in logical argumentation, but rather in the shock, or the failure, of recognition.[120]

What is key, here, and what so often goes neglected in Hegel scholarship, is the emphasis on Hegelian phenomenology as a formal innovation—and a formal innovation that works to give a certain experience. Jameson then describes the shock of this experience, and its inextricability from, even its identity with, the dialectic:

> There is a breathlessness about this shift from the normal object-oriented activity of the mind to such dialectical self-consciousness—something of the sickening shudder we feel in an elevator's fall or in the sudden dip in an airliner. That recalls us to our body much as this recalls us to our mental positions as thinkers and observers. The shock indeed is basic, and constitutive of the dialectic as such: without this transformational moment, without this initial conscious transcendence of an older, more naïve position, there can be no question of any genuinely dialectical coming to consciousness.[121]

What I have emphasized in this final chapter, is that this speculative experience provided by the formal innovation of Hegel's phenomenology also offers a solution to the tendency of criticism and critique to transcendental reduction—in addition to offering a solution to what Jameson identifies as the organizational dilemma represented by the holism of the dialectic. To understand the dialectic from the outside is to formalize it as a schema, to understand it only from a transcendental standpoint. To truly grasp the dialectic requires the critic to experience it, even live it. By emphasizing the shocking, even "sickening" experience of a truly dialectical criticism, through which we are brought to self-consciousness not via logical argumentation but via the sudden, ironic reversal of what we had once held to be true, criticism might be moved beyond its detached, diagnostic mode.[122]

Jameson's subsequent reflections on dialectical criticism across the remainder of this enormous chapter are themselves presented phenomenologically (as opposed to polemically or schematically). Nonetheless, the method developed might be generally and briefly described as a kind of historicizing and (more particularly) periodizing mode of analysis which "isolates" the text before placing it in its context of a "succession of alternative structural realizations."[123] Jameson also stresses the essential metacritical character of dialectical criticism, which must, as it interprets its object, provide an interpretation and justification of its own existence, of its own theoretical and historical presuppositions—what he defines elsewhere as "metacommentary."[124] Crucially, the thing that differentiates this mode of dialectical criticism from both other historicisms and the due diligence of other self-reflexive metacritiques is that Jameson understands all cultural texts, ultimately, as imaginary attempts to resolve irreconcilable social contradictions. One the one hand, this means for Jameson that all cultural texts can be and perhaps to some extent always are ideologically mystifying, employing what he goes on to describe in *The Political Unconscious* as "strategies of containment"—strategies which, while identifying social contradictions (however unconsciously), seek to spuriously sublimate them into a more coherent and manageable narrative or image (whether moral, religious, or artistic).[125] Jameson even accuses Hegel's notion of absolute spirit of being a containment strategy, as prematurely sublimating the unthinkable yet real impossibility of collective praxis in the present into an ultimately aesthetic placeholder.[126]

On the other hand, the understanding of all cultural texts as imaginary attempts to resolve irreconcilable social contradictions also means, for Jameson, that all cultural texts can have and perhaps to some extent always do have a radical utopian impulse: a drive to overcome these contradictions. This is what allows him in *The Political Unconscious* to analyze Joseph Conrad's *Lord Jim* and *Nostromo* not as merely reducible to a particular historical period or to the product of their author's much-debated motivations and prejudices but instead as displaying a concrete textual structure of interrelating and overlapping periods and discourses, belying a desperate attempt to move beyond their historical-political determinations. "Seen as ideology and Utopia all at once, Conrad's stylistic practice can be grasped as a symbolic act which, seizing on the Real in all of its reified resistance, at one and the same time projects a unique sensorium of its own, a libidinal resonance no doubt historically determinate, yet whose ultimate ambiguity lies in its attempt to stand beyond history."[127] For Jonathan Culler, this is what makes Jameson particularly refreshing today, "at a time when critics, young and old, seem all too eager to condemn this or that text for its complicity with the various evils of our modernity."[128] Perhaps this paints Jameson as more of a reparative reader than he is. While Jameson would certainly identify a residual utopian impulse in even the most retrograde cultural products—from the advertising slogan to even expressions of antisemitism—this does not mean, of course, that Jameson would say that these things are *not* complicit with the evils of modernity, as containing, mystifying, and aestheticizing its contradictions. What a dialectical criticism does achieve, however, is a mode of interpretation equipped to identify and delineate both components, without engaging merely in acts of moral celebration or condemnation. Every text contains within it a tension—a tension between an often unacknowledged registration of social contradiction and a utopian impulse. It is in the identification of this tension that dialectical criticism, for Jameson, finds its critical force.

To a large extent, this mode of criticism coheres closely with the idea of speculative reading elaborated in this book and particularly in this concluding chapter—that is, one where the critical force of a literary work and its interpretation is to be located in the experience of the contradiction between the subjectivity represented in and by the work (analogous to what Jameson refers to as its utopian impulse) and the simultaneous discovery of its disavowed social and political determination—in the experience of the identity and lack of identity between subject and substance (to use Hegelian terminology). While not wanting to undermine Jameson's importance and the at times breathtaking intricacy and sophistication of his readings, where I believe his criticism is lacking is the downgraded status he affords to what he describes earlier in *Marxism and Form* as the "basic shock" of dialectical thinking. In *The Political Unconscious*, this shock is no longer constitutive of the dialectic but instead described as an "unavoidable experiential accompaniment" to it—derived from the unfortunate requirement to be constantly and repeatedly "decentering" the individual subject or reader by confronting them with (social, political) determinations extrinsic to conscious experience.[129] While Jameson here "grants" this experiential component, he is also hasty to minimize it, for he argues that even the experience of the individual consciousness's decentering is itself too closely related to individual experience and to the persistence of categories too closely related to the individual subject; when what a truly Marxist-Hegelian criticism should be aiming for, he argues, is a "view of meaning as a collective process."[130] The "experiential accompaniment" of the dialectic for Jameson, then, is merely evidence that even the dialectical disclosure of the individual experience's determination does not in itself offer any transcendence or escape from it—just as, he writes, "the most lucid subjects of psychoanalysis" never really "achieve the habit of lucidity and self-knowledge."[131] This is a more substantial account of the experience of the dialectic than the one on offer in *Marxism and Form*. It is for a start grounded more firmly in Marx, for whom the disclosure of the fetish-character (the mediation) of the (immediate) commodity is not sufficient to overcome it (I'll return to this point later). It is also, however, a methodological sidelining of it.

The problem with merely "granting" the dialectic with an unfortunate "experiential accompaniment" is that it is precisely this experience of stuckness—of natural consciousness coming to realize its political determination but nonetheless the inescapability of it—that lends the dialectic its critical force. Jameson, however, in his critical practice, rarely seeks to emphasize and intensify this feeling—the "sickening" experience of jolting from naive immediate experience to the discovery of its mediation and the irreconcilable tension between the two—opting instead to intensify his focus on the decidedly nonexperiential mediation, determination, and unconscious which is uncovered. Jameson stresses in the conclusion to *The Political Unconscious* that "the approach to the Real [our political unconscious] is at best fitful, the retreat from it into this or that form of intellectual comfort perpetual"[132]—and yet it is the moment of encounter with this Real of our political determination which is totally outside conscious experience that Jameson seeks to capture. I have argued in this book, on the contrary, that in order to discover this mediation or determination, consciousness must not hide from the naivete of "immediate" experience, but instead must follow its path. This is because its only when we most intensely and immediately experience (in reading, for example) that the critical revelation of this immediate experience's mediation might be most unbearable—that the speculative experience might be most intensely felt.

Jameson, however, in being anxious to mediate this immediacy *in advance*, consistently reverts to a place of critical detachment from his text, where the determination of this experience is treated (in a neo-Kantian fashion) as its criterion of "validity" or its quasi-transcendental a priori. This is perhaps even conceded by Jameson in a recent 2022 article, on the occasion of the fortieth anniversary of *The Political Unconsciousness*, where he describes "our unconscious, political or otherwise, as a matter of deeper categories, to use Kant's useful term—underlying categories that shape our conscious thought and interpretations of groups, the self, and indeed art and literature."[133] This may be trivially true, but the problem is the implied methodology: like Kant himself, Jameson risks positing and hypostasizing the dichotomies between consciousness and its (unconscious) conditions of possibility, between subjectivity and objectivity, without traversing their speculative identity and nonidentity, without following the path. A truly speculative Hegelian reading would *not* renounce immediacy in advance. Hegel himself never does. In the *Phenomenology*, for example, each "shape of spirit" that we occupy is a point of departure on the way to knowledge that considers itself to be immediate. However, it is only by following the path of this immediacy, through traversing the experience, that we discover what this certainty disavows.

Unsurprisingly perhaps, Jameson's methodologically diagnostic approach to literary theory which often has little to say about the value of the immediate experience of the text means that he is often picked upon by practitioners of postcritique as an exemplar of the critical paradigm. In particular, Stephen Best and Sharon Marcus, in the editorial introduction to their 2009 issue of *Representations* on "surface reading," direct most of their polemical ire for "symptomatic reading" at Jameson's *The Political Unconscious*. In it, they present Jamesonian criticism as an authoritarian and elitist practice for which both the writer and reader of literary texts are ideologically brainwashed, requiring the "heroic" literary critic to "free the hidden truth hidden in the depths of the text." Not only does it "[usurp] the place of the author," they argue, but even the place of God; the Jamesonian critic believes that they alone "can transcend the blinkered point of view of mankind."[134]

Of course, as should already be clear, this is a misreading, or at the very least an extreme overstatement. To reiterate, Jameson "grants" the dialectic with an experiential "accompaniment" precisely because the disclosure of the workings of our unconscious (political or otherwise) *does not* in itself offer any transcendence from it—and this irreconcilable tension between our individual experience and its determination is itself experiential. The designation of Jameson as emblematic of crude criticism, overwriting its text with extraneous, distracting, and often elaborately constructed historical detail, is especially ironic given that, as Leo Robson has identified, "Jameson has made a number of allusions to the sort of claims put forth by post-critique."[135] For example, Felski equates critique with "vulgar sociology,"[136] while Jameson too warns against "a vulgar-sociological or content approach to works of art."[137] Jameson recognized in 1971, long before the dawn of this most recent postcritical moment, that "exegesis, interpretation, commentary have fallen into disrepute."[138] Robson compellingly makes the case that, far from brushing off the affective and experiential possibilities of a text or artwork, Jameson often refreshes the experience with reference to his immediate aesthetic experience, or else through his style.[139] For instance, in his regular book reviews, Jameson "has developed a voice that sometimes resembles that of a wry belletrist with unusual command of technical language, at others that of a fire-breathing theorist with more than a dash of the fan boy."[140] And yet, one can understand how such a caricaturing and selective reading of Jameson as evidenced by Best and Marcus might arise given that Jameson also claims, at times in an almost Gnostic register, that the interpretation of texts "consists in rewriting a given text in terms of a particular interpretative master code" or "Ur-narrative"—that is, in light of an "ultimate hidden or unconscious meaning."[141]

What, though, is Best and Marcus's proposed alternative? Just as we saw that Latour's rejection of Kantian critique leads him to endorse an uncritical naive realism, Best and Marcus argue that the job of the critic is not to diagnose symptoms, but to far more modestly articulate "what is evident, perceptible, apprehensible in texts; what is neither hidden nor in hiding."[142] As I have already argued, such a criticism does not move beyond the antinomies of critique, but is a disavowal or (to repeat Felski's own term) "circumvention" of them. If critique, as they claim, is too closely tied to disclosing the conditions of the possibility of meaning at the expense of that meaning itself, then postcritique is even more doggedly tied to appearances at the expense of an understanding of what conditions and shapes their appearing.

In a revealing article from 2016, entitled "Marxist Criticism and Hegel," Jameson concedes that the "weak link" of much contemporary criticism is this awkward move between text and context—or, as we might understand them, text and conditions of possibility—that postcritique has emphasized. "Indeed," he writes,

> As far as Marxist literary criticism is concerned, I think it can be generally agreed that its most embarrassing move tends to be this (unavoidable) shifting of gears in which we pass from literary analysis to Marxian interpretation and find ourselves obliged to evoke the social and political meaning of the text in terms of the classes, historical contradictions, political and economic background, the conjectures and forces and ideologies, capitalist alienation, commodification, and ideological occultation and repression, all of which lurk behind the aesthetic curtain and are suddenly unveiled in all their impoverished extraliterary nakedness like the wizard of Oz.[143]

This is precisely the "unavoidable" shift between text and context that is criticized by postcritics such as Best and Marcus (and Latour, Felski, Love, et al.). The difference is, of course, that they do indeed avoid it. In the words of Latour, taken up by Felski as the title of one of her chapters in *The Limits of Critique*: "Context stinks!"[144] What is context according to Latour? "It's a way of stopping the description when you are too tired or lazy to go on."

Jameson goes on to invoke his own method of critique in "a much older work" (i.e., *The Political Unconscious*), only to admit self-deprecatingly that the methodology on offer there "is a solution that does not solve, or even paper over, the crucial moment of transition, the embarrassing link of the move from text to context."[145] He then, however, turns to another possible solution, developed from the logic of essence in Hegel's *Logic*. This particular method for literary criticism proposes that, by "following a number of logical preconditions for the work back in time, we lay in place what had already to be—socially, historically, formally, existentially, or psychologically—before reconstructing the actual production of the thing in itself, its emergence into Existence and its appearance, its reception and meaning for Actuality."[146] But despite having abstracted this methodological procedure from a passage in Hegel, this could far more easily be read as a statement of detached Kantian criticism—once again, this is a methodology which instructs us to take the work as a given, then reconstruct it by identifying its conditions of possibility. Jameson proposes here to overcome the awkward moment of transition between text and context by reducing or "rewriting" the text in terms of its horizons of "validity" (to return once again to Lotze's neo-Kantian terminology)—the criteria of its possible meaning.

Speculative Reading and the Critique of Political Economy

Before moving on, it is worth elaborating my above suggestion that this speculative experience—which involves naively following the path of immediacy—is already essential to Marx's critical method. Certainly, Marx's critical method (as with Hegel's) is directed toward discovering the disavowed mediation of any ostensible immediacy. But the way this method proceeds (again, as with Hegel) also makes the immediacy of the experience of reading an essential, formative moment of the critique.

This is best demonstrated with reference to Marx's critique of the fetish-character of the commodity. As Rose writes, Marx's "theory of commodity fetishism is the most [Hegelian] speculative moment in Marx's exposition of capital. It comes nearest to demonstrating in the historically specific case of commodity producing society how substance is ([mis-]represented as) subject, how necessary illusion arises out of productive activity."[147] This point is shared by Lukács and Adorno among others who, as Rose demonstrates in her early *Marxist Modernism* lectures, sought to generalize this theory of the fetish-character of commodities into a Marxist theory of culture.[148] I want to suggest, with reference to Keston Sutherland's groundbreaking but overlooked reading of this passage from Marx, that the speculative character of this moment in Marx's work not only extends to its phenomenological mode of exposition and the speculative experience of reading that it yields but that it is contingent upon them—and that both of these have been to school in Hegel's own phenomenology, for which (as I have sought to demonstrate throughout this book) the experiential content has an educative, even political intent.

In his essay "Marx in Jargon," Sutherland argues that the "concept" or "theory" of "commodity fetishism" has been severely misunderstood. First, "*der Fetischcharakter der Ware*" is "the fetish-*character* of commodities." To understand it as "the *fetishism* of commodities," as the official mistranslation would have it, is to suggest that the fetishism is merely a mode of apprehension, or else an epistemological problem, rather than an irreducible and insurmountable feature of the character of commodities themselves.[149] This has led to the second misunderstanding, whereby the fetish-character has been understood as a conceptual or theoretical problem of signification or understanding rather than a problem with social reality itself.[150]

What, then, is the fetish-character if not a concept or a theory? By philologically reconstructing Marx's writing, Sutherland demonstrates that it is in fact the subject of a satirical drama at the expense of his bourgeois reader. *Der Fetisch* as articulated by Marx is a term derived and *détourned* from the work of the eighteenth-century, aristocratic French ethnographer Charles de Brosses. Throughout his 1760 essay on *Du Culte des Dieux Fétische*, de Brosses performatively dramatizes a sense of "astonishment" on behalf of all enlightened modern European readers at the primitive phenomenon of fetish worship—of the worship of inanimate objects and animals by so-called savages. He writes: "one cannot prevent oneself from being *astonished* by the fact that nations and ages [*siècles*] so remote from each other should agree on the same idea."[151] This "astonishment" does not, as Giorgio Agamben has *theorized* it, evince de Brosses's "forgetfulness of the original status of objects"[152] but is rather, as Sutherland shows, evidence of a "form of polite, literary socializing among equals, a way of dramatizing and giving confessional literary color to his recognition of the kindred intelligence of his reader."[153] This practice of literary astonishment is "*irresistible* in the sense that it fulfils a moral imperative and serves as evidence of civilized sensibility."[154] De Brosses's drama is thus a satire at the expense of a "barbaric" figure, aimed at establishing "sympathetic mutuality" between members of the same class, "on the grounds of their common difference from the stupid and the unenlightened."[155]

What is particularly essential, here, is that "fetishism in *Du Culte des Dieux Fétisches* is not a 'concept'; it is, rather, the subject of a drama"—a drama which "depends on a specific historical *dramatis personae* sharing specific relations."[156] By translating "fetishism" into a concept of a theory, this irreducibly literary character is overlooked.

Despite not mentioning Hegel here, Sutherland's account of Marx's subsequent *détournment* of de Brosses's literary astonishment and *fétischisme* exemplifies the ironic, even satiric force of the dialectic, of all speculative experience. In Marx's *Capital*, the barbarian figure is not ultimately (as it was for de Brosses) a mere subject of ridicule; a means for polite, albeit racist, literary socializing among smug, self-important equals. Instead, the barbarian figure is *Capital*'s reader. The figure who is incapable of disenchanting or conquering the fetish-character of the commodity is first invoked as either "an infant, or a barbarian or a cannibal." Thus, "the stage is set, in this prologue to theoretical disillumination, for a literary conversation that will illuminate sympathetic mutuality between Marx and his readers."[157] And yet, once promised, this sense of security, certainty, community, and superiority—of all the comfort and confidence that comes with critical detachment—we are rudely and radically denied it. We are denied the sympathetic mutuality of the community of readers who can judge this barbarian figure; for this barbarian figure, we are shocked and disgusted to find, is us. As Sutherland puts it, echoing Marx's own horrific metaphor: despite our initial false assurance, we soon discover that "we are instead the person, like the infant vampire who licks clean the cauldron of *Gallerte*, sucking the blood off his milk teeth, who is real by negative virtue of not yet being impossible."[158] This is because the fetish-character of the commodity is not something that will be disenchanted and therefore vanquished through a process of analysis or logical argumentation, as it is so often implied. It is instead the assurance of the fact "that you are eating your brothers and sisters and that no act of deconstruction ... will get humanity out of your mouth."[159] The resulting "stupefaction" of the reader, to use Sutherland's word, constitutive of speculative experience as such, is the same one as theorized by Rose which, by "demonstrat[ing] the domination of abstraction ... urges *us* to transform ethical life by re-cognizing the law of its determination." The significant difference between this articulation of stupefaction and the "shock" of the dialectic as described by Jameson, is that it defends a moment of naive immediacy in the interpretation of commodities—and by extension all cultural "texts"—which means that when the moment of mediation or determination is disclosed ("mediation" or "determination" seeming such sanitized words now for what is in truth the self-cannibalization of humanity in consumption and exchange), the intensity of the unbearability of this truth is radicalized. By recognizing the law of our determination—that is, by recognizing this necessary implication in a system of universal suffering—we, the reader, are faced with a dead end for which there is no theoretical solution. It is the revelation of this determination that produces the only truly Marxist ethical injunction, which is revolution.[160]

This is the truth of the Hegelian irony theorized in the first chapter of this book, a dramatic irony to which we are not privy until it is too late. As Sutherland (and also Marx) shows, a speculative experience is one in which we are led into a sense of security and certainty, only to be rudely, even violently, confronted with what that comfort disavows. It is also emblematic of the refusal of any methodological distinction between the subject and object of critique and also of any neat dichotomy of objective determinations and their subjective mediations. The subject of the speculative satire is both the critic's pretensions to detachment but also the disavowed barbarism of the bourgeois reader. In fact, they are the same thing.

The Remains of the Day

For Marx, it is essential that the true nature of the commodity (and, by extension, of commodity producing society) cannot be known in advance of the critique nor demonstrated merely through a detached, disinterested process of logical argumentation or deduction. Instead, it must come to be known through a naive experience of terrible discovery—and self-discovery.

This is analogous to Rose's reading of Kazuo Ishiguro's novel *The Remains of the Day* (1989) and its 1993 film adaptation directed by James Ivory, as exemplifying (albeit at the level of representation) a phenomenological recollection of fascism. While the film of *Schindler's List* (for example) may succeed in "informing" audiences about fascism and therefore "overcomes knowledge-resistance to the Holocaust," the problem with being satisfied with this is that "as Freud argued, knowledge-resistance is the first and easiest of the five resistances to overcome."[161] More crucially, overcoming knowledge-resistance does no work to confront the spectator with their own possible implication with that which is up on screen. The spectator remains a spectator, and so they remain emotionally and politically unchallenged—or worse, edified. This is what Rose describes as "Holocaust piety"[162]: Fascism is rendered as a thing that others in the past or elsewhere are susceptible to, most likely because they are probably already evil, or else stupid—in short, most likely because they are *not like me*—and the Holocaust becomes an "ineffable" event of diabolical and inexplicable evil to which we should respond only with silence or prayer. For Rose, this is simply a defense mechanism: "the witness of 'ineffability,' that is, nonrepresentability, is *to mystify something we dare not understand*, because we fear that it may be all too understandable, all too continuous with what we are—human, all too human."[163]

Likewise, to return to Marx, if "commodity fetishism" is reduced to a pure theory or else a conceptual problem of signification, it may appear to overcome a certain knowledge-resistance about the inner workings of a commodity producing society, but at the same time, by proceeding with methodological detachment, the critic is allowed to feel comfortable, even superior, in their self-assumed enlightenment. For Marx, this ultimately self-defensive reflex is the epitome of bourgeois ideology. In Sutherland's words, it is this self-defense mechanism which "occludes real social contradiction by reductively neutralizing satire"[164]—this time not into pious silence or impious laughter but into manageable and readily consumable concepts.

The Remains of the Day, meanwhile, is "a film in which the representation of Fascism ... engage[s] with the fascism of representation";[165] a film in which the representation of fascism implicates the very "political culture which we identify as our own, and hence an emotional economy which we cannot project and disown."[166] This is principally because the central character's implication in fascism is not known in advance (and indeed, might seem at the beginning to be impossibly remote), and is only revealed once we have been allowed to develop an identification with him. The film (and novel) tells the story of the dedication of a head butler (a "bondsman," Rose adds, with a nod to Hegel) to a British lord; a servant who gradually "finds himself in the contradiction of the ethic of service." This contradiction is twofold. First, there is the ethical injunction to dedicate oneself to "the noblest Lord"; which is followed by the contradicting injunction for "disinterested, unquestioning commitment" once the pledge of service has been made. Second, there is the ethical ideal of dignity, which when realized in unstinting, dispassionate service, necessarily forgoes the dignity of self-realization (whether in love, identity, or politics).[167] In Rose's words: "The attractions of German Nazism are present in microcosm in the organization of the aristocratic household as a fascist corporation."[168] Crucially, we gradually discover that this microcosm is not merely allegorical but literal, as "the noblest Lord" to whom he has dedicated everything turns out, as the servant-narrator can barely bring to terms, to be invested in encouraging the British political class to support the Nazis.

The servant's realization of his wasted life at the end of the narrative—

tangible but hardly articulated—offers him no comfort or transcendence. It does offer him, however, "*the remains of the day*"[169]—a comprehension. These are the same remains of the day that speculative thinking offers us, arriving, as it always does, too late, to make us realize for example that the remains we are consuming in capitalist exchange are the gelatinated "expenditure of human brains, muscles, nerves, hands, and so on."[170] These remains of the day offer no theoretical solution but an intellectual dead end. ("Bourgeois reader, this dead end is intended for you.")[171] Likewise, our own true because experienced comprehension of fascism in reading or watching *The Remains of the Day* does not offer us comfort in the confidence of our own moral superiority. "Instead of emerging with sentimental tears, which leave us emotionally and politically intact," as Rose puts it, "we emerge with the dry eyes of a deep grief, which belongs to the recognition of our ineluctable grounding in the norms of the emotional and political culture represented, and which leave us with the uncertainty of the remains of the day."[172]

What is thematized in this novel (call it "the shock of recognition," "stupefaction," speculative experience) is also represented in its narrative form and so reproduced in its reading experience. By returning to Hegel, however, we can see that it is a speculative experience that might be implicit in the speculative experience of reading as such, of any work or text. In reading speculatively, we recollect not only the ironic truth of the text, but the ironic coexistence of real life with real abstraction. Crucially, however, this criticism is not conducted by the critic alone but the reader in cooperation with the text. While a Marxist criticism in a neo-Kantian mode may point behind the text to its objective determination or criteria of "validity," it is only through the speculative experience of the unbearable disjunction between the fetters of this determination and our subjective freedom as represented in and by the text and our reading of it (our expression, feeling, passion, hatred, and love; the utopian impulse implied by any ideological containment strategy) that we have any hope of saving the life that this determination squanders: of recognizing the rose in the cross of the present, of preserving subjective freedom in the realm of the substantial. This is done not by dismissing the immediacy of the reading experience in advance as mere false consciousness but by naively following it. For it is only through the experience of the extremity of the contradiction of this feeling with the impersonal operations of capital which are totally and forever extrinsic to it that the horror of these operations might be more fully known. To retrieve Hegelian speculative experience for literary theory might therefore reveal and sustain the irony of life lived under the dominion of its opposite.

Hegel's Defense of Poetry

It must follow then that the works in which this speculative experience might be most powerfully felt and fully realized are those which *do not* renounce in advance the immediacy and intensity of experience for the abstractions of form and impersonality—what might pass for mediation without immediacy. Hegel is certainly a thinker of mediation, and yet mediation for Hegel is always a process which must begin from that which takes itself to be *im*-mediate. We learn *only by experience* that we meant something other than we meant to mean, that "immediacy itself is essentially mediated."[173] Hegel's great insight is that when we aim first for mediation without immediacy, what we get is all the more immediate—and, worse, an immediacy which is satisfied with itself. We are left with "monotonous formalism" and "lifeless determinations" (*PhG* §51)—moralism, vulgar sociology, crude descriptive historicism, graphs, maps, trees.

This is why lyric poetry, for Hegel, is among the highest and most spiritual forms of artistic expression. Again, the cliché of Hegel as the ultimate thinker of mediation and objectivity for whom *Geist* names a necessarily social collectivity might seem to suggest that lyric, as the most personal, particular, and subjective—in a word, the most immediate—should be the lowest art form. And yet, it is poetry which Hegel describes in his lectures on aesthetics as "the absolute and true art of the spirit and its expression as spirit."[174] Lyric poetry, in particular, is described as totally fulfilling the artistic vocation of "self-expression and ... the apprehension of the mind in its own self-expression"—and it is afforded this place precisely because it begins *immediately*.[175]

Lyric poetry for Hegel finds its raw material in subjectivity and particularity, but the processes of lyric expression and lyric reading (which at their best could be described as speculative) are for this reason one of mediation and universalization. Lyric poetry begins by taking up what is there before the poet—the particularity of their inner life, thoughts, and feelings. In this way, it is not unlike the *Phenomenology* or the *Logic*, which also begin from what is apparently most pure, immediate, certain, without any further determination. And yet, lyric poetry expresses the particularity of this subjectivity precisely in order to move beyond it. It represents for Hegel the "emergence from self [which] means only liberation from that immediate, dumb, void of ideas concentration of the heart which now opens out to self-expression and therefore grasps and expresses in the form of self-conscious insights and ideas what formerly was only felt."[176] Hegel is therefore resolutely un-Keatsian. Unheard melodies are *not* sweeter. The germ of the poem which exists in the poet's head is always and forever of no interest, significance, or profundity, unless this germ spreads through expression and reading. The immediacy and particularity of the lyric poet's interior life *is* stupid and boring, for Hegel. However, the particular power of lyric poetry is that, like speculative thinking itself, it presupposes no mediation in advance but discovers and actuates it through experience. It is precisely through the intensity of its particular immediacy, that lyric poetry achieves mediation and universality.[177]

Why do we read William Wordsworth or Sylvia Plath or Sean Bonney? Is it because we want to find out more about the lives, thoughts, or feelings of these particular historical individuals? To have them pieced together and finally worked out before us? To be able to say: "Ah! There they are!" — No. That's what biographies are for. As Hegel puts it, in reading lyric poetry "we have no inclination at all to get to know his [the poet's] particular fancies, his amours, his domestic affairs, or the history of his uncles and aunts"[178]—even when the poems we read are most concerned with such particular details. To read lyric in this biographical way can even amount to something of a betrayal, for it is to neglect that it is the distinct capacity of lyric expression to intimate the possibility of transcending the confines of one's present finite existence. As Jacqueline Rose puts it with reference to Plath: biographical readings "have to wrestle with the fact that for the writer, the lived life was the point of departure rather than, as it is for the biographer, the place at which there is a desperate need to arrive. At worst it is a kind of insult: Don't think that this life, for all your efforts, will ever be anything other than the thing you truly are."[179] The force of lyric is that, like speculative thinking, it allows for the possibility that we might mean more than we meant to, that what "is" to the letter might go beyond itself.

This is ultimately what differentiates Hegel's *Phenomenology* from Wordsworth's *Prelude*, both works which, through a great labor of recollection, represent and actuate the growth of mind, or spirit. For Wordsworth, the freshness and the glory of the immediacy of early childhood or of youthful revolutionary fervor are forever lost, crushed by the weight of custom and maturity, and it is only via melancholic poetic recollection that the infinite nature of these lose moments might be intimated. For Hegel, meanwhile, it is only in the moment of recollection and relinquishment, or kenosis—*Erinnerung* and *Entäuserung*—that these otherwise particular moments of immediacy gain any lasting significance at all.

Does lyric poetry really offer "liberation" from a particular, finite existence, as Hegel puts it? In Marx's terms, does it really allows us to transcend the "dot-like" isolation of life under capital, where subjects are reduced to mere "bearers" of their economic function? No. Marx's abandonment of lyric poetry and his critique of philosophy (which only interprets the world when the point is to change it) is provoked precisely by the speculative realization that no work of analysis, interpretation, or art (not even the most sublime lyric poem) is sufficient to reverse or overcome the fetish-character of commodities and the alienation of humanity into the living death of real abstraction.[180] Anything less than this amounts to an unreflective containment strategy, an imaginary attempt to resolve real contradiction: Romantic idealism. However, as Adorno argues in his essay "On Lyric Poetry and Society," in what is effectively a speculative rereading of Hegel's account, lyric poetry is still the highest form of spiritual self-expression, even under capital where the falsity of lyric—that is, its presentation of unalienated, unmediated, infinite subjectivity—is most manifest. And this is because, precisely through presenting the illusion of pure subjective expression, it intensifies and concentrates the contradiction and irony of an alienated life: "Even lyric works in which no trace of conventional and concrete existence, no crude materiality remains, the greatest lyric works in our language, owe their quality to the force with which the 'I' creates the illusion of nature emerging from alienation. Their pure subjectivity, the aspect of them that appears seamless and harmonious, bears witness to its opposite, to suffering in an existence alien to the subject and to love for it as well."[181] Lyric as a form of immediate self-expression *is* a containment strategy, with a utopian, idealist impulse—but it is in traversing this immediacy that the fact of its mediation is made most painful. As Adorno puts it elsewhere: "Works unfold not only through interpretation and critique but also through their rescue, which aims at the truth of false consciousness."[182] Lyric at its most passionate may represent a false consciousness, but the truth of this false consciousness is that it testifies most explicitly to the contradiction between humanity and capital, to the fact that humanity is at once capital's *Menschenmaterial* and capital's "eternal irony"—that is, the troublesome subjective particular which refuses to be finally subsumed into a false universality. As Sutherland writes, poetry is not "an ideal plateau of already free and unenclosed expression, or a virtual world beyond the impediments, suffering and division of labour," as it might appear to present itself—"it is a perpetual exertion of imagination and of desire: the subject at full stretch."[183] Great lyric poetry, even in its falsity, is unable to lie.[184]

This is why Anahid Nersessian finds Keats, for example, to be one of the most politically radical poets in the English language. Not because of his alleged Jacobin sympathies, which would again rely too heavily on his biography and not on the poetry. (Besides, as Nersessian notes, Keats has little if anything to say about the political hot topics of his day such as the Napoleonic wars, the Industrial Revolution, slavery, or the Peterloo Massacre.) Instead, for Nersessian: "Keats's radicalism lies elsewhere, in his style."[185] The passionate intensity of Keats's lyrics, the life and love expressed by them, make explicit the eternal irony of an alienated life. It does not in itself overcome the pain of this alienation, but it does "make it unforgettable."[186] Keats's dream is Marx's dream: "that the basic agony of having a body might be expropriated or stolen away from all unnecessary and debilitating uses of human life and remade into the condition of a shared freedom."[187] Is this dream a utopia? An abstract universal or aesthetic placeholder? Perhaps. Lyric poetry is the expression and yearning of an unalienated life yet arises in an alienated society, so it necessarily contains an abstract imperative.[188] For desiring subjects, abstraction is unavoidable. But it is the experience of this contradiction between what passes for living and life, of the contradiction of subjective freedom in the realm of the substantial, that Hegel describes as speculative—it is the experience which "demonstrates the domination of abstraction" and therefore "urges us to transform ethical life."[189] Nersessian's speculative reading of Keats realizes this ironic truth. "This," she writes, "in Sean Bonney's ineradicable words, is what I've heard: 'for "love / of beauty" say fuck the police.'"[190]

Knausgaard's Struggle

In her book on *Immediacy, or The Style of Too Late Capitalism* which I mentioned at the beginning of this book, Anna Kornbluh scorns all works of immediate self-expression as merely complicit in an ideological conceit which seeks to naturalize the individual and the present. While she does not substantially address lyric as a genre, she does ascribe the poet Anne Boyer's awards success to her use of "the prosaic lyrical 'I' that has become the defining mode of me-generations, both the baby boomers and the millennials."[191] Kornbluh favors instead the detached third person as "an extraordinary construction of a mode of thought unavailable to us in everyday lived experience, in our own stupid envelopes. Third person stretches away from phenomenal subjectivity, toward speculative objectivity. It enacts a kind of thinking unavailable anywhere else—and that's the magic."[192] Kornbluh neglects to address, however, what makes this imagined always already mediated third person outside the parameters of our "stupid envelopes" any less of a containment strategy. If anything (although I would hesitate to write off any narrative mode in advance), one could argue that the third person is *more* covert about overwriting its process of mediation—of how and from where that voice emerged. In this sense, Kornbluh is right. The third person is "magic"—a trick or illusion whose secret is obscured.

By dismissing all immediacy in advance and demanding instead a style of mediation, Kornbluh does not mediate immediacy, she merely judges it. What she offers is not a critique of immediacy but an immediate morality in the sense that Hegel criticized: "a general prescription, not located in the social relations which underlie it, and hence incapable of providing any sustained and rigorous analysis of those relations"[193]—a presupposition which prohibits reading altogether. By emphasizing the priority of mediation over immediacy as a methodological principle, Kornbluh neglects that true mediation is a process which begins from that which takes itself to be immediate.

The majority of Kornbluh's ire against immediacy as literary style is reserved for the contemporary proliferation of so-called autofiction: work which represents, in her words, "a revolt against character, form, and fictionality itself."[194] For Kornbluh, autofiction is both symptomatic and reinforcing of the ideology of too late capitalism, its immediacy "shedding literature's potential to immanently criticize the known world."[195] She argues that its ostensible presentism and resistance to representation suggests a resignation to the world as it "is," while its first personalism reflects an atomized world of individuals and an obsession with identity. Although a number of vastly different writers fall subject to this criticism (Rachel Cusk, Anne Boyer, Olivia Laing, Tao Lin, Maggie Nelson, and Sheila Heti are all discussed), it is Karl Ove Knausgaard who receives most attention. Indeed, if there is any writer whose theme is his "particular fancies, his amours, his domestic affairs, or the history of his uncles and aunts" (to repeat from Hegel), it could be Knausgaard, whose 3,600-page, six-volume novel series *My Struggle* documents in painstaking, hypnotic detail and unreflective, unadorned prose the banalities of his life: eating cornflakes, changing diapers, cleaning, cooking, making coffee, reading, smoking, checking emails; punctuated by some more dramatic experiences: his father's slow death from alcoholism, a moment of hysterical self-cutting, throwing up at a party in Björk's apartment in Reykjavik.[196]

In the words of Ben Lerner: "Knausgaard isn't really quotable. There's too much lengthy digression and extremely—at times almost absurdly—detailed description; one would have to excerpt pages and pages, not a sentence or paragraph, to give an accurate sense of the effect.... [H]e appears to just write down everything he can recall (and he appears to recall everything)."[197] He shirks character for the "reality" of people ("Tonje isn't a 'character.' She is Tonje. Linda isn't a character. She is Linda.") and third-person narrativity for the immediacy of pure voice ("I wanted to just *say* it, you know. As it is").[198] What's more, Knausgaard wrote the entire series without edits or rewrites, and in less than two years (the 550-page fifth book was written in eight weeks). For Kornbluh, Knausgaard's writing and success (for instance, selling half a million copies in Norway by 2014, a country of just five million people) is emblematic of our cultural fascination with immediacy, of capitalist realism at its most extreme: "Nothing more than what phenomenally exists can be produced; all that remains is fluid, effulgent, sui generis exchange. Fiction, narrative, impersonality, and collectivity withdraw; reality, voice, personality, and atomism ascend. To get at value, get rid of mediation."[199]

Is it possible, though, that by reading Knausgaard with critical distance, with presupposed judgments of his narrative first person and hyperrealism, that Kornbluh reads Knausgaard *immediately*—or else, that she reads off her own immediate prejudgment and so precludes a reading of the work itself? In reading *My Struggle*, are we *really* concerned with getting to the *real* Knausgaard (the *real* Tonje, the *real* Linda)? Shouldn't we instead affirm "the fact"—to repeat from Jacqueline Rose—"that for the writer, the lived life was the point of departure"? Isn't it Kornbluh's insufficiently immediate reading, not Knausgaard's immediate prose, which says, "Don't think that this life"—this *struggle*—"for all your efforts, will ever be anything other than the thing you truly are"?

In an interview, Knausgaard claims: "When I'm at dinner parties, I don't say anything. I think what I have to say is stupid. It's not worth anything. I prefer not to say anything."[200] This claim might sound facetious given his prodigious output, but I believe him. The substantial content of *My Struggle* is indeed unremarkable, and Knausgaard never comes across as an especially interesting person with unique perspectives or insights, nor does he come across like he wants us to think of him as such. And yet, as he goes on to describe his writing process: "I let go of myself or my own opinions and just follow the text and see what happens.... Of course, it is me, but it has something else, and that's the motor in the writing. That's how things come into being.... When I'm writing, there is something that belongs to the process of writing."[201] Kornbluh gives the impression that what *My Struggle* consists of is the immediate self-expression of an immediately conceived self, when it is instead analogous to the process of mediating that immediacy in Hegel's sense: a process of letting oneself go, of one's own presuppositions, and just following the path. When it comes to *My Struggle*, it is the act of writing (or, for us, of reading) which mediates the immediate detail, not because it attempts to conceive of the mediation in advance, but because, in the words of Hegel, it "sets aside every reflection, simply to take up *what is there before us.*"[202]

What is the effect or result of this mediation? It is not to imbue the minutiae of everyday life with an aura of mystique or to reveal some more fundamental yet ineffable substrata beneath phenomena. It is neither a work of New Age mindfulness, encouraging a full presence and attention to the profundity of "the little things"; nor a work of Heideggerian disclosure. As I have already noted, Knausgaard's prose is plain. He does not seek to transform that which he describes, nor to elevate it, nor to defamiliarize it. It is not a work of Steinian domestic modernism, making the immediate-everyday strange. While for Gertrude Stein, potatoes are "in the preparation of cheese, in the preparation of crackers, in the preparation of butter, in it,"[203] for Knausgaard: "I forked the last bit of potato, yellow against the white plate, and raised it to my mouth. While I was chewing I gathered the remaining pieces of meat on my plate, loaded them onto my fork with the knife, together with some onion from the salad, swallowed, and lifted the rest to my mouth."[204] He certainly appears to fulfill his ambition of "just saying it as it is"—apparently unmediated. Jameson wonders in his review of the final volume of *My Struggle* "why we take such satisfaction in the notation of all these daily things."[205] We might wonder too how (if at all) these daily things can be said to be mediated if they are left untransformed, if Linda is Linda, and a potato is a potato?

One answer might be that, in spite of the sheer force of the particularity and specificity of these moments, we begin to recognize ourselves in them—not because they are experiences that we have necessarily had, but because they are experiences as such. As Martin Hägglund argues: "The transformative effect of Knausgaard's writing does not depend on sharing his cultural background or personal circumstances. You are a potential addressee of his work by virtue of being a time-bound, practically committed agent who can be moved to explore and deepen your commitment to the life you are leading."[206] Just as lyric poetry, for Hegel, is universal by merit of its total immersion in the particular "I," because by reading it speculatively we recognize in the subjectivity of the poem a subjectivity as such, something that we too share, so Knausgaard's struggle becomes our own not because it is mediated or universalized in advance but, on the contrary, because it begins by being his struggle alone. Knausgaard justifies his autobiographical writing like this: "the life I led was not my own. I tried to make it mine, this was my struggle."[207] The irony, however, is that in the process of writing his life down, not only did he make his private life totally public and therefore *not* his own in the sense that he exposed it for all to read, he also universalized his life in the very gesture of writing the word "I." As Hegel puts it: "The *I* that expresses itself is *brought to a hearing*; it is an infection in which it has immediately made its transition into a unity with those for which it is there" (*PhG* §507). "The I, which is *this I* and no other ... is just as much the immediately *mediated*, or the sublated, *universal* I" (*PhG* §799). However much one tries to express their particular self and no other, they are spreading their subjectivity like a contagion insofar as they are read by others who recognize themselves—who recognize themselves not in the particular content of *this* "I" but in its pure negativity *as* an "I." For Knausgaard, as with Hegel, I can know myself and take ownership of myself only by recollecting and relinquishing myself, by giving myself up to others (*PhG* §808).

Another answer is intimated by Jameson: "It is what a different postwar theoretical philosophy called redemption; all these insignificant moments of an insignificant daily life are here redeemed, by the ordinary, undistinctive sentences which write them down.... Knausgaard has written them down, and written about writing them, and this is the story, not of his own experiences, but of the writing of these non-reflexive sentences, about which we do not even feel his writer's cramp or his aching shoulder, his blurred vision."[208] This is a nod to Adorno, who in the "Finale" of his *Minima Moralia*, writes: "The only philosophy which can be responsibly practiced in face of despair is the attempt to contemplate all things as they would present themselves from the standpoint of redemption."[209] Importantly, I think, and against what Jameson seems to be saying to the letter, the moments and things of Knausgaard's insignificant life are not *actually* redeemed for us, here, now, by being written down. No sublation in reality has occurred. No work of writing or reading will be sufficient to redeem us from the finitude of what Adorno calls "damaged life." But perhaps Knausgaard may have written them, and perhaps we may read them, from the *standpoint* of redemption. This is not an unconditional or transcendental standpoint removed from what is. ("The more passionately thought denies its conditionality for the sake of the unconditional, the more unconsciously and so calamitously, it is delivered up to the world.")[210] Rather, we may speculatively reread it as the standpoint of speculative experience, where the contradiction between our subjective freedom (of thinking, writing, reading, even perhaps of loving) and the objective unfreedom of damaged, alienated life, is made most manifest. Writing freely about writing his unfreedom, our unfreedom: this is Knausgaard's mediation, his struggle.

In an essay on the author Jon Fosse, though he could equally have been writing about himself, Knausgaard claims: "No one has written more perceptively about Jon Fosse's literature than Lev Tolstoy in *War and Peace*, in the passage where the main character, Prince Andrei, is moved to tears when listening to a piece of music and endeavors to understand why. He finds reason in the terrible contrast between the illimitable infinity within him and the constraint of his worldly materiality."[211] "Speculative experience" names what it is to encounter this terrible contrast, between the infinitude of the spirit and the finite constraints of the letter, and to follow it—to its end.

Acknowledgments

This book owes a great debt to the inspiration, support, and encouragement of many friends and colleagues. In particular, I am grateful for Rebecca Comay, Christian Gelder, Josh Jewell, Louis Klee, Anahid Nersessian, and Keston Sutherland, who all offered invaluable advice or help at crucial moments. The book was also significantly improved following comments from two anonymous readers for the University of Chicago Press. More than anyone, Ross Wilson guided, encouraged, and inspired me in writing this book. He has been a great mentor and example, and I cannot thank him enough. Thanks, also, to all of my students at the University of Cambridge, who inspired me and from whom I learned a lot.

Much of the material in this book was tried out in presentations at various conferences and colloquia. Some of the questions I was asked and the discussions I had ended up shaping my writing in important ways. I am particularly grateful to the organizers and audiences of the Arts and Humanities Research Council International Conferences at the University of Cambridge (2019-20), The Poetics of Phenomenology workshop at the University of Tübingen (2020), the Warwick Continental Philosophy Conference (2021), and the Center for Research in Modern European Philosophy Graduate Conference (2021).

I am thankful for the support of my family, who are always a source of happiness and comfort. My greatest thanks, finally, go to Brontë, whose encouragement sustains me daily. I am grateful for her integrity, kindness, and love.

* * *

A section of chapter 3 appeared previously as "'The Letter Kills, but the Spirit Gives Life'" in *Critical Horizons* 24, no. 3 (2023): 266-81, © 2023 Critical Horizons Pty Ltd., reprinted by permission of Taylor & Francis Ltd. (https://www.tandfonline.com) on behalf of Critical Horizons Pty Ltd.; and a section of chapter 4 appeared previously as "The Limits of Recognition" in *Angelaki* 27, no. 6 (2022): 21–30, © 2022 Informa UK Limited, trading as Taylor & Francis Group, reprinted by permission of Taylor & Francis Ltd. (https://www.tandfonline.com/)

Notes

Preface

1. Paul de Man, "Sign and Symbol in Hegel's *Aesthetics*," in *Aesthetic Ideology*, ed. Andrzej Warminski, 91–104 (Minneapolis: University of Minnesota Press, 1996), 92–93.

2. G. W. F. Hegel, *The Phenomenology of Spirit*, trans. by Terry Pinkard (Cambridge: Cambridge University Press, 2018). References to this work will be given, as above, in-text by paragraph number with the abbreviation *PhG*. Where citations of Hegel's works give both English and German sources, unless otherwise specified, the German will be referenced by volume and page number from G. W. F. Hegel, *Werke in zwanzig Bänden*, 20 vols., ed. Eva Moldenhauer and Karl Markus Michel (Frankfurt a.M.: Suhrkamp, 1986), with the abbreviation *Werke*.

3. See Gillian Rose, "Does Marx Have a Method?" (unpublished lecture recording, University of Sussex, 1987). Transcript forthcoming in a special issue of *Thesis Eleven* on the work of Gillian Rose.

4. Anna Kornbluh, *Immediacy, or The Style of Too Late Capitalism* (London: Verso, 2024), 7.

5. Kornbluh critiques a number of writers who, in spite of their differences, she identifies as exhibiting immediacy as literacy style, including Karl Ove Knausgaard, Rachel Cusk, Anne Boyer, Olivia Laing, Tao Lin, and Maggie Nelson. Kornbluh, *Immediacy*, 65–112. In a footnote she also lists César Aira, J. M. Coetzee, Teju Cole, Akwaeke Emezi, Takashi Hiraide, Chris Kraus, Hitomi Kanehara, Franciso Goldman, and Sherman Alexie. Kornbluh, *Immediacy*, 68n9.

6. Kornbluh, *Immediacy*, 8.

7. Kornbluh, *Immediacy*, iv. Qtd. from G. W. F. Hegel, *Lectures on the Philosophy of Religion: One Volume Edition; The Lectures of 1827*, ed. Peter C. Hodgson, trans. R. F. Brown, P. C. Hodgson, and J. M. Stewart (Oxford: Oxford University Press, 2006), 157.

8. A joke told by Slavoj Žižek can be repurposed here: "At that time, military patrols had the right to shoot without warning at people walking on the streets after curfew (ten o'clock); one of the two soldiers on patrol sees somebody in a hurry at ten minutes to ten and shoots him *immediately* [my emphasis]. When his colleague asks him why he shot when it was only ten to ten, he answers: 'I knew the fellow—he lived far from here and in any case would not be able to reach his home in ten minutes, so to simplify

matters, I shot him now.'" This is the same as how Kornbluh's criticism of immediacy proceeds: She condemns immediacy *immediately*—she shoots before it's ten o'clock—without working through it, without the very process of mediation she calls for. Slavoj Žižek, *The Sublime Object of Ideology* (London: Verso, 2008), xxx. This joke was "told" to me by an anonymous reader.

9. Kornbluh, *Immediacy*, 196.

10. See G. W. F. Hegel, "Philosophical Dissertation on the Orbits of the Planets (1801), Preceded by the 12 Theses Defended on August 27, 1801," trans. Pierre Adler, *Graduate Faculty Philosophy Journal* 12 (1987): 276.

11. G. W. F. Hegel, *Aesthetics: Lectures on Fine Art*, 2 vols., trans. T. M. Knox (Oxford: Clarendon Press, 1988), 2:601.

12. As Theodor W. Adorno notes: "For Hegel mediation is never a middle element between extremes ... instead, mediation takes place in and the through the extremes, in the extremes themselves. This is the radical aspect of Hegel, which is incompatible with any advocacy of moderation." Theodor W. Adorno, *Hegel: Three Studies*, trans. Shierry Weber Nicholsen (Cambridge, MA: MIT Press), 8.

13. G. W. F. Hegel, *Lectures on the History of Philosophy*, 3 vols., trans. E. S. Haldane (Lincoln: University of Nebraska Press, 1995), 1:400.

14. Hegel, *Lectures on the History of Philosophy*, 1:400; G. W. F. Hegel, *The Science of Logic*, trans. George di Giovanni (Cambridge: Cambridge University Press, 2010), 47.

15. The importance of recollection for Hegel's thinking is becoming an important theme in Hegel scholarship. See in particular: Angelica Nuzzo, *Memory, History, Justice in Hegel* (London: Palgrave Macmillan, 2012); and Valentina Ricci and Federico Sanguinetti, eds, *Hegel on Recollection: Essays on the Concept of "Erinnerung" in Hegel's System* (Newcastle: Cambridge Scholars Publishing, 2013). It also receives considerable discussion in Robert B. Brandom's recent *A Spirit of Trust: A Reading of Hegel's "Phenomenology"* (Cambridge, MA: Harvard University Press, 2019), which I critique below.

16. An interesting parallel might be found in T. S. Eliot's conception of the literary canon: "What happens when a new work is created is something that happens to all the works of art which preceded it. The existing monuments form an ideal order among themselves, which is modified by the introduction of the new (the really new) work of art among them." T. S. Eliot, "Tradition and the Individual Talent (1917)," in *Selected Essays*, 13–22 (London: Faber and Faber, 1932), 15. Slavoj Žižek also discusses this essay with reference to Hegel in *Less Than Nothing: Hegel and the Shadow of Dialectical Materialism* (London: Verso, 2013) 209.

17. Rebecca Comay and Frank Ruda, *The Dash—The Other Side of Absolute Knowing* (Cambridge, MA: MIT Press, 2018), 3.

18. Benedetto Croce, *What is Living and What is Dead in the Philosophy of Hegel*, trans. Douglas Ainslie (London: Macmillan, 1915).

19. "Life" is becoming one of the most debated topics of Hegel scholarship, especially concerning its depiction in the *Logic*, and its import for critical and social theory. See in particular: J. M. Bernstein, "To Be Is to Live, to Be Is to Be Recognized," in *Torture and Dignity: An Essay on Moral Injury* (Chicago: University of Chicago Press, 2015), 175–217; Karen Ng, "Ideology Critique from Hegel and Marx to Critical Theory," *Constellations* 22, no. 3 (2015): 393–404; Martin Hägglund, *This Life: Why Mortality Makes Us Free* (London: Profile Books, 2019); Karen Ng, *Hegel's Concept of Life: Self-Consciousness, Freedom, Logic* (Oxford: Oxford University Press, 2020); Jensen Suther, "Back to Life?

The Persistence of Hegel's Idealism (A Response to Karen Ng, *Hegel's Concept of Life: Self-Consciousness, Freedom, Logic*)," *boundary* 2, September 23, 2020.

20. Hegel, *Logic*, 382.

21. G. W. F. Hegel, *Philosophy of Nature*, trans. A. V. Miller (Oxford: Oxford University Press, 1970), 441.

22. Jacques Derrida, *Glas*, trans. John P. Leavey, Jr., and Richard Rand (Lincoln: University of Nebraska Press, 1986), 116a.

23. J. M. Bernstein, *The Fate of Art: Aesthetic Alienation from Kant to Derrida and Adorno* (University Park: Pennsylvania State University Press, 1992), 274.

24. See in particular: Rita Felski, *The Limits of Critique* (Chicago: University of Chicago Press, 2015); Stephen Best and Sharon Marcus, "Surface Reading: An Introduction," *Representations* 108, no. 1 (2009): 1–21; Heather Love, "Close Reading and Thin Description," *Public Culture* 25, no. 3 (2013): 401–34; all of which will be discussed in more detail in the concluding chapter of this book.

Introduction

1. Michel Foucault, "The Discourse on Language," in *"The Archeology of Knowledge" and "The Discourse on Language,"* trans. A. M. Sheridan Smith, 215–37 (New York: Pantheon Books, 1972), 235.

2. Maurice Blanchot, *The Writing of the Disaster*, trans. Ann Smock (Lincoln: University of Nebraska Press, 1995), 46.

3. Werner Hamacher, *pleroma—Reading in Hegel*, trans. Nicholas Walker and Simon Jarvis (London: Athlone Press, 1998), 1.

4. See, for instance, Slavoj Žižek, *Disparities* (London: Bloomsbury, 2016), 3. Adorno writes that Croce's "loathsome question" of Hegel "makes the impudent claim that because one has the dubious fortune to live later, and because one has a professional interest in the person one is to talk about, one can sovereignly assign the dead person his place, thereby in some sense elevating oneself above him.... The converse question is not even raised: what the present means in the face of Hegel; whether perhaps the reason one imagines one has attained since Hegel's absolute reason has not in fact long since regressed behind the latter and accommodated to what merely exists." Adorno, *Hegel*, 1.

5. Jacques Derrida, *Positions*, trans. Alan Bass (Chicago: University of Chicago Press, 1981), 40.

6. Derrida, *Positions*, 77.

7. Jacques Derrida, *Of Grammatology*, trans. Gayatri Chakravorty Spivak (Baltimore: Johns Hopkins University Press, 1997), 24–26.

8. Derrida, *Of Grammatology*, 18.

9. Gillian Rose, *Hegel Contra Sociology* (London: Verso, 2009), 1.

10. Judith Butler, *Subjects of Desire: Hegelian Reflections in Twentieth-Century France* (New York: Columbia University Press, 2012), xxvi.

11. Catherine Malabou, *The Future of Hegel: Plasticity, Temporality and Dialectic*, trans. Lisabeth During (London: Routledge, 2009).

12. Žižek, *Less Than Nothing*, 194.

13. Comay and Ruda, *The Dash*, 2.

14. On the importance of Hegel to *Knowledge and Human Interests*, see Garbis Kor-

tian, *Metacritique: The Philosophical Argument of Jürgen Habermas*, trans. John Raffan (Cambridge: Cambridge University Press, 1980). On the question of Habermas's relationship to Hegel see especially: Robert B. Pippin, "Hegel, Modernity, and Habermas," *The Monist* 74, no. 3 (1991): 329–57; Douglas Moggach, "Hegel and Habermas," *The European Legacy* 2, no. 3 (1997): 550–56; Kenneth Baynes, "Freedom and Recognition in Hegel and Habermas," *Philosophy and Social Criticism* 28, no. 1 (2002): 1–17; and Robert B. Brandom, "Towards Reconciling Two Heroes: Habermas and Hegel," *Argumenta* 1, no. 1 (2015): 29–42. While Baynes and Brandom, as with Kortian, emphasize the confluences between Hegel and Habermas, Moggach and Pippin emphasize the differences, particularly with reference to Habermas's misreadings of Hegel.

15. See especially Axel Honneth, *The Struggle for Recognition: The Moral Grammar of Social Conflicts*, trans. Joel Anderson (Cambridge: Polity Press, 2005). For the best critical accounts of Honneth's reading of Hegel, see Karin de Boer, "Beyond Recognition? Critical Reflections on Honneth's Reading of Hegel's *Philosophy of Right*," *International Journal of Philosophical Studies* 21, no. 4 (2013): 534–58; and Robert B. Pippin, "Reconstructivism: Honneth's Hegelianism," *Philosophy and Social Criticism* 40, no. 8 (2014): 725–41. Honneth's Hegelianism and its utilization by Rita Felski's postcritical literary theory will receive a more thorough analysis in the concluding chapter of this book.

16. Robert B. Brandom, *Tales of the Mighty Dead: Historical Essays in the Metaphysics of Intentionality* (Cambridge, MA: Harvard University Press, 2002), 102.

17. Brandom, *A Spirit of Trust*, 2.

18. Brandom, *A Spirit of Trust*, 2.

19. Brandom, *A Spirit of Trust*, 1.

20. Brandom, *A Spirit of Trust*, 532.

21. Brandom, *Tales of the Mighty Dead*, 95.

22. Brandom, *Tales of the Mighty Dead*, 101.

23. Stephen Houlgate, "Phenomenology and *De Re* Interpretation: A Critique of Brandom's Reading of Hegel," *Hegel Bulletin* 29 (2015): 30–47. See also Stephen Houlgate, review of *A Spirit of Trust: A Reading of Hegel's "Phenomenology"* by Robert B. Brandom, *Notre Dame Philosophical Reviews*, April 14, 2020, https://ndpr.nd.edu/reviews/a-spirit-of-trust-a-reading-of-hegels-phenomenology/.

24. Allen Speight, *Hegel, Literature and the Problem of Agency* (Cambridge: Cambridge University Press, 2001).

25. Katrin Pahl, *Tropes of Transport: Hegel and Emotion* (Evanston, IL: Northwestern University Press, 2012), 6.

26. See Pahl, *Tropes of Transport* and Speight, *Hegel, Literature and the Problem of Agency*, 15.

27. See especially: Comay, "Hegel's Last Words," in *The Dash*, 65–86; and Robert B. Pippin, "The Status of Literature in Hegel's *Phenomenology of Spirit*: On the Lives of Concepts," in *Philosophy by Other Means: The Arts in Philosophy and Philosophy in the Arts* (Chicago: University of Chicago Press, 2021), 39–55.

28. See, for instance: Jennifer Ann Bates, *Hegel and Shakespeare on Moral Imagination* (New York: SUNY Press, 2010); Keston Sutherland, "*Sub Songs* versus the Subject: Critical Variations on a Distinction between Prynne and Hegel," in *On the Late Poetry of J. H. Prynne*, ed. Joe Luna and Jow Lindsay Walton (Brighton: Hi Zero & Sad Press, 2014), 123–42; Joe Moshenska, "Why Can't Spenserians Stop Talking About Hegel? A Response to Gordon Teskey," *Spenser Review* 44 (2014); Wayne Deakin, *Hegel and the*

English Romantic Tradition (London: Palgrave Macmillan, 2015), which discusses Samuel Taylor Coleridge, William Wordsworth, Percy Bysshe Shelley, and Mary Shelley; Angelia Nuzzo, *Approaching Hegel's Logic, Obliquely: Melville, Molière, Beckett* (New York: SUNY Press, 2018), which, in addition to those named in the title, also discusses Giacomo Leopardi and Elizabeth Bishop; Eva Ruda, ed., *Beckett and Dialectics: Be it Something or Nothing* (London: Bloomsbury Academic, 2021), particularly Rebecca Comay, "Senile Dialectic," 61–104; and Jensen Suther, "Spirit Disfigured: The Persistence of Freedom in the Modernist Novel" (PhD diss., Yale University, 2019).

29. M. A. R. Habib, *Hegel and the Foundations of Literary Theory* (Cambridge: Cambridge University Press, 2018), 14.

30. G. W. F. Hegel, *Lectures on the Philosophy of Religion: One Volume Edition: The Lectures of 1827*, ed. Peter C. Hodgson, trans. R. F. Brown, P. C. Hodgson, and J. M. Stewart (Oxford: Oxford University Press, 2006), 83n17. Addition from 1831 lecture.

31. Andrew Cole, *The Birth of Theory* (Chicago: University of Chicago Press, 2014), 19.

32. Adorno, *Hegel*, 83.

33. Susan Buck-Morss, *Hegel, Haiti, and Universal History* (Pittsburgh: University of Pittsburgh Press, 2009), 20. This book was developed from the earlier article, Susan Buck-Morss, "Hegel and Haiti," *Critical Inquiry* 26, no. 4 (2000): 821–65.

34. Slavoj Žižek, *First as Tragedy, Then as Farce* (London: Verso, 2009), 111.

35. Adorno, *Hegel*, 89.

36. Adorno, *Hegel*, 11, 148.

37. Martin Heidegger, *Hegel's Phenomenology of Spirit*, trans. Parvis Emad and Kenneth Maly (Bloomington: Indiana University Press, 1988), 36. These lectures were delivered at the University of Freiburg in 1930–31 and first published in German in 1980.

38. Heidegger, *Hegel's Phenomenology of Spirit*, 36.

39. Heidegger, *Hegel's Phenomenology of Spirit*, 82.

40. Malabou, *The Future of Hegel*, 181.

41. See 2 Corinthians 3:6. *The Holy Bible: New Revised Standard Version with Apocrypha* (Oxford: Oxford University Press, 1995).

42. Malabou, *The Future of Hegel*, 181.

43. Malabou, *The Future of Hegel*, 181.

44. Malabou, *The Future of Hegel*, 183.

45. Malabou, *The Future of Hegel*, 167.

46. Rose, *Hegel Contra Sociology*, 1.

47. G. W. F. Hegel, *Elements of the Philosophy of Right*, ed. Allen W. Wood, trans. H. B. Nisbet (Cambridge: Cambridge University Press, 2003), 21.

48. This coinage, *Punktualität* in the German, is from Marx's *Grundrisse: Foundations of the Critique of Political Economy (Rough Draft)*, trans. Martin Nicolaus (London: Penguin Books, 1993), 485. I owe my knowledge of it to Keston Sutherland's lecture, "Poetry and Subjective Infinity," online video recording, Vimeo, April 7, 2014, https://vimeo.com/91328990.

49. Theodor W. Adorno, *Minima Moralia: Reflections from Damaged Life*, trans. by E. F. N. Jephcott (London: Verso, 2005), 19.

50. For more on Marx and gelatine, or *Gallerte*, see Keston Sutherland, "Marx in Jargon," in *Stupefaction: A Radical Anatomy of Phantoms* (London: Seagull Books, 2011), 26–90.

174 Notes to Pages 15–24

51. Sutherland, "Poetry and Subjective Infinity."

52. V. I. Lenin, *Imperialism: The Highest Stage of Capitalism: A Popular Outline*, trans. Yuri Sdobnikov, vol. 22 of *Lenin: Collected Works* (Moscow: Progress Publishers, 1974), 185–304.

53. Rose, *Hegel Contra Sociology*, 235.

54. Karl Marx and Friedrich Engels, *The Holy Family, or Critique of Critical Criticism*, trans. Richard Dixon and Clemens Dutt, in vol. 4 of *Marx/Engels Collected Works (MECW)* (London: Lawrence & Wishart, 1975), 37. This is also the epigraph to Sutherland's lecture "Poetry and Subjective Infinity."

Chapter One

1. Hegel, *Aesthetics*, 1:67, 68, 160, 161, 161, 223, 243, 244.
2. Hegel, *Aesthetics*, 1:159–60.
3. Hegel, *Aesthetics*, 1:601.
4. Hegel, *Aesthetics*, 1:160.
5. Søren Kierkegaard, *The Concept of Irony, with Continual Reference to Socrates*, in vol. 2 of *Kierkegaard's Writings*, ed. and trans. Howard V. Hong and Edna H. Hong (Princeton, NJ: Princeton University Press, 1989), 265.
6. Jeffrey Reid, *The Anti-Romantic: Hegel Against Ironic Romanticism* (London: Bloomsbury, 2014), 1. This volume is Reid's revision and translation of his earlier *L'antiromantique: Hegel contre le romantisme ironique* (Laval: Presses de l'Univeristé Laval, 2007).
7. De Man, "The Concept of Irony," in *Aesthetic Ideology*, 164.
8. De Man, "The Concept of Irony," in *Aesthetic Ideology*, 168.
9. Kierkegaard, *The Concept of Irony*, 265.
10. Hegel, *Aesthetics*, 1:160.
11. Butler, *Subjects of Desire*, 7–8.
12. Butler, *Subjects of Desire*, 76.
13. Richard Rorty, *Consequences of Pragmatism (Essays: 1972–1980)* (Minneapolis: University of Minnesota Press, 1994), 148.
14. John McGowan, *Postmodernism and Its Critics* (New York: Cornell University Press, 1991), 177.
15. Gillian Rose, *Mourning Becomes the Law: Philosophy and Representation* (Cambridge: Cambridge University Press, 1996), 6–7.
16. Rorty, *Consequences of Pragmatism*, 148.
17. Rose, *Mourning Becomes the Law*, 13.
18. De Man lists these as primary functions of irony in "The Concept of Irony," 165.
19. Günter Wohlfart, *Der spekulative Satz: Bemerkungen zum Begriff der Spekulation bei Hegel* (Berlin: Walter de Gruyter, 1981), v. My translation.
20. Stephen Houlgate, *The Opening of Hegel's 'Logic': From Being to Infinity* (West Lafayette, IN: Purdue University Press, 2006), 94.
21. Fred Rush, *Irony and Idealism: Rereading Schlegel, Hegel, and Kierkegaard* (Oxford: Oxford University Press, 2016), 159.
22. Rush, *Irony and Idealism*, 165.
23. Friedrich Schlegel, "Ideas," in *The Early Political Writings of the German Roman-*

tics, ed. and trans. Frederick C. Beiser, 123-40 (Cambridge: Cambridge University Press, 1999), 131.

24. Adorno, *Hegel*, 89.
25. Adorno, *Hegel*, 95.
26. Theodor W. Adorno, *Drei Studien zu Hegel*, in vol. 5 of *Gesammelte Schriften*, ed. Rolf Tiedemann, 247-383 (Frankfurt a.M.: Suhrkamp, 2003), 331.
27. Adorno, *Drei Studien zu Hegel*, 5:326; my emphasis.
28. Hegel, *Werke*, vol. 3, *Phänomenologie des Geistes*, 75.
29. Hegel, *Werke*, vol. 3, *Phänomenologie des Geistes*, 68.
30. G. W. F. Hegel, *Encyclopedia of the Philosophical Sciences in Basic Outline*, part 1, *Science of Logic*, trans. Klaus Brinkmann and Daniel O. Dahlstrom (Cambridge: Cambridge University Press, 2010), §10, p. 38.
31. Donald Phillip Verene, *Hegel's Recollection: A Study of Images in the "Phenomenology of Spirit"* (Albany: SUNY Press, 1985), 14.
32. Hegel, *Logic*, 59.
33. Rose, *Hegel Contra Sociology*, 160.
34. For example, W. T. Stace writes that Hegel's philosophy proceeds in "triads of thesis, antithesis, synthesis." When he finds that Hegel's works do not consistently follow this "ideal method," he claims: "These irregularities do not indicate, however, that our description of the dialectic method is wrong. What they do show is that Hegel has not himself been able to carry out his own dialectic method with absolute consistency in all cases. This is of course an imperfection in his system." W. T. Stace, *The Philosophy of Hegel: A Systematic Exposition* (New York: Dover, 1955), 97. For a critique of this stereotype, with reference to Stace, see Gustav E. Mueller, "The Hegel Legend of 'Thesis-Antithesis-Synthesis,'" in *The Hegel Myths and Legends*, ed. Jon Stewart (Evanston, IL: Northwestern University Press, 1996), 301-5.
35. Translation slightly altered.
36. Hegel, *Werke*, vol. 3, *Phänomenologie des Geistes*, 77.
37. Hegel, *Logic*, 47.
38. Brandom, *A Spirit of Trust*. This example is first developed on pp. 76-80, and then reprised on pp. 89-92.
39. Brandom, *A Spirit of Trust*, 91-92.
40. Brandom, *A Spirit of Trust*, 362.
41. Brandom, *A Spirit of Trust*, 101.
42. Brandom, *A Spirit of Trust*, 3.
43. Brandom, *A Spirit of Trust*, 96.
44. Hegel, *Encyclopedia Logic*, §48, p. 93.
45. Hegel, *Logic*, 382-83.
46. Samuel Beckett, "What Is the Word?," in *Poems: 1930-1989*, 113-15 (London: Calder Publications, 2002), 113.
47. Hegel, *Encyclopedia Logic*, §24, p. 61.
48. "The Absolute itself is the identity of identity and non-identity; being opposed and being one are both together in it." G. W. F. Hegel, *The Difference Between Fichte's and Schelling's System of Philosophy*, trans. H. S. Harris and Walter Cerf (Albany: SUNY Press, 1977), 156.
49. Hegel, *Lectures on the History of Philosophy*, 1:400.

50. Hegel, *Werke*, vol. 18, *Vorlesungen über die Geschichte der Philosophie I*, 460.
51. Hegel, *Werke*, vol. 3, *Phänomenologie des Geistes*, 54.
52. Malabou, *The Future of Hegel*, 177.
53. Rose, *Hegel Contra Sociology*, 52.
54. Hegel, *Werke*, vol. 3, *Phänomenologie des Geistes*, 58–59. Žižek recovers the latent concept of *"absoluter Gegenstoss,"* translated as "absolute recoil," from Hegel's logic of reflection to describe the emergence of a thing out of its own loss or failure. "When positedness is self-sublated, an essence is no longer directly determined by an external Other, by its complex set of relations to its otherness, to the environment into which it emerged. Rather, it determines itself, it is 'within itself the absolute recoil upon itself'— the gap, or discord, that introduces dynamism into it is absolutely immanent." Slavoj Žižek, *Absolute Recoil: Towards a New Foundation of Dialectical Materialism* (London: Verso, 2014), 4.
55. Hegel to von Knebel, August 30, 1807. G. W. F. Hegel, *The Letters*, trans. Clark Butler and Christiane Seiler (Bloomington, IN: Indiana University Press, 1984), 145.
56. Adorno, *Hegel*, 83.
57. Translation slightly altered.
58. Hegel, *Philosophy of Right*, §166.
59. For Hegel on Antigone see *PhG*, §§436, 469; *Philosophy of Right*, §144; *Aesthetics*, 2:1217–18.
60. Adorno, *Hegel*, 83.
61. Julia Kristeva, *Julia Kristeva Interviews*, ed. Ross Mitchell Guberman (New York: Columbia University Press, 1966), 45.
62. Alain Badiou, *Logics of Worlds: Being and Event II*, trans. Alberto Toscano (London: Continuum, 2009), 324.
63. Marx and Engels, *The Holy Family*, 37.
64. Quoted in Rose, *Hegel Contra Sociology*, 51, 86–87. Rose's own translations.
65. Theodor W. Adorno, *Critical Models: Interventions and Catchwords*, trans. Harry W. Pickford (New York: Columbia University Press, 2005), 7.
66. See Mladen Dolar, "The Phrenology of Spirit," in *Supposing the Subject*, ed. Joan Copjec (London: Verso, 1994), 64–83; and Žižek, *The Sublime Object of Ideology*, 234–37.
67. Žižek, *The Sublime Object of Ideology*, 235.
68. Hamacher, *pleroma*, 6.
69. Judith Butler, "Commentary on Joseph Flay's 'Hegel, Derrida, and Bataille's Laughter,'" in *Hegel and His Critics: Philosophy in the Aftermath of Hegel*, ed. William Desmond, 174–78 (Albany: SUNY Press, 1989), 175.
70. Butler, "Commentary on Joseph Flay's 'Hegel, Derrida, and Bataille's Laughter,'" 175.
71. See Josiah Royce, *Lectures on Modern Idealism* (New Haven: Yale University Press, 1919), 147; Jean Hyppolite, *Genesis and Structure of Hegel's "Phenomenology of Spirit*,*"* trans. Samuel Cherniak and John Heckman (Evanston, IL: Northwestern University Press, 1974), 11–12; M. H. Abrams, *Natural Supernaturalism: Tradition and Revolution in Romantic Literature* (New York: W. W. Norton, 1971), 225–37.
72. Hegel, *Encyclopedia Logic*, §81, p. 130; *Logic*, 737.
73. Rebecca Comay, "Resistance and Repetition: Hegel and Freud," in *Hegel and Resistance: History, Politics and Dialectics*, ed. Bart Zantvoort and Rebecca Comay, 35–57 (London: Bloomsbury, 2019), 50.

74. Rush, *Irony & Idealism*, 165.
75. Isobel Armstrong, *The Radical Aesthetic* (Hoboken, NJ: Wiley, 2000), 62.
76. Jacques Derrida, *Points ... Interviews, 1974-1994*, ed. Elisabeth Weber, trans. Peggy Kamuf (Stanford: Stanford University Press, 1995), 321.
77. Gillian Rose, *Judaism and Modernity: Philosophical Essays* (London: Verso, 2017), 10.
78. Luke 9:62.
79. Keston Sutherland, "Wrong Poetry," in *Stupefaction*, 91; with quotation from *PhG*, §57.
80. This is comparable to what Lisa Robertson (after Hannah Arendt, and with reference to Pauline Réage's *Histoire d'O*) calls "nilling." For Robertson, in the act of reading there must be a willed surrender of agency which verges on the masochistic. See Lisa Robertson, "Lastingness: Réage, Lucrèce, Arendt," in *Nilling: Prose Essays on Noise, Pornography, The Codex, Melancholy, Lucretius, Folds, Cities and Related Aporias* (Toronto: Bookthug, 2012), 28.
81. Hegel's student Karl Ludwig Michelet, qtd. in Terry Pinkard, *Hegel: A Biography* (Cambridge: Cambridge University Press, 2000), 203.
82. Simon Jarvis, "Prosody as Cognition," *Critical Quarterly* 40, no. 4 (1998): 3-15.
83. Adorno, *Hegel*, 53.
84. Brandom, *Tales of the Mighty Dead*, 106.
85. These terms are defined in full in Brandom, *Tales of the Mighty Dead*, 94-107. Brandom proposes *de dicto* and *de re* as possible modes of interpretation for reading any philosopher; Hegel is mentioned as an example throughout without acknowledging the vitally unique status given to reading in his philosophy.
86. Brandom, *Tales of the Mighty Dead*, 98-99.
87. Brandom, *Tales of the Mighty Dead*, 101.
88. Brandom, *Tales of the Mighty Dead*, 102.
89. Robert B. Brandom, *Articulating Reasons: An Introduction to Inferentialism* (Cambridge, MA: Harvard University Press, 2009), 205n7.
90. Brandom, *Tales of the Mighty Dead*, 103.
91. Stephen Houlgate, "Phenomenology and *De Re* Interpretation," 31.
92. Brandom, *Tales of the Mighty Dead*, 102.
93. Comay and Ruda, *The Dash*, 5, quoting *PhG*, §87, and *Logic*, 47.

Chapter Two

1. Marcel Proust, *In Search of Lost Time*, vol. 1, *Swann's Way*, trans. C. K. Scott Moncrieff and Terence Kilmartin, rev. D. J. Enright (New York: Modern Library, 1992), 116.
2. Hegel, *Werke*, vol. 3, *Phänomenologie des Geistes*, 590. This is why, for Hegel, the philosophy of nature involves the passivity of an external observer: it "has, as it were, simply to watch how nature itself sublates its externality." G. W. F. Hegel, *Philosophy of Mind*, trans. W. Wallace and A. V. Miller, rev. Michael Inwood (Oxford: Oxford University Press, 2017), 14.
3. Timothy Bahti, *Allegories of History: Literary Historiography after Hegel* (Baltimore: Johns Hopkins University Press, 1992), 81.
4. Hegel, *Werke*, vol. 3, *Phänomenologie des Geistes*, 548, 591.
5. Hegel, *Werke*, vol. 3, *Phänomenologie des Geistes*, 590.

6. Terry Pinkard, "Translator's Note," in *PhG*, xlii.
7. Hegel, *Werke*, vol. 3, *Phänomenologie des Geistes*, 590.
8. Matthew 27:46.
9. 1 Corinthians 11:24. These words also appear with some variation in Matthew 26:26; Mark 14:22; Luke 22:19.
10. Hegel, *Werke*, vol. 3, *Phänomenologie des Geistes*, 591.
11. Theodor W. Adorno, *Negative Dialectics*, trans. E. B. Ashton (London: Routledge, 2004), 23.
12. Hegel, *Werke*, vol. 3, *Phänomenologie des Geistes*, 591.
13. See Matthew 27:33; Mark/Markus 15:22; Luke/Lukas 23:33; John/Johannes 19:17. *Die Bibel: Lutherübersetzung* (Peabody, MA: Hendrickson, 2018). The term for Golgotha in the original Biblical Greek, Γολγοθα, is a simplified pronunciation of the Aramaic *golgolta*, which corresponds to the Hebrew gulgōleṯ (גֻּלְגֹּלֶת), meaning "skull." "Calvary" is the anglicized form of the Latin *calvāria*, also meaning "skull." *OED Online*, s.v. "golgotha (n.)," https://www.oed.com/view/Entry/79828?redirectedFrom=golgotha#eid.
14. A similar point has been made by Bahti: "We re-mark as well that the *Schädelstätte*, Golgotha, is 'both' sublation or allegory—trading the body for the spirit, while promising thereby resurrection of the body—*and* the literal place of the skull, the material left-over, left over." *Allegories of History*, 90.
15. Hegel, *Werke*, vol. 3, *Phänomenologie des Geistes*, 18.
16. Hegel, *Werke*, vol. 3, *Phänomenologie des Geistes*, 590. Translation altered, changing "picture" to "image." Where Pinkard, following J. B. Baillie, has translated *Bild* as "picture," I will follow A. V. Miller and Michael Inwood to give "image." This is in order to correlate with translations of other German philosophical texts (from Kant to Fichte, Schelling, and others from Hegel, and to Benjamin and Adorno) in which *Bild* is usually translated as "image," thus preserving a certain genealogy; and also to preserve the etymological links between *Bild* (image) and *Einbildungskraft* (imagination). These etymological links extend in the German: *bilden* is to form, which is to develop, hence *Bildung*, culture, formation. See G. W. F. Hegel, *The Phenomenology of Mind*, 2 vols., trans. by J. B. Baillie (London: Swan Sonnenschein, 1910), 2:821; *Phenomenology of Spirit*, trans. by A. V. Miller (Oxford: Oxford University Press, 1977); *The Phenomenology of Spirit*, trans. Michael Inwood (Oxford: Oxford University Press, 2018).
17. Hegel, *Werke*, vol. 3, *Phänomenologie des Geistes*, 128–29. This is the felicitous translation suggested by Verene, which is translated by Baillie (1:152–56), Miller, Pinkard, and Inwood as "inverted world": "The English term 'topsy-turvy' is an apt word for this image. The first element of the English world is related to the word 'top' and the second to 'to turn over.' Topsy-turvy is the top where the bottom should be; the object is reversed." Verene, *Hegel's Recollection*, 44.
18. Hegel, *Werke*, vol. 3, *Phänomenologie des Geistes*, 120, 127. This is Miller and Inwood's translation, translated by Pinkard as "motionless realm of laws," and Baillie as both "quiescent" and "changeless kingdom of laws" (1:143, 151).
19. Hegel, *Werke*, vol. 3, *Phänomenologie des Geistes*, 175.
20. Hegel, *Werke*, vol. 3, *Phänomenologie des Geistes*, 262.
21. Hegel, *Werke*, vol. 3, *Phänomenologie des Geistes*, 386.
22. Hegel, *Werke*, vol. 3, *Phänomenologie des Geistes*, 436.
23. Hegel, *Werke*, vol. 3, *Phänomenologie des Geistes*, 531.
24. Hegel, *Werke*, vol. 3, *Phänomenologie des Geistes*, 548.

25. Robert B. Pippin, *After the Beautiful: Hegel and the Philosophy of Pictorial Modernism* (Chicago: University of Chicago Press, 2015), 16.

26. F. W. J. Schelling, *System of Transcendental Idealism*, trans. Peter Heath (Charlottesville: University Press of Virginia, 2001), 233.

27. "Oldest System Programme of German Idealism (1796)," trans. Andrew Bowie, in *Aesthetics and Subjectivity: From Kant to Nietzsche*, by Andrew Bowie, 2nd ed., 334–35 (Manchester: Manchester University Press, 2006), 334.

28. G. W. F. Hegel, *Natural Law: The Scientific Ways of Treating Natural Law, Its Place in Moral Philosophy, and Its Relation to the Positive Sciences of Law*, trans. T. M. Knox (Philadelphia, PA: University of Pennsylvania Press, 1975), 55–56; "Über die wissenschaftlichen Behandlungsarten des Narturrechts, seine Stelle in der praktischen Philosophie und sein Verhältnis zu den positiven Rechtswissenschaften," in *Werke*, vol. 2, *Janaer Schriften*, 435. Translation altered, changing "picture" for "image" (*Bild*).

29. Hegel, *Werke*, vol. 2, *Janaer Schriften*, 127.

30. See Catherine Malabou, "'Idealism': A New Name for Metaphysics; Hegel and Heidegger on *A Priori Synthesis*," in *German Idealism Today*, ed. Markus Gabriel and Anders Moe Rasmussen (Berlin: De Gruyter, 2017), 189–202.

31. Rolf-Peter Hortsmann, "The Reception of the *Critique of Pure Reason* in German Idealism," in *The Cambridge Companion to Kant's "Critique of Pure Reason*,*"* ed. Paul Guyer, 329–45 (Cambridge: Cambridge University Press, 2010), 341.

32. Malabou, "Idealism," 193.

33. Malabou, "Idealism," 194.

34. Malabou, "Idealism," 190.

35. Hegel, *Werke*, vol. 3, *Phänomenologie des Geistes*, 575.

36. Pinkard and Inwood opt for "representation" and occasionally "representational thought/thinking," while Miller also uses "picture-thinking." Baillie usually translates to "idea" or "presentation."

37. Hegel, *Encyclopedia Logic*, §3, p. 31.

38. Hegel, *Encyclopedia Logic*, §2, p. 29.

39. Hegel, *Logic*, 735.

40. Hegel, *Philosophy of Mind*, §§572–73, p. 267.

41. Fredric Jameson, *The Hegel Variations: On the "Phenomenology of Spirit"* (London: Verso, 2010), 119.

42. Hegel, *Encyclopedia Logic*, §3, p. 1.

43. Hegel, *Lectures on the Philosophy of Religion*, 145–47.

44. Hegel, *Lectures on the Philosophy of Religion*, 144–45. Variations of this phrase can be found throughout Hegel's work post-*PhG*. For example, in the *Encyclopedia Logic*, §20, p. 52: "It can generally be said that philosophy does nothing but transform representations into thoughts—and, indeed, beyond that, the mere thought into the concept."

45. Hegel, *Werke*, vol. 3, *Phänomenologie des Geistes*, 591. The lines of poetry are a misquotation (deliberate or otherwise) of the final couplet of Schiller's 1782 poem "Die Freundschaft": "Aus dem Kelch des ganzen Seelenreiches / Schäumt ihm—die Unendlichkeit"; "From out of the chalice of the whole realm of the soul / Foams for Him—infinity." Translation from Verene, *Hegel's Recollection*, 6.

46. Comay, "Hegel's Last Words," in *The Dash*, 70; quoting from Hegel's *Aesthetics*, 1:89; *Werke*, vol. 13, *Vorlesungen über die Ästhetik I*, 123. The full sentence reads: "At

this highest stage [i.e., poetry], art now transcends itself, in that it forsakes the element of a reconciled embodiment of the spirit in sensuous form and passes over from the poetry of the imagination [*Poesie der Vorstellung*] to the prose of thought [*Prosa des Denkens*]."

47. Jameson, *The Hegel Variations*, 116.

48. Jacques Derrida, "To Forgive: The Unforgivable and the Imprescriptible," in *Questioning God*, ed. John Caputo, Mark Dooley, and Michael Scanlon, 21–51 (Bloomington: Indiana University Press, 2001), 46.

49. Hyppolite, *Genesis and Structure*, 573.

50. "On February 5, 1807, two weeks after Hegel, now virtually penniless, had finished a new Preface for the book [the *Phenomenology of Spirit*], the housekeeper and landlady of the house where Hegel was living, Christiana Charlotte Johanna Burkhardt, gave birth to his illegitimate son, Ludwig. With no money, no real paying job, and a child by a woman who was married to some one who had recently abandoned her, Hegel's situation was now desperate." Pinkard, *Hegel Biography*, 229–30.

51. Hegel to Niethammer, October 13, 1806, *The Letters*, 114–15.

52. Speight, *Hegel, Literature and the Problem of Agency*, 133.

53. William Shakespeare, *The Tempest*, in *The Oxford Shakespeare: The Complete Works*, 2nd ed., ed. W. J. Craig (London: Oxford University Press, 1966), 1–23 (5.1.50–51; epilogue.1).

54. Translation altered. Hegel, *Werke*, vol. 3, *Phänomenologie des Geistes*, 262.

55. This is true of Baillie (1:337), Miller, and Pinkard. The one exception is Inwood, who opts for "pissing."

56. Verene, *Hegel's Recollection*, 87.

57. Dolar, "Phrenology of Spirit," 70.

58. Verene, *Hegel's Recollection*, 104.

59. Verene, *Hegel's Recollection*, 112.

60. Verene, *Hegel's Recollection*, 112.

61. Verene, *Hegel's Recollection*, xii.

62. See Jacques Derrida, "The Pit and the Pyramid: Introduction to Hegel's Semiology," in *Margins of Philosophy*, trans. Alan Bass (Brighton: Harvester Press, 1982), 69–108; and de Man, "Sign and Symbol in Hegel's *Aesthetics*." Derrida "commemorates" the latter of these in his lecture "The Art of *Mémoires*," trans. Jonathan Culler, in *Memoires for Paul de Man* (New York: Columbia University Press, 1988), 45–88. For a critique of de Man's reading, see Raymond Geuss, "A Response to Paul de Man," *Critical Inquiry* 10, no. 2 (1983): 375–82. In the wake of Derrida and de Man, the section of the *Encyclopedia* on *Gedächtnis* has also received discussion in John Sallis, "Ending(s): Imagination, Presentation, Spirit," in *Spacings: Of Reason and Imagination in Texts of Kant, Fichte, and Hegel* (Chicago: University of Chicago Press, 1987), 132–58; and David Farrell Krell, "Of Pits and Pyramids," in *Of Memory, Reminiscence, and Writing: On the Verge* (Bloomington: Indiana University Press, 1990), 204–39. See also, more recently, Jennifer Ann Bates, *Hegel's Theory of Imagination* (Albany: State University of New York Press, 2004), particularly chapter 5, "The Communicative Imagination," 81–102.

63. Derrida, *Of Grammatology*, 26.

64. Hegel, *Philosophy of Mind*, §451, p. 184; *Werke*, vol. 10, *Enzyklopädie der philosophischen Wissenschaften im Grundrisse; Dritter Teil: Die Philosophie des Geistes*, 257.

65. Hegel, *Philosophy of Mind*, §451, p. 185.

66. Hegel, *Philosophy of Mind*, §451, p. 185; *Werke*, vol. 10, *Enzyklopädie der philosophischen Wissenschaften im Grundrisse; Dritter Teil: Die Philosophie des Geistes*, 258.
67. Hegel, *Philosophy of Mind*, §452, p. 186.
68. Hegel, *Philosophy of Mind*, §452, p. 186.
69. Hegel, *Philosophy of Mind*, §453, p. 187.
70. Hegel, *Philosophy of Mind*, §453, p. 187.
71. "As sight is the most highly developed sense, the name φαντασία [*phantasia*] (imagination) has been formed from φάος [*phaos*] (light) because it is not possible to see without light." Aristotle, "On the Soul," in *The Complete Works of Aristotle: The Revised Oxford Translation*, 2. vols., ed. Jonathan Barnes, 641–92 (Princeton: Princeton University Press, 1991), 1:682 (429a).
72. Bates, *Hegel's Theory of Imagination*, 62.
73. G. W. F. Hegel, *The Philosophy of Spirit (1805–1806)*, in *Hegel and the Human Spirit: A Translation of the Jena Lectures on the Philosophy of Spirit (1805–6) with Commentary*, by Leo Rauch, 83–183 (Detroit: Wayne State University Press, 1983), 87.
74. Hegel, *The Philosophy of Spirit (1805–1806)*, 87.
75. Hegel, *The Philosophy of Spirit (1805–1806)*, 87.
76. Verene, *Hegel's Recollection*, 2.
77. Hegel, *Werke*, vol. 3, *Phänomenologie des Geistes*, 590.
78. Hegel, *Werke*, vol. 3, *Phänomenologie des Geistes*, 591.
79. See Ludwig Wittgenstein, *Tractatus Logico-Philosophicus*, trans. D. F. Pears and B. F. McGuinness (London: Routledge, 2001), 89.
80. Comay and Ruda, *The Dash*, 51.
81. Hegel, *Werke*, vol. 3, *Phänomenologie des Geistes*, 32.
82. Rebecca Comay, *Mourning Sickness: Hegel and the French Revolution* (Stanford: Stanford University Press, 2011), 86–87, 95.
83. Hegel, *Philosophy of Mind*, §449, p. 183.
84. Hegel, *Philosophy of Mind*, §449, p. 183.
85. Drew Milne, "The Beautiful Soul: From Hegel to Beckett," *Diacritics* 32, no. 1 (2002): 70.
86. See, respectively, Susan Buck-Morss, *Hegel, Haiti, and Universal History*; Cole, *The Birth of Theory*; Alexandre Kojève, *Introduction to the Reading of Hegel: Lectures on the "Phenomenology of Spirit,"* ed. Allan Bloom, trans. James H. Nichols Jr. (Ithaca, NY: Cornell University Press, 1980). On "man and wife": Derrida suggests that Hegel derived the master-slave dialectic from his reading of Rousseau's account of the "the battle between men and women" in *Emile*, where Rousseau writes: "If he takes a wife from a lower class, natural and civil law are in accordance and all goes well. When he marries a woman of higher rank it is just the opposite case; the man must choose between diminished rights or imperfect gratitude; he must be ungrateful or despised. Then the wife, laying claim to authority, makes herself a tyrant over her lawful head; and the master, who has become a slave, is the most ridiculous and miserable of creatures. Such are the unhappy favorites whom the sovereigns of Asia honor and torment with their alliance; people tell us that if they desire to sleep with their wife they must enter by the foot of the bed." Derrida, *Of Grammatology*, 176; Jean-Jacques Rousseau, *Emile; or, Education*, trans. Barbara Foxley (London: J. M. Dent, 1911), 370.
87. I owe this list of possible referents to Milne, "The Beautiful Soul," 70. However, Milne also writes, and I agree, that "a balance needs to be struck ... between recon-

structing the historical intelligibility of Hegel's terms and assessing the truth of his argument" (69); "More is required than an oscillation between conceptual paraphrases and philological reconstructions of sundry contextual 'backgrounds'" (75).

88. Slavoj Žižek, "A Short Note on Hegel and the Exemplum of Christ," *Crisis & Critique* 8, no. 2 (2021): 433.

89. Žižek, "A Short Note on Hegel and the Exemplum of Christ," 433.

90. See Hannah Arendt, *Eichmann in Jerusalem: A Report on the Banality of Evil* (London: Penguin, 2006).

91. Žižek, "Hegel and the Exemplum," 433. Žižek develops his argument, and this point in particular, from Pierre Bayard, *Comment parler des faits qui ne se sont pas produits?* (Paris: Minuit, 2020).

92. Hegel, *Lectures on the Philosophy of Religion*, 149.

93. Hegel, *Aesthetics*, 1:404.

94. Jacques Derrida, "White Mythology: Metaphor in the Text of Philosophy," in *Margins of Philosophy*, 213.

95. Louis Althusser, "Preface to *Capital* Volume 1," in *Lenin and Philosophy, and Other Essays*, trans. Ben Brewster, 45–65 (New York: NYU Press, 2001), 48–49.

96. Keston Sutherland, "The Poetics of *Capital*," in *Capitalism: Concept, Idea, Image*, ed. Peter Osborne, Éric Alliez, and Eric-John Russell, 203–18 (London: CRMEP Books, 2019), 218.

97. Scott, Robert, "Suffering and the Feeling of Suffering in Marx's *Capital*," *Textual Practice* 36 (2022): 76–93.

98. Fredric Jameson, *Representing "Capital": A Commentary on Volume One* (London: Verso, 2011), 68.

99. Sutherland, "Marx in Jargon," 42; translating from Karl Marx, *Das Kapital* (2nd German ed., 1872), in *Marx-Engels-Gesamtausgabe* (Berlin: Dietz, 1989 [1975]), 2.8.70.

100. Sutherland, "Marx in Jargon," 42, with quotation from the sixth volume of the popular encyclopedia *Meyers Konversations-Lexikon* (1888).

101. Sutherland, "Marx in Jargon," 40.

102. Hegel, *Philosophy of Right*, 23.

103. Qtd. in T. M. Knox, "Explanatory Notes," in *Outlines of the Philosophy of Right* by G. W. F. Hegel, trans. T. M. Knox, ed. and rev. Stephen Houlgate, 324–63 (Oxford: Oxford University Press, 2008), 328n16.

104. Hegel, *Philosophy of Right*, 23.

105. Gillian Rose, *The Broken Middle: Out of our Ancient Society* (Oxford: Blackwell, 1992), xi.

106. As Socrates says to Meno: "Since the soul both is immortal and has been born many times, and has seen both what is here and what is in Hades, and in fact all things, there is nothing it has not learned." Therefore, "there is no reason why someone who has recollected only one thing—which is what people call 'learning'—should not discover everything else, as long as one is brave and does not give up on the search. For seeking and learning turn out to be wholly recollection." Plato, *Meno*, in *"Meno" and "Phaedo,"* ed. David Sedley and Alex Long, 1–41 (Cambridge: Cambridge University Press, 2011), 15.

107. Ernst Bloch, *Subjekt-Objekt: Erläuterungen zu Hegel* (Frankfurt a.M.: Suhrkamp, 1962), 503; qtd. and trans. in Ricci and Sanguinetti, eds., introduction to *Hegel on Recollection*, xiii.

108. Ernst Bloch, *The Principle of Hope*, 3 vols., trans. Neville Plaice, Stephen Plaice, and Paul Knight (Oxford: Basil Blackwell, 1986), 1:270.

109. "The philosophers have only *interpreted* the world in various ways; the point is to *change* it." Karl Marx, "Theses on Feuerbach [Original version]," in *MECW* 5 (1976): 5.

110. Heidegger, *Hegel's Phenomenology*, 82.

111. Derrida, "White Mythology," 269. *Relever* is Derrida's translation of *aufheben*, sublate; *relève, Aufhebung*, sublation.

112. Hamacher, *pleroma*, 15.

113. Hamacher, *pleroma*, 227.

114. Derrida, *Of Grammatology*, 26; my emphasis.

115. "All these developments are governed by the opposition *Auswendig/Inwendig* and by that of *Entäußerung* and *Erinnerung*." Derrida, "The Pit and the Pyramid," 95n23. Michael Inwood, too, in the glossary to his translation of the *Phenomenology*, writes that "*Erinnerung* is the converse of *Entäußerung*." Inwood, "Glossary of Some Key Terms," in *The Phenomenology of Spirit*, trans. Inwood, 327.

116. Hegel, *Logic*, 753. *Encyclopedia Logic*, §244, p. 303; *Werke*, vol. 8, *Enzyklopädie der philosophischen Wissenschaften im Grundrisse; Erster Teil: Die Wissenschaft der Logik*, 393. This implicitly scatological imagery has prompted Slavoj Žižek, in an essay entitled "Hegel and Shitting: The Idea's Constipation," to quip: "What critics of Hegel's voracity need is, perhaps, a dosage of a good laxative." In *Hegel's Infinite: Religion, Politics, and Dialectic*, ed. Slavoj Žižek and Creston Davis, 221–35 (New York: Columbia University Press, 2011), 231.

117. Rose, *The Broken Middle*, xi.

118. Hegel, *Werke*, vol. 7, *Grundlinien der Philosophie des Rechts*, 28; my emphasis.

119. Hegel, *Aesthetics*, 1:18–19.

120. Comay, *Mourning Sickness*, 96. Comay goes on to describe Hegel's critique of Kantian and early post-Kantian morality: "The various strands can be difficult to unravel in Hegel's narrative, and again, Hegel's caricature is offensive, and again, it doesn't matter," 103.

121. Adorno, *Minima Moralia*, 49.

122. See Sigmund Freud, "Remembering, Repeating and Working-Through (Further Recommendations on the Technique of Psycho-Analysis II) (1914)," in *The Case of Schreber, Papers on Technique and Other Works*, vol. 12 of *The Standard Edition of the Complete Psychological Works of Sigmund Freud*, ed. and trans. by James Strachey (London: Hogarth Press, 1958), 145–56.

123. Malabou, *The Future of Hegel*, 146.

124. Malabou, *The Future of Hegel*, 146.

125. Hegel, *Encyclopedia Logic*, 5.

126. Malabou, *The Future of Hegel*, 151.

127. Brandom, *A Spirit of Trust*, 438.

128. Brandom, *A Spirit of Trust*, 438.

129. Brandom, *A Spirit of Trust*, 628.

130. Brandom, *A Spirit of Trust*, 19.

131. Brandom, *A Spirit of Trust*, 631.

132. Brandom, *A Spirit of Trust*, 632.

133. In his review of *A Spirit of Trust*, Žižek compares Brandom's reparative attitude to that of the American Republican Senator Tom Cotton who caused an uproar when he

"forgivingly recollected" America's historical use of slavery as a "necessary evil" for the establishment of the union which would then go on to "abolish" slavery. Slavoj Žižek, "Hegel: The Spirit of Distrust," in *Reading Hegel*, by Slavoj Žižek, Frank Ruda, and Agon Hamza, 13-100 (Cambridge: Polity, 2022), 35.

134. Brandom, *A Spirit of Trust*, 747.
135. Brandom, *A Spirit of Trust*, 747.
136. See Theodor W. Adorno, "The Meaning of Working Through the Past," in *Critical Models*, 89-104.
137. Brandom, *A Spirit of Trust*, 753.
138. I first wrote this chapter in the summer of 2020 in the week when antiracism protestors toppled a commemorative statue of Colston and cast it into Bristol Harbour.
139. Brandom, *A Spirit of Trust*, 632.

Chapter Three

1. This repeats Hegel's account of the standards of a good historian from his *Philosophy of Mind*, 183, referenced in the previous chapter.
2. Comay, *Mourning Sickness*, 96.
3. 2 Corinthians/2 Korinther 3:6.
4. See John H. Smith, *The Spirit and Its Letter: Traces of Rhetoric in Hegel's Philosophy of "Bildung"* (New York: Cornell University Press, 1988).
5. See Frederick C. Beiser, *German Idealism: The Struggle Against Subjectivism, 1781-1801* (Cambridge, MA: Harvard University Press, 2022), 295; Terry Pinkard, *German Philosophy 1760-1860: The Legacy of Idealism* (Cambridge: Cambridge University Press, 2002), 98; and Paul W. Franks, *All or Nothing: Systematicity, Transcendental Arguments, and Skepticism in German Idealism* (Cambridge, MA: Harvard University Press, 2005), 268.
6. Hegel, *Lectures on the Philosophy of Religion*, 93. Incidentally, this argument could be used as yet another example of the insufficiency of Brandom's *de re* hermeneutics for reading Hegel—a hermeneutics which proceeds "from the facts *as she* [the reader] *takes them to be*," from "the inferential context provided by her own commitments," as "the best any of us could do." Brandom, *Tales of the Mighty Dead*, 101.
7. Hegel, *Lectures on the Philosophy of Religion*, 93.
8. Hegel, *Lectures on the Philosophy of Religion*, 93-94. G. W. F. Hegel, *Vorlesungen über die Philosophie der Religion*, 3 vols., ed. Walter Jaeschke (Hamburg: Felix Meiner, 1993), 1:77.
9. Hegel, *Letters*, 35. Translation slightly altered. G. W. F. Hegel, *Briefe von und an Hegel*, 4 vols., ed. Johannes Hoffmeister (Hamburg: Felix Meiner, 1969), 1:24.
10. In Kant's own words: "For if the moral law commands that we *ought* to be better human beings now, it inescapably follows that we must be *capable* of being better human beings." *Religion within the Boundaries of Mere Reason*, trans. Allen Wood and Georgie di Giovanni (Cambridge: Cambridge University Press, 1998), 70. "The action must be possible under natural conditions if the ought is directed to it." *Critique of Pure Reason*, trans. Paul Guyer and Allen W. Wood (Cambridge: Cambridge University Press, 1998), 540.
11. G. W. F. Hegel, *Early Theological Writings*, trans. T. M. Knox (Philadelphia: University of Pennsylvania Press, 1971), 143.

12. Hegel's limited and prejudiced conception of Judaism is also evident in §340 of the *Phenomenology*: "As it can be said of the Jewish people that precisely because they immediately stand before the gates of salvation, they are both supposed to be and actually have been the most corrupted of all peoples. What this people should be in and for themselves, this being-themselves [*Selbstwesenheit*], is what to themselves they are not; instead, they shift it off into an other-worldly beyond of themselves. Through this self-relinquishing [*Entäußerung*], they make a higher existence *possible* for themselves which they could achieve if only they could again take their object back into themselves rather than if they had remained within the immediacy of being" (Hegel, *Werke*, vol. 3, *Phänomenologie des Geistes*, 257). As Donatella Di Cesare puts it: "In Hegel's view, Judaism had evaded and continued to evade the Christian *Aufhebung*. It did not let itself be taken over or sublimated—as it should have.... Since Judaism resisted this, and did not permit the spirit to overcome 'alienation,' 'returning' to itself, it was excluded from the dialectic of universal history." Donatella Di Cesare, *Heidegger and the Jews: The Black Notebooks*, trans. Murtha Baca (Cambridge: Polity, 2018), 38. For a speculative retrieval of Judaism against its misrepresentation as "the sublime Other of modernity," see Gillian Rose's essay collection *Judaism and Modernity*.

13. Hegel, *Early Theological Writings*, 213, with quotation from Kant's *Critique of Practical Reason*. The edition that Knox quotes from is Immanuel Kant, *"Critique of Practical Reason" and Other Works on the Theory of Ethics*, trans. Thomas Kingsmill Abbott (London: Longmans, Green and Co., 1923), 175-76.

14. As did Lacan, but with a difference. As Žižek identifies, while Adorno and Horkheimer identify the sadistic truth of Kant, Lacan offers a Kantian Sade. See Slavoj Žižek, "Kant and Sade: The Ideal Couple," *Lacanian Ink* 13 (1998): 12-25. For a more detailed comparison, see Rebecca Comay, "'Adorno avec Sade ...,'" *differences* 17, no. 1 (2006): 6-19. See also Theodor W. Adorno and Max Horkheimer, "Excursus II: Juliette or Enlightenment and Morality," in *Dialectic of Enlightenment: Philosophical Fragments*, ed. Gunzelin Schmid Noerr, trans. Edmund Jephcott (Stanford: Stanford University Press, 2002), 63-93; and Jacques Lacan, "Kant with Sade," in *Écrits*, trans. Bruce Fink (London: W. W. Norton, 2006), 645-68.

15. Comay, *Mourning Sickness*, 95.

16. Hegel, *Letters*, 43. Translation slightly altered for clarity.

17. As he would go onto write in his *Logic*, 91: "The individual name is something meaningless, in the sense that it does not express a universal, and for the same reason appears as something merely posited and arbitrary; just as proper names, too, can be arbitrarily assumed, given or also altered." While Hegel's account of names is not just limited to proper names, this position can account in part for the near total absence of proper names in the *Phenomenology of Spirit*.

18. Indeed, the tension between faith and law which Marcion found throughout Paul's epistles led him not only to emend scripture but to abolish parts of it. For its dependency on law, Marcion regarded the Old Testament as the work of the devil. He also rejected all Gospels except Luke's, purging it of all references to the Hebrew Bible. See John Barton, *A History of the Bible: The Book and Its Faiths* (London: Penguin Books, 2020), 182.

19. F. W. J. Schelling, "Lectures on the Method of Academic Study (1803)," trans. E. S. Morgan, in *The Schelling Reader*, ed. Benjamin Berger and Daniel Whistler, 361-70 (London: Bloomsbury, 2020), 368.

20. Hegel, *Letters*, 43; *Briefe*, 1:33.

21. J. G. Fichte, *Attempt at a Critique of All Revelation*, ed. Allen Wood, trans. Garrett Green (Cambridge: Cambridge University Press, 2010), 23.

22. J. G. Fichte, *Early Philosophical Writings*, trans. and ed. Daniel Breazeale (Ithaca, NY: Cornell University Press, 1988), 329.

23. For more, see Claude Piché, "The Letter is Particularly Lethal in the *Wissenschaftslehre*," and Kien-how Goh, "The Ideality of Idealism: Fichte's Battle against Dogmatic Kantianism," both in *Fichte and Transcendental Philosophy*, ed. Tom Rockmore and Daniel Breazeale, 85–102, 128–42 (London: Palgrave Macmillan, 2014); and Matthew C. Altman, "The Letter and the Spirit: Kant's Metaphysics and Fichte's Epistemology," in *The Palgrave Fichte Handbook*, ed. Steven Hoeltzel (London: Palgrave Macmillan, 2019), 421–42.

24. Friedrich Heinrich Jacobi, "David Hume on Faith, or Idealism and Realism: A Dialogue—Preface and also Introduction to the Author's Collected Philosophical Works," in *The Main Philosophical Writings and the Novel "Allwill,"* trans. George di Giovanni, 253–338 (Montreal and Kingston: McGill-Queen's University Press, 1994), 338.

25. Jacobi, "David Hume on Faith, or Idealism and Realism," 338.

26. Slavoj Žižek has argued something similar: "Fichte's reaction to Jacobi's criticism of Kant is paradigmatic of how a true philosopher proceeds, fearlessly running against the grain of the predominant common sense." *Less Than Nothing*, 179. For another account of the relationship between Fichte and Jacobi see also, Dieter Henrich, *Between Kant and Hegel: Lectures on German Idealism*, ed. David S. Pacini (Cambridge, MA: Harvard University Press, 2003), 111–12.

27. Qtd. in Peter Fenves, *Late Kant: Towards Another Law of the Earth* (London: Routledge, 2003), 114–15.

28. Kant, *Critique of Pure Reason*, 102.

29. J. G. Fichte, *Foundations of Transcendental Philosophy*, trans. and ed. Daniel Breazeale (Ithaca, NY: Cornell University Press, 1998), 474.

30. Fichte, *Early Philosophical Writings*, 192–93.

31. Fichte, *Early Philosophical Writings*, 100.

32. Hegel, *The Difference Between Fichte's and Schelling's*, 79.

33. See for example Altman, "The Letter and the Spirit," 421.

34. Hegel, *Werke*, vol. 3, *Phänomenologie des Geistes*, 168.

35. Stefania Achella, "Memory and Fate: Recollection in Hegel's Philosophy of Religion," in *Hegel on Recollection*, 187.

36. Comay, *Mourning Sickness*, 113.

37. See for instance, Gillian Rose, "The Comedy of Hegel and the *Trauerspiel* of Modern Philosophy," in *Mourning Becomes the Law*, 64, 70–71. Rose develops this concept from Freud via Laurence A. Rickels, *Aberrations of Mourning* (Minneapolis: University of Minnesota Press, 2011).

38. Comay, *Mourning Sickness*, 113.

39. Hegel also critiques Catholicism and the Crusades in his *Lectures on the Philosophy of History*, trans. J. Sibree (London: H. G. Bohn, 1857), 405–15.

40. Hegel, *Letters*, 283.

41. See especially Plato, *Phaedrus*, ed. Harvey Yunis (Cambridge: Cambridge University Press, 2011).

42. Hegel to Döderlein, April 29, 1817, in *Letters*, 365.

43. It must be noted, however, and as I will elaborate below, this latter descriptor in particular—"manipulated"—is not one Luther would have liked, believing his Biblical translations, tracts, and sermons to be indelibly true to the spirit of God's word, however deviant they may be from any historical-philological "letter." For instance, when Luther receives complaints for translating Paul's epistle to the Romans 3:28 to say that "a person is justified without the works of law, but by faith *alone*" (this word "alone" [*sola*] does not appear in the original), he replies: "Since your papist wishes to make such a fuss about the world 'sola' ('alone'), go straight back to him and say, 'Dr Martin Luther wishes to keep it as it is, and says that a papist and a donkey are one and the same.' *Sic volo, sic iubeo, sit pro ratione voluntas* (I desire it, I command it, may my will be reason enough)." One can imagine Hegel responding with similarly disgruntled hubris at pedants bemoaning his misquotation of Schiller at the end of the *Phenomenology*, for instance. Martin Luther, *An Open Letter on Translating*, trans. Howard Jones (Oxford: Taylor Institution Library, 2017), 11. As Jones notes, the Latin is a quotation from the Roman satirist Juvenal's *Satire 6*, line 223.

44. For a different discussion of this letter, used to elucidate the differences between Hegel and Adorno, see Gillian Rose, "From Speculative to Dialectical Thinking—Hegel and Adorno," in *Judaism and Modernity*, 53-64.

45. Hegel, *Letters*, 280.

46. Kant, *Critique of Pure Reason*, 99.

47. Hegel, *Letters*, 281.

48. Hegel, *Letters*, 281.

49. Adorno and Horkheimer, *Dialectic of Enlightenment*, 66.

50. Kant, *Critique of Pure Reason*, 493.

51. Georg Lukács, *History and Class Consciousness: Studies in Marxist Dialectics*, trans. Rodney Livingstone (Cambridge, MA: MIT Press, 1971), 48.

52. Theodor W. Adorno, *Kant's "Critique of Pure Reason,"* ed. Rolf Tiedemann, trans. Rodney Livingstone (Stanford: Stanford University Press, 2001), 6.

53. Badiou, *Logics of Worlds*, 535.

54. Hegel, *Encyclopedia Logic*, §48, p. 93.

55. Hegel, *Encyclopedia Logic*, §4, p. 92.

56. Hegel, *Letters*, 281-82.

57. This use of the word "parallax" is with reference to Žižek's development of the term as a concept. See especially Slavoj Žižek, *The Parallax View* (Cambridge, MA: MIT Press, 2006).

58. Hegel, *Encyclopedia Logic*, §48, p. 94.

59. "Philosophy's 'grey in grey'... would turn hubris not into humility but into motile configuration." Rose, *The Broken Middle*, xi.

60. Hegel, *Letters*, 282.

61. Hegel, *Logic*, 12.

62. Fichte, *Early Philosophical Writings*, 193.

63. Fichte, *Early Philosophical Writings*, 392. June 27, 1795, 392-96. Fichte writes a scathing letter to Schiller upon the latter's rejection of his "Letters concerning the Spirit and the Letter within Philosophy" for *Die Horen* (Schiller's new journal).

64. Hegel, *Lectures on the Philosophy of Religion*, 82-83.

65. Hegel, *Lectures on the Philosophy of Religion*, 84.

66. Hegel, *Lectures on the Philosophy of Religion*, 83.

67. Hegel, *Lectures on the Philosophy of Religion*, 469-70.

68. Graham Ward, "How Hegel became a Philosopher: Logos and the Economy of Logic," *Critical Research on Religion* 1, no. 3 (2013): 271.

69. John Milbank, "The Theological Critique of Philosophy in Hamann and Jacobi," in *Radical Orthodoxy: A New Theology*, ed. John Milbank, Catherine Pickstock, and Graham Ward, 21-37 (London: Routledge, 1999), 23. For Schleiermacher on the "dead letter" of empiricism and worldly knowledge against the living spirit of religion, see, for example, Friedrich Schleiermacher, *On Religion: Speeches to its Cultured Despisers*, trans. Richard Crouter (Cambridge: Cambridge University Press, 2010), 9.

70. Hegel, *Lectures on the Philosophy of Religion*, 78-79.

71. Hegel to von Altenstein, April 3, 1826, in *Letters*, 531.

72. Hegel to Tholuck, July 3, 1826, in *Letters*, 520; my emphasis.

73. G. W. F. Hegel, "Address on the Tercentenary of the Submission of the Augsburg Confession (25 June 1830)," in *Political Writings*, ed. Laurence Dickey and H. B. Nisbet, trans. by H. B. Nisbet, 186-96 (Cambridge: Cambridge University Press, 1999), 189.

74. Hegel, *Logic*, 348.

75. I include Paul himself in this list for, as Regina Schwartz has stated, the "story of biblical interpretation begins in the Bible, where the prophets rework the exodus narratives, the New Testament interprets the 'Old' (the construction of these categories was itself a major interpretative event), and Paul offers allusive remarks about the letter and the spirit that are to influence subsequent patristic principles of exegesis." Regina M. Schwartz, "Introduction: On Biblical Criticism," in *The Book and the Text: The Bible and Literary Theory*, ed. Regina M. Schwartz, 1-15 (London: Basil Blackwell, 1990), 4. For a book-length study of Paul's *gramma-pneuma* distinction, both in its original context and its aftermaths in these and other thinkers, see Paul S. Fiddes and Günter Bader, eds, *The Spirit and the Letter: A Tradition and a Reversal* (London: Bloomsbury, 2013). See also Keith D. Stanglin, *The Letter and Spirit of Biblical Interpretation: From the Early Church to Modern Practice* (Grand Rapids, MI: Baker Academic, 2018).

76. Augustine of Hippo, *On the Spirit and the Letter*, trans. W. J. Sparrow Simpson (London: Society for Promoting Christian Knowledge, 1925), 39-42.

77. Roemer/Romans 3:28; my emphasis.

78. Hegel, *Early Theological Writings*, 223.

79. Hegel, *Early Theological Writings*, 212.

80. Friedrich Nietzsche, *Daybreak: Thoughts on the Prejudices of Morality*, trans. R. J. Hollingdale (Cambridge: Cambridge University Press, 2003).

81. Alain Badiou, *Saint Paul: The Foundation of Universalism*, trans. Ray Brassier (Stanford: Stanford University Press, 2003), 79. For a further discussion of the question of Paul and law in Badiou's thought (compared and contrasted to Slavoj Žižek's), see Adam Kotsko, "Politics and Perversion: Situating Žižek's Paul," in *Žižek and Law*, ed. Laurent de Sutter, 31-41 (Abingdon: Routledge, 2015), 31-33.

82. Martin Luther, *Luther's Works*, vol. 39, *Church and Ministry*, ed. Eric W. Gritsch (St Louis, MO: Concordia; and Philadelphia: Fortress Press, 1970), 188.

83. One exception is Randall C. Gleason, "'Letter' and 'Spirit' in Luther's Hermeneutics," *Bibliotheca Sacra* 157 (2000): 468-85. I owe my knowledge of Luther's treatment of 2 Corinthians 3:6 to this article.

84. Qtd. in Frederic W. Farrar, *History of Interpretation* (London: Macmillan, 1886), 342-53.

85. *Luther's Works*, vol. 39, *Church and Ministry*, 175; a reference to Matthew 7:26.
86. *Luther's Works*, vol. 39, *Church and Ministry*, 186.
87. Alan M. Olson, *Hegel and the Spirit: Philosophy as Pneumatology* (Princeton: Princeton University Press, 1992), 127.
88. *Luther's Works*, vol. 39, *Church and Ministry*, 182.
89. Frank Ruda, *Abolishing Freedom: A Plea for Contemporary Fatalism* (Lincoln: University of Nebraska Press, 2016), 15. This is the crux of Luther's debate with Erasmus of Rotterdam on the question of free choice. For Luther, the experience of freedom is analogous to Paul's conversion experience on the road to Damascus. As Ruda puts it, "I experience faith only when I encounter God, and I am thus forced to renew myself." See also E. Gordon Rupp and Philip S. Watson, eds, *Luther and Erasmus: Free Will and Salvation* (Louisville, KY: Westminster, 1996).
90. Karl Barth, *The Epistle to the Romans*, trans. Edwyn C. Hoskyns (London: Oxford University Press, 1933), 6-7. See also Gleason, "'Letter' and 'Spirit,'" 485.
91. Hegel to Voss, in *Letters*, 107.
92. Luther, *Open Letter on Translating*, 17.
93. Hegel to Voss, in *Letters*, 107.
94. Hegel, *Encyclopedia Logic*, §244, p. 303; *Werke Enzyklopädie der philosophischen Wissenschaften im Grundrisse; Erster Teil: Die Wissenschaft der Logik*, 393.
95. Hegel, *Philosophy of Right*, 21.

Chapter Four

1. Rose, *Hegel Contra Sociology*, 1.
2. Peter Osborne, "Hegelian Phenomenology and the Critique of Reason and Society," *Radical Philosophy* 32 (1982): 8-15.
3. Rose, *Hegel Contra Sociology*, 235.
4. Rose, *Hegel Contra Sociology*, 15.
5. Rose, *Hegel Contra Sociology*, 2.
6. Rose, *Hegel Contra Sociology*, 6. This is perhaps an overstatement. See note 10 below.
7. Rose, *Hegel Contra Sociology*, 7.
8. Qtd. with an altered translation in Rose, *Hegel Contra Sociology*, 9, from Rudolf Hermann Lotze, *Microcosmos: An Essay Concerning Man and His Relation to the World*, 2 vols., trans. Elizabeth Hamilton and E. E. Constance Jones (Edinburgh: T. & T. Clark, 1894), 2:575.
9. Rose, *Hegel Contra Sociology*, 9. As David Sullivan notes, Heidegger was the first philosopher to identify the extent of Lotze's influence on neo-Kantianism (and also Husserlian phenomenology). With his introduction of the terminology of validity and values (Heidegger argues), Lotze established the prejudice that philosophy should aspire to be a pure and general logic, "an ideal network of propositions," distinct from "the empirical reality of things." Martin Heidegger, *Logic: The Quest of Truth*, trans. Thomas Sheehan (Bloomington: Indiana University Press, 2010),50. See David Sullivan, "Hermann Lotze," in *The Stanford Encyclopedia of Philosophy*, first published January 12, 2005; substantive revision November 2, 2018, https://plato.stanford.edu/archives/win2018/entries/hermann-lotze/. Lotze's influence on neo-Kantianism is also discussed in Thomas E. Willey, *Back to Kant: The Revival of Kantianism in German*

Social and Historical Thought, 1860-1914 (Detroit: Wayne State University Press, 1978), 40-57; and Frederick C. Beiser, *The Genesis of Neo-Kantianism: 1796-1880* (Oxford: Oxford University Press, 2014), 192-96.

10. Rose, *Hegel Contra Sociology*, 10.
11. Rose, *Hegel Contra Sociology*, 14.
12. Rose, *Hegel Contra Sociology*, 15.
13. Rose, *Hegel Contra Sociology*, 15.
14. Rose, *Hegel Contra Sociology*, 15.
15. Rose, "Does Marx Have a Method?"
16. Rose, *Hegel Contra Sociology*, 47-48.
17. Rose, *Hegel Contra Sociology*, 231.
18. Qtd. in Rose, *Hegel Contra Sociology*, 51. Rose's translation.
19. Rose, *Hegel Contra Sociology*, 52.
20. Karl Marx, *Capital: A Critique of Political Economy*, trans. Ben Fowkes (London: Penguin Books, 1982), 138.
21. Hegel, *Philosophy of Right*, 22. The full quotation reads: "To recognize reason as the rose in the cross of the present and thereby to delight in the present—this rational insight is the *reconciliation* with actuality which philosophy grants to those who have received the inner call *to comprehend*, to preserve their subjective freedom in the realm of the substantial, and at the same time to stand with their subjective freedom not in a particular and contingent situation, but in what has being in and for itself."
22. Fredric Jameson, *Marxism and Form: Twentieth-Century Dialectical Theories of Literature* (Princeton, NJ: Princeton University Press, 1974), 306.
23. Rose, *Hegel Contra Sociology*, 199. Rose argues that this is the trace of a necessary yet disavowed imperative or *Sollen* of Hegel's thought. As "philosophy is the concept of real recognition" yet "arises in a society where real recognition has not been achieved," philosophy necessarily "reinforces the primacy of the concept, and falls into the terms of a dichotomy which it seeks to transform. It thus contains an abstract imperative, a moment of *Sollen*." Rose, *Hegel Contra Sociology*, 84.
24. Habib, *Hegel and the Foundations of Literary Theory*, ix.
25. Rose, *Hegel Contra Sociology*, 2.
26. See Paul Ricoeur, *Freud and Philosophy: An Essay on Interpretation*, trans. Denis Savage (New Haven: Yale University Press, 2008), 32-36.
27. Rita Felski, "Postcritical," in *Further Reading*, ed. Matthew Rubery and Leah Price, 135-43 (Oxford: Oxford University Press, 2020), 135.
28. Gillian Rose, "Interview with Gillian Rose," transcribed and ed. Vincent Lloyd, *Theory, Culture & Society*, 25 (2008): 208; my emphasis. The interviewer is Andy O'Mahony. It was first broadcast on RTE Radio on November 4, 1995.
29. Kant, *Critique of Pure Reason*, 704.
30. Robyn Marasco, *The Highway of Despair: Critical Theory After Hegel* (New York: Columbia University Press, 2015), 25-26.
31. See Marx and Engels, *The Holy Family*.
32. Rose, *Hegel Contra Sociology*, 1.
33. Willi Goetschel, *Constituting Critique: Kant's Writing as Critical Praxis*, trans. Eric Schwab (Durham, NC: Duke University Press, 1994), 1.
34. See Stephen Best and Sharon Marcus, "Surface Reading: An Introduction," *Representations* 108, no. 1 (2009): 1-21.

35. See Franco Moretti, "Conjectures on World Literature," *New Left Review*, 1 (2000), 54–68; and Franco Moretti, *Distant Reading* (London: Verso, 2013).

36. See N. Katherine Hayles, "How We Read: Close, Hyper, Machine," *ADE Bulletin* 150 (2010): 62–79.

37. See Love, "Close Reading and Thin Description."

38. See Timothy Bewes, "Reading with the Grain: A New World in Literary Criticism," *differences* 21, no. 3 (2010): 1–33.

39. See Toril Moi, *Revolution of the Ordinary: Literary Studies after Wittgenstein, Austin, and Cavell* (Chicago: University of Chicago Press, 2017).

40. See, for example, Bruno Latour, *Reassembling the Social: An Introduction to Actor-Network-Theory* (Oxford: Oxford University Press, 2005). ANT is also central to Rita Felski's articulation of postcritique. See, for instance, Felski, *The Limits of Critique*, 151–85.

41. Graham Harman, "The Well-Wrought Broken Hammer: Object-Oriented Literary Criticism," *New Literary History* 43, no. 2 (2012): 183–203.

42. Andrew H. Miller, "Implicative Criticism, or The Display of Thinking," *New Literary History* 44, no. 3 (2013): 345–60.

43. See in particular the work of Andrew Piper, such as *Enumerations: Data and Literary Study* (Chicago: University of Chicago Press, 2018).

44. John Guillory, *Professing Criticism: Essays on the Organization of Literary Study* (Chicago: University of Chicago Press, 2022), 101.

45. Felski, *The Limits of Critique*, 1.

46. Felski, *The Limits of Critique*, 5.

47. See Ricoeur, *Freud and Philosophy*, 32–36. With this characterization of critique, Felski also draws on the work of Eve Kosofsky Sedgwick and her account of "paranoid" reading. See Eve Kosofsky Sedgwick, "Paranoid Reading and Reparative Reading, or, You're So Paranoid, You Probably Think This Essay is About You," in *Touching Feeling: Affect, Pedagogy, Performativity* (Durham, NC: Duke University Press, 2003), 123–52.

48. Felski, *The Limits of Critique*, 1.

49. Felski, *The Limits of Critique*, 9.

50. Felski, *The Limits of Critique*, 10.

51. Felski, *The Limits of Critique*, 2.

52. Bruno Latour, "Why Has Critique Run out of Steam? From Matters of Fact to Matters of Concern," *Critical Inquiry* 30 (2004): 225–48.

53. Hegel, *Philosophy of Right*, 23.

54. As already noted, this link was first made by Sedgwick, along with her introduction of the idea of "paranoia" into literary critical discourse. However, as Bruce Robbins argues, despite her influence on the trend, her work is not so easily described as postcritical. Robbins argues that "Felski misreads Sedgwick, who is well worth taking back from Felski." Similarly, Merve Emre has indicted postcritique for its "flagrant" misreading of Sedgwick. Sedgwick is not simply against paranoid or suspicious readings. Instead, for Sedgwick the crucial question is what can a reader do *after* the paranoid reading has disclosed that which has been disavowed: "Paranoid performativity may have something more to offer than impotence." See Bruce Robbins, "Not So Well Attached," *PMLA* 132 (2017): 373; and Merve Emre, *Paraliterary: The Making of Bad Readers in Postwar America* (Chicago: University of Chicago Press, 2017), 222.

55. Goetschel, *Constituting Critique*, 1.

56. Drew Milne, "Introduction: Criticism and/or Critique," in *Modern Critical*

Thought: An Anthology of Theorists Writing on Theorists, ed. Drew Milne, 1–22 (Hoboken, NJ: Blackwell, 2003), 5; with reference to Kant, *Critique of Pure Reason*, 100–101.

57. Milne, "Criticism and/or Critique."

58. Michel Foucault, "What is Enlightenment?," trans. Catherine Porter, amended by Robert Hurley, in *Essential Works of Foucault, 1954-1984*, vol. 1, *Ethics: Subjectivity and Truth*, ed. Paul Rabinow, 303–19 (London: Penguin Books, 2000), 315. See Milne, "Criticism and/or Critique," 7.

59. Felski, *The Limits of Critique*, 5.

60. Gilles Deleuze, *Nietzsche and Philosophy*, trans. Hugh Tomlinson (London: Continuum, 2005), 83–84.

61. Sally Sedgwick, *Hegel's Critique of Kant: From Dichotomy to Identity* (Oxford: Oxford University Press, 2012), 155.

62. Sedgwick, *Hegel's Critique of Kant*, 156.

63. This is Rose's phrase: "This unsettled and unsettling approach, which is not a 'position' because it will not *posit* anything, and refuses any beginning or end, would yet induce repetition forwards—a beginning in the middle." Rose, *The Broken Middle*, 155.

64. Hegel, *Philosophy of Right*, 21.

65. Foucault, "What is Enlightenment?," 315.

66. For more detailed accounts of Foucault's disavowed neo-Kantianism, see Gillian Rose, *Dialectic of Nihilism: Post-Structuralism and Law* (Oxford: Blackwell, 1984), 171–207; and Craig Brandist, "Neo-Kantianism in Cultural Theory: Bakhtin, Derrida and Foucault," *Radical Philosophy* 102 (2000): 6–16. Both explicate Foucault's neo-Kantianism with explicit reference to the Marburg and Heidelberg Schools of sociology.

67. See, for example, Felski, *The Limits of Critique*, 150.

68. Bruno Latour, "The Politics of Explanation: an Alternative," in *Knowledge and Reflexivity: New Frontiers in the Sociology of Knowledge*, ed. Steve Woolgar, 155–77 (London: Sage, 1988), 155.

69. Latour, "The Politics of Explanation: an Alternative," 155.

70. Latour, "The Politics of Explanation: an Alternative," 173.

71. Latour, "Why Has Critique Run out of Steam?," 231–32.

72. Latour, "The Politics of Explanation," 173.

73. Rita Felski, *Hooked: Art and Attachment* (Chicago: University of Chicago Press, 2020), 9.

74. Hegel, *Logic*, 47.

75. Felski, *Hooked*, 10.

76. Three out of four of these lectures are available to watch on the Trinity College, University of Cambridge website, accessed May 8, 2024, https://www.trin.cam.ac.uk/about/public-lectures/clark/.

77. Rita Felski, "Recognizing Class," *New Literary History* 52, no. 1 (2021): 97.

78. Rita Felski, "Good Vibrations," *American Literary History* 32, no. 2 (2020): 406.

79. Amanda Anderson, *The Way We Argue Now: A Study in the Cultures of Theory* (Princeton, NJ: Princeton University Press, 2005), 141. Qtd. in Felski, "Recognizing Class," 97.

80. Felski, "Recognizing Class," 101.

81. Rita Felski, "Remix: On Literature and Theory," Clark Lectures 2021, online video recording, YouTube, uploaded February 23, 2021, https://www.youtube.com/watch?v=o56TpkAbhKE.

82. Felski, "Remix."
83. For example, Robbins describes Felski's project as moving literary scholarship "closer to fandom, a profession that is closer to the industry's dollars-and-cents metric and its rhetoric of helpful and largely positive advice to the would-be consumer." Robbins, "Not So Well Attached," 372. Likewise, Robert T. Tally Jr. argues that postcritique "compromises the very position of the literary critic or professor entirely, championing an approach to literature that removes both expertise and even knowledge from the process, and encourages readers to trust their own affective reaction to whatever 'brand' of literature seems most commercially attractive to them at any given moment." Robert T. Tally Jr., "Reading Adorno by the Pool; or, Critical Theory in a Postcritical Era," *symplokē* 27 (2019): 287.
84. Felski, "Remix."
85. Felski, "Recognizing Class," 96.
86. Didier Eribon, *Returning to Reims*, trans. Michael Lucey (London: Allen Lane, 2018), 170.
87. Axel Honneth, *The Struggle for Recognition*, 132. My emphases.
88. Felski, "Recognizing Class," 99. See Jacques Lacan, "The Mirror Stage as Formative of the *I* Function as Revealed in Psychoanalytic Experience," in *Écrits*, 75–81; Louis Althusser, "Ideology and Ideological State Apparatuses," in *On the Reproduction of Capitalism: Ideology and Ideological State Apparatuses*, trans. G. M. Goshgarian (London: Verso, 2014), 232–72.
89. Axel Honneth, *Recognition: A Chapter in the History of Ideas*, trans. Joseph Ganahl (Cambridge: Cambridge University Press, 2021), 128n45.
90. Honneth, *Recognition*, 175–76.
91. Felski, "Recognizing Class," 101.
92. G. W. F. Hegel, *"System of Ethical Life" and "First Philosophy of Spirit,"* trans. H. S. Harris and T. M. Knox (Albany: State University of New York Press, 1979). The *System of Ethical Life*, usually dated 1802, went unpublished until 1913.
93. Honneth, *The Struggle for Recognition*, 5.
94. Honneth, *The Struggle for Recognition*, 5.
95. Felski makes reference to Charles Taylor, "The Politics of Recognition," in *Multiculturalism: Examining the Politics of Recognition*, ed. Amy Gutmann (Princeton, NJ: Princeton University Press, 1994), 25–73; Nancy Fraser, "Rethinking Recognition," *New Left Review* 3 (2000): 107–20; and Nancy Fraser and Axel Honneth, *Redistribution or Recognition? A Political-Philosophical Exchange*, trans. Joel Golb, James Ingram, and Christiane Wilke (London: Verso, 2003).
96. Felski, "Recognizing Class," 98.
97. Rose, *Hegel Contra Sociology*, 44.
98. Honneth, *The Struggle for Recognition*, 172.
99. Honneth, *The Struggle for Recognition*, 186n40.
100. For an account of Rose's theory of recognition with broader comparison to other prominent alternatives, see Kate Schick, "Re-Recognizing Recognition: Gillian Rose's 'Radical Hegel' and Vulnerable Recognition," *Telos* 173 (2015): 87–105.
101. Rose, *Hegel Contra Sociology*, 64.
102. Hegel, *System of Ethical Life*, 101–2.
103. Rose, *Hegel Contra Sociology*, 77.
104. Hegel, *System of Ethical Life*, 102.

105. Rose, *Hegel Contra Sociology*, 60. It is important to note that while Hegel is arguing that only "relative" (i.e., not absolute) ethical life and misrecognition are possible under bourgeois property relations, he is not advocating for communism—that is, for the abolition of private property and class society. The final section of the *System of Ethical Life* imagines a different property relation designed merely to counterbalance bourgeois property relations with a system of mutual dependence between different social groups. This system is still based on the stratification of society into agricultural, acquisitive, and administrative classes. Rose's reading defends Hegel nonetheless, arguing: "By acknowledging the contradictions of bourgeois enterprise and private property, Hegel hoped to surmount and contain them. He developed a notion of absolute ethical life which does not deny and suppress, nor reproduce, real relations, lack of identity" (75).

106. Marx, *Capital*, 165. Translation slightly altered. Fowkes renders *phantasmagorische* as "fantastic." This is a mistranslation. As Rose notes: "The epithet 'phantasmagoric' stresses the personifications as well as the strangeness of the form in which the relations between men appear. 'Phantasmagoria' means a crowd or succession of dim or doubtfully real persons. The word was coined in England in 1802 and was taken over later into German." Gillian Rose, *The Melancholy Science: An Introduction to the Thought of Theodor W. Adorno* (London: Verso, 2014), 40.

107. Felski, "Recognizing Class," 101.

108. Rose, *Judaism and Modernity*, 35.

109. Axel Honneth, *Pathologies of Reason: On the Legacy of Critical Theory*, trans. James D. Ingram (New York: Columbia University Press, 2009), 19.

110. Felski, "Recognizing Class," 99.

111. Marx, *Capital*, 799.

112. Marx and Engels, *The Holy Family*, 36–37.

113. Eribon, *Returning to Reims*, 82, 84.

114. Marx and Engels, *The Holy Family*, 37.

115. Walter Benjamin, "The Work of Art in the Age of Mechanical Reproduction," in *Illuminations*, trans. Harry Zohn, ed. Hannah Aredent, 217–52 (New York: Schocken Books, 2007), 241.

116. Eribon, *Returning to Reims*, 115.

117. Here, I reformulate Rose's indictment of the two major, apparently opposing strands of sociology, both of which are reducible to a neo-Kantian paradigm. She writes: "Structural sociology is 'empty,' action theory is 'blind.' The former imposes abstract postulates on social reality and confirms by simplifying the contradictions of dominant law. The latter confirms social reality as a mass of random meanings in its immediate mode of representation." *Hegel Contra Sociology*, 228–29. This, in turn, parodies Kant's famous formulation from the *Critique of Pure Reason*, 193–94 that "thoughts without content are empty, intuitions without concepts are blind."

118. Jameson, *Marxism and Form*, 306.

119. Fredric Jameson, *The Modernist Papers* (London: Verso, 2016), ix.

120. Jameson, *The Modernist Papers*, ix.

121. Jameson, *The Modernist Papers*, 308.

122. This "sickening" experience of dialectical criticism might be productively compared to the Russian Formalist concept of "defamiliarization" which Jameson would go onto write about in his following book, *The Prison-House of Language: A Critical*

Account of Structuralism and Russian Formalism (Princeton, NJ: Princeton University Press, 1972).

123. Jameson, *Marxism and Form*, 319.

124. Fredric Jameson, "Metacommentary," *PMLA* 86 (1971): 9-18.

125. See especially Jameson, *The Political Unconscious*, 37-39.

126. Jameson, *The Political Unconscious*, 38. See also Fredric Jameson, *Valences of the Dialectic* (London: Verso, 2009), 100-101. This is quite close to what Rose argues in *Hegel Contra Sociology*, although she credits Hegel with a bit more self-consciousness. For Rose, Hegel can only think the absolute abstractly and subjectively, but unlike Kant and Fichte who do so fetishistically or (in the words of Jameson) as a containment strategy, Hegel self-consciously theorizes this very failure and its historical determination. "Once we realize this we can think the absolute by acknowledging the element of *Sollen* in such a thinking, by acknowledging the subjective element, the limits on our thinking the absolute. This is to think the absolute and fail to think it quite differently from Kant and Fichte's thinking and failing to think it." Rose, *Hegel Contra Sociology*, 218.

127. Jameson, *The Political Unconscious*, 226.

128. Jonathan Culler, "Synchronous Coexistence and Temporal Overlay," *PMLA* 137 (2022): 517-20.

129. Jameson, *The Political Unconscious*, 274.

130. Jameson, *The Political Unconscious*, 275.

131. Jameson, *The Political Unconscious*, 274.

132. Jameson, *The Political Unconscious*, 274.

133. Fredric Jameson, "Criticism and Categories," *PMLA* 137 (2022): 563-67.

134. Best and Marcus, "Surface Reading," 15.

135. Leo Robson, "Jameson After Post Critique," *New Left Review* 144 (November/December 2023).

136. Felski, *The Limits of Critique*, 171.

137. Fredric Jameson, "Symptoms of Theory or Symptoms for Theory?," *Critical Inquiry* 30 (Winter 2004): 407.

138. Jameson, "Metacommentary," 9.

139. For the former, Robson highlights in particular the beginning of Jameson's 1979 essay on modern painting (De Kooning, Cézanne, and Gertsch): "What I like to look at in De Kooning's paintings is the yellow. I like to look at the yellow parts of even those paintings I don't think much of. Next to the yellow, I like to look at the pink. Finally the grey. For me the name De Kooning means the chance to stare at these painted colors, not works of art or experiences of form, and certainly not the various figurative pretexts, although the remnants of the faces of women are certainly unavoidable." See Jameson, "Towards a Libidinal Economy of Three Modern Papers," in *The Modernist Papers*, 255.

140. Robson, "Jameson After Post Critique." Some of these book reviews are recently collected in Fredric Jameson, *Inventions of a Present: The Novel in its Crisis of Globalization* (London: Verso, 2024).

141. Jameson, *The Political Unconscious*, 6.

142. Jameson, *The Political Unconscious*, 9.

143. Fredric Jameson, "Marxist Criticism and Hegel," *PMLA* 131 (2016): 432.

144. See Felski, *The Limits of Critique*, 151-85.

145. Felski, *The Limits of Critique*, 151-85.

146. Felski, *The Limits of Critique*, 437.

147. Rose, *Hegel Contra Sociology*, 232.

148. Gillian Rose, *Marxist Modernism: Introductory Lectures on Frankfurt School Critical Theory*, ed. Robert Lucas Scott and Gordon Finlayson (London: Verso, 2024).

149. Sutherland, "Marx in Jargon," 33–34.

150. Incidentally, and as Sutherland also notes, this misunderstanding of *der Fetischcharakter* is implied by Jameson when he writes that "if commodity fetishism can in one way be usefully described as 'the effacement of the traces of production from the object,' then aesthetic dereification will naturally enough be identified as the will to conceal those traces." Fredric Jameson, *Signatures of the Visible* (London: Routledge, 1992), 188. Qtd. in Sutherland, "Marx in Jargon," 84n37.

151. Charles de Brosses, *Du Culte des Dieux Fétiches, ou Parallèle de l'ancienne Religion de l'Egypte avec la Religion actuelle de Nigritie* (Westmead: Gregg International, 1972), 237. Qtd. in and trans. in Sutherland, "Marx in Jargon," 58.

152. Giorgio Agamben, *Stanzas: Word and Phantasm in Western Culture*, trans. Ronald L. Martinez (Minneapolis: University of Minnesota Press, 1993), 35. Qtd. in Sutherland, "Marx in Jargon," 57.

153. Sutherland, "Marx in Jargon," 58.

154. Sutherland, "Marx in Jargon," 59.

155. Sutherland, "Marx in Jargon," 59.

156. Sutherland, "Marx in Jargon," 62.

157. Sutherland, "Marx in Jargon," 68.

158. Sutherland, "Marx in Jargon," 70.

159. Sutherland, *Stupefaction*, 13.

160. As already noted: Rose argues that this represents the trace of a necessary yet disavowed imperative or *Sollen* of Hegel's thought. See 195n126.

161. Rose, *Mourning Becomes the Law*, 42.

162. Rose, *Mourning Becomes the Law*, 43.

163. Rose, *Mourning Becomes the Law*, 43. A more up-to-date example (which probably can't be credited with informing anyone about anything) might be Taika Waititi's comedy *Jojo Rabbit* (2019), in which the only people who could possibly be seduced by fascism are represented as bumbling morons, and therefore the tone is one of smugly superior de Brossesian smug astonishment, aimed only at establishing "sympathetic mutuality" between members of the same class, "on the grounds of their common difference from the stupid and the unenlightened" (to reuse Sutherland's words). We often see similar instances of de Brossesian astonishment today in liberal-left responses to supporters of, for instance, Donald Trump or Brexit.

164. Sutherland, "Marx in Jargon," 50.

165. Rose *Mourning Becomes the Law*, 51.

166. Rose *Mourning Becomes the Law*, 54.

167. Rose *Mourning Becomes the Law*, 51.

168. Rose *Mourning Becomes the Law*, 52.

169. Rose *Mourning Becomes the Law*, 53.

170. Marx, *Capital*, 134.

171. Sutherland, "Marx in Jargon," 76.

172. Rose, *Mourning Becomes the Law*, 54.

173. Hegel, *Lectures on the Philosophy of Religion*, 157.
174. Hegel, *Aesthetics*, 2:626.
175. Hegel, *Aesthetics*, 2:1113.
176. Hegel, *Aesthetics*, 2:1112.
177. For an excellent, concise account of Hegel on lyric, see Jonathan Culler, *Theory of the Lyric* (Cambridge, MA: Harvard University Press, 2017), 92–109. See John Keats, "Ode on a Grecian Urn": "Heard melodies are sweet, but those unheard / Are sweeter."
178. Hegel, *Aesthetics*, 2:1121.
179. Jacqueline Rose, "'This Is Not a Biography,'" *London Review of Books* 24, no. 16 (August 22, 2002).
180. For Marx's abandonment of writing poetry, see Keston Sutherland, "Marx's Defence of Poetry," *World Picture* 10 (Spring 2015): 1–15.
181. Theodor W. Adorno, "On Lyric Poetry and Society," in *Notes to Literature*, 2 vols., ed. Rolf Tiedemann, trans. Shierry Weber Nicholsen (New York: Columbia University Press, 1991), 1:41.
182. Theodor W. Adorno, *Aesthetic Theory*, ed. Gretel Adorno, Rolf Tiedemann, and Robert Hullot-Kentor, trans. Robert Hullot-Kentor (London: Continuum, 1997), 130.
183. Keston Sutherland, "Statement for 'Revolution and/or Poetry,'" *Revolution and/or Poetry*, October 15, 2013, https://revolutionandorpoetry.wordpress.com/2013/10/15/keston-sutherlands-statement-for-revolution-andor-poetry/.
184. Adorno, *Aesthetic Theory*, 130.
185. Anahid Nersessian, *Keats's Odes: A Lover's Discourse* (Chicago: The University of Chicago Press, 2021), 5.
186. Nersessian, *Keats's Odes*, 7.
187. Nersessian, *Keats's Odes*, 16.
188. See Rose, *Hegel Contra Sociology*, 84: "Philosophy is … the concept of real recognition, that is, abstract, because it arises in a society where real recognition has not been achieved.… It thus contains an abstract imperative, a moment of *Sollen*."
189. Rose, *Hegel Contra Sociology*, 199.
190. Nersessian, *Keats's Odes*, 16, with quotation from Sean Bonney, "Corpus Hermeticum: On the Revolutions of the Heavenly Spheres," in *Letters Against the Firmament* (London: Enitharmon Press, 2015), which quotes in turn from Keats's letter to Fanny Brawne on July 8, 1819: "All my thoughts, my unhappiest days and nights have I find not at all cured me of my love of Beauty, but made it so intense that I am miserable that you are not with me: or rather breathe in that dull sort of patience that cannot be called Life."
191. Kornbluh, *Immediacy*, 107.
192. Kornbluh, *Immediacy*, 79.
193. Rose, *Hegel Contra Sociology*, 36.
194. Kornbluh, *Immediacy*, 71.
195. Kornbluh, *Immediacy*, 69.
196. These latter events occur in volumes 1, 2, and 4, respectively.
197. Ben Lerner, "Each Cornflake," Review of *My Struggle*, vol. 3, *Boyhood Island*, by Karl Ove Knausgaard, *London Review of Books* 36, no. 10 (May 22, 2014).
198. Karl Ove Knausgaard, *My Struggle*, vol. 6, *The End*, trans. Martin Aitken and Don Bartlett (London: Harvill Secker, 2018), 1009–10; Karl Ove Knausgaard, "Karl

Ove Knausgaard Became a Literary Sensation Exposing His Every Secret: Readers Love Him, He Hates Himself," interview by Evan Hughes, *New Republic* (April 7, 2014); qtd. in Kornbluh, *Immediacy*, 66.

199. Kornbluh, *Immediacy*, 68.

200. Karl Ove Knausgaard, "865. Karl Ove Knausgaard," *Otherppl with Brad Listi*, podcast, September 2023, https://open.spotify.com/episode/0zOTUIpQoXGoqaobszMeYg?si=84c8081a64f64d7c.

201. Knausgaard, "865. Karl Ove Knausgaard."

202. Hegel, *Logic*, 47.

203. Gertrude Stein, *Tender Buttons* (New York: Claire Marie, 1914), 51.

204. Karl Ove Knausgaard, *My Struggle*, vol. 2, *A Man in Love*, trans. Don Bartlett (London: Vintage, 2013), 346.

205. Fredric Jameson, "Itemised," review of *My Struggle*, vol. 6, *The End*, by Karl Ove Knausgaard, *London Review of Books* 40, no. 21 (November 8, 2018).

206. Hägglund, *This Life*, 92.

207. Knausgaard, *My Struggle*, vol. 2, *A Man in Love*, 60.

208. Jameson, "Itemised."

209. Adorno, *Minima Moralia*, 247.

210. Adorno, *Minima Moralia*, 247.

211. Karl Ove Knausgaard, "Karl Ove Knausgaard on the Writing of Jon Fosse," *Literary Hub*, September 30, 2019, https://lithub.com/karl-ove-knausgaard-on-the-writing-of-jon-fosse/; with reference to Leo Tolstoy, *War and Peace*, trans. Anthony Briggs (London: Penguin Books, 2007), 508.

Bibliography

Abrams, M. H. *Natural Supernaturalism: Tradition and Revolution in Romantic Literature*. New York: W. W. Norton, 1971.
Achella, Stefania. "Memory and Fate: Recollection in Hegel's Philosophy of Religion." In *Hegel on Recollection: Essays on the Concept of "Erinnerung" in Hegel's System*, edited by Valentina Ricci and Federico Sanguinetti, 179-98. Newcastle: Cambridge Scholars Publishing, 2013.
Adorno, Theodor W. *Aesthetic Theory*. Edited by Gretel Adorno, Rolf Tiedemann, and Robert Hullot-Kentor. Translated by Robert Hullot-Kentor. London: Continuum, 1997.
———. *Critical Models: Interventions and Catchwords*. Translated by Harry W. Pickford. New York: Columbia University Press, 2005.
———. *Drei Studien zu Hegel*. In volume 5 of *Gesammelte Schriften*, edited by Rolf Tiedemann, 247-383. Frankfurt a.M.: Suhrkamp, 2003.
———. *Hegel: Three Studies*. Translated by Shierry Weber Nicholsen. Cambridge, MA: MIT Press.
———. *Kant's "Critique of Pure Reason."* Edited by Rolf Tiedemann. Translated by Rodney Livingstone. Stanford: Stanford University Press, 2001.
———. "The Meaning of Working Through the Past." In *Critical Models: Interventions and Catchwords*, translated by Harry W. Pickford, 89-104. New York: Columbia University Press, 2005.
———. *Minima Moralia: Reflections from Damaged Life*. Translated by E. F. N. Jephcott. London: Verso, 2005.
———. *Negative Dialectics*. Translated by E. B. Ashton. London: Routledge, 2004.
———. "On Lyric Poetry and Society." In *Notes to Literature*, 2 vols. Edited by Rolf Tiedemann. Translated by Shierry Weber Nicholsen. New York: Columbia University Press, 1991.
Adorno, Theodor W., and Max Horkheimer. *Dialectic of Enlightenment: Philosophical Fragments*. Edited by Gunzelin Schmid Noerr. Translated by Edmund Jephcott. Stanford: Stanford University Press, 2002.
Agamben, Giorgio. *Stanzas: Word and Phantasm in Western Culture*. Translated by Ronald L. Martinez. Minneapolis: University of Minnesota Press, 1993.

Althusser, Louis. "Ideology and Ideological State Apparatuses." In *On the Reproduction of Capitalism: Ideology and Ideological State Apparatuses*, translated by G. M. Goshgarian, 232–72. London: Verso, 2014.

———. "Preface to *Capital* Volume 1." In *Lenin and Philosophy, and Other Essays*, translated by Ben Brewster, 45–65. New York: NYU Press, 2001.

Altman, Matthew C. "The Letter and the Spirit: Kant's Metaphysics and Fichte's Epistemology." In *The Palgrave Fichte Handbook*, edited by Steven Hoeltzel, 421–42. London: Palgrave Macmillan, 2019.

Anderson, Amanda. *The Way We Argue Now: A Study in the Cultures of Theory*. Princeton, NJ: Princeton University Press, 2005.

Arendt, Hannah. *Eichmann in Jerusalem: A Report on the Banality of Evil*. London: Penguin, 2006.

Aristotle. "On the Soul." In volume 1 of *The Complete Works of Aristotle: The Revised Oxford Translation*, edited by Jonathan Barnes, 641–92. Princeton: Princeton University Press, 1991.

Armstrong, Isobel. *The Radical Aesthetic*. Hoboken, NJ: Wiley, 2000.

Augustine of Hippo. *On the Spirit and the Letter*. Translated by W. J. Sparrow Simpson. London: Society for Promoting Christian Knowledge, 1925.

Badiou, Alain. *Logics of Worlds: Being and Event II*. Translated by Alberto Toscano. London: Continuum, 2009.

———. *Saint Paul: The Foundation of Universalism*. Translated by Ray Brassier. Stanford: Stanford University Press, 2003.

Bahti, Timothy. *Allegories of History: Literary Historiography after Hegel*. Baltimore: Johns Hopkins University Press, 1992.

Barth, Karl. *The Epistle to the Romans*. Translated by Edwyn C. Hoskyns. London: Oxford University Press, 1933.

Barton, John. *A History of the Bible: The Book and Its Faiths*. London: Penguin Books, 2020.

Bates, Jennifer Ann. *Hegel and Shakespeare on Moral Imagination*. New York: SUNY Press, 2010.

———. *Hegel's Theory of Imagination*. Albany: State University of New York Press, 2004.

Bayard, Pierre. *Comment parler des faits qui ne se sont pas produits?* Paris: Minuit, 2020.

Baynes, Kenneth. "Freedom and Recognition in Hegel and Habermas." *Philosophy and Social Criticism* 28, no. 1 (2002): 1–17.

Beckett, Samuel. "What Is the Word?" In *Poems: 1930–1989*, 113–15. London: Calder Publications, 2002.

Beiser, Frederick C. *German Idealism: The Struggle Against Subjectivism, 1781–1801*. Cambridge, MA: Harvard University Press, 2022.

Benjamin, Walter. "The Work of Art in the Age of Mechanical Reproduction." In *Illuminations*, translated by Harry Zohn, edited by Hannah Arendt, 217–52. New York: Schocken Books, 2007.

Bernstein, J. M. *The Fate of Art: Aesthetic Alienation from Kant to Derrida and Adorno*. University Park: Pennsylvania State University Press, 1992.

———. "To Be Is to Live, to Be Is to Be Recognized." In *Torture and Dignity: An Essay on Moral Injury*, 175–217. Chicago: University of Chicago Press, 2015.

Best, Stephen, and Sharon Marcus. "Surface Reading: An Introduction." *Representations* 108, no. 1 (2009).
Bewes, Timothy. "Reading with the Grain: A New World in Literary Criticism." *differences* 21, no. 3 (2010): 1–33.
Blanchot, Maurice. *The Writing of the Disaster*. Translated by Ann Smock. Lincoln: University of Nebraska Press, 1995.
Bloch, Ernst. *The Principle of Hope*, 3 vols. Translated by Neville Plaice, Stephen Plaice, and Paul Knight. Oxford: Basil Blackwell, 1986.
——. *Subjekt-Objekt: Erläuterungen zu Hegel*. Frankfurt a.M.: Suhrkamp, 1962.
Bonney, Sean. "Corpus Hermeticum: On the Revolutions of the Heavenly Spheres." In *Letters Against the Firmament*. London: Enitharmon Press, 2015.
Brandist, Craig. "Neo-Kantianism in Cultural Theory: Bakhtin, Derrida and Foucault." *Radical Philosophy* 102 (2000): 6–16.
Brandom, Robert B. *Articulating Reasons: An Introduction to Inferentialism*. Cambridge, MA: Harvard University Press, 2009.
——. *A Spirit of Trust: A Reading of Hegel's "Phenomenology."* Cambridge, MA: Harvard University Press, 2019.
——. *Tales of the Mighty Dead: Historical Essays in the Metaphysics of Intentionality*. Cambridge, MA: Harvard University Press, 2002.
——. "Towards Reconciling Two Heroes: Habermas and Hegel." *Argumenta* 1, no. 1 (2015): 29–42.
Buck-Morss, Susan. "Hegel and Haiti." *Critical Inquiry* 26, no. 4 (2000): 821–65.
——. *Hegel, Haiti, and Universal History*. Pittsburgh: University of Pittsburgh Press, 2009.
Butler, Judith. "Commentary on Joseph Flay's 'Hegel, Derrida, and Bataille's Laughter.'" In *Hegel and His Critics: Philosophy in the Aftermath of Hegel*, edited by William Desmond, 174–78. Albany: SUNY Press, 1989.
——. *Subjects of Desire: Hegelian Reflections in Twentieth-Century France*. New York: Columbia University Press, 2012.
Cole, Andrew. *The Birth of Theory*. Chicago: University of Chicago Press, 2014.
Comay, Rebecca. "'Adorno avec Sade....'" *differences* 17, no. 1 (2006): 6–19.
——. *Mourning Sickness: Hegel and the French Revolution*. Stanford, CA: Stanford University Press, 2011.
——. "Resistance and Repetition: Hegel and Freud." In *Hegel and Resistance: History, Politics and Dialectics*, edited by Bart Zantvoort and Rebecca Comay, 35–57. London: Bloomsbury, 2019.
——. "Senile Dialectic." In *Beckett and Dialectics: Be it Something or Nothing*, edited by Eva Ruda, 61–104. London: Bloomsbury Academic, 2021.
Comay, Rebecca, and Frank Ruda. *The Dash—The Other Side of Absolute Knowing*. Cambridge, MA: MIT Press, 2018.
Croce, Benedetto. *What is Living and What is Dead in the Philosophy of Hegel*. Translated by Douglas Ainslie. London: Macmillan, 1915.
Culler, Jonathan. "Synchronous Coexistence and Temporal Overlay." *PMLA* 137 (2022): 517–20.
——. *Theory of the Lyric*. Cambridge, MA: Harvard University Press, 2017.
Deakin, Wayne. *Hegel and the English Romantic Tradition*. London: Palgrave Macmillan, 2015.

de Boer, Karin. "Beyond Recognition? Critical Reflections on Honneth's Reading of Hegel's *Philosophy of Right*." *International Journal of Philosophical Studies* 21, no. 4 (2013): 534–58.

de Brosses, Charles. *Du Culte des Dieux Fétiches, ou Parallèle de l'ancienne Religion de l'Egypte avec la Religion actuelle de Nigritie*. Westmead: Gregg International, 1972.

Deleuze, Gilles. *Nietzsche and Philosophy*. Translated by Hugh Tomlinson. London: Continuum, 2005.

de Man, Paul. "The Concept of Irony." In *Aesthetic Ideology*, edited by Andrzej Warminski, 163–84. Minneapolis: University of Minnesota Press, 1996.

———. "Sign and Symbol in Hegel's *Aesthetics*." In *Aesthetic Ideology*, edited by Andrzej Warminski, 91–104. Minneapolis: University of Minnesota Press, 1996.

Derrida, Jacques. "The Art of *Mémoires*," translated by Jonathan Culler. In *Memoires for Paul de Man*, 45–88. New York: Columbia University Press, 1988.

———. *Glas*. Translated by John P. Leavey Jr. and Richard Rand. Lincoln: University of Nebraska Press, 1986.

———. *Of Grammatology*. Translated by Gayatri Chakravorty Spivak. Baltimore: Johns Hopkins University Press, 1997.

———. "The Pit and the Pyramid: Introduction to Hegel's Semiology." In *Margins of Philosophy*, translated by Alan Bass, 69–108. Brighton: Harvester Press, 1982.

———. *Points... Interviews, 1974-1994*. Edited by Elisabeth Weber, translated by Peggy Kamuf. Stanford: Stanford University Press, 1995.

———. *Positions*. Translated by Alan Bass. Chicago: University of Chicago Press, 1981.

———. "To Forgive: The Unforgivable and the Imprescriptible." In *Questioning God*, edited by John Caputo, Mark Dooley, and Michael Scanlon, 21–51. Bloomington: Indiana University Press, 2001.

———. "White Mythology: Metaphor in the Text of Philosophy." in *Margins of Philosophy*, translated by Alan Bass, 207–71. Brighton: Harvester Press, 1982.

Di Cesare, Donatella. *Heidegger and the Jews: The Black Notebooks*. Translated by Murtha Baca. Cambridge: Polity, 2018.

Die Bibel: Lutherübersetzung. Peabody, MA: Hendrickson, 2018.

Dolar, Mladen. "The Phrenology of Spirit." In *Supposing the Subject*, edited by Joan Copjec, 64–83. London: Verso, 1994.

Eliot, T. S. "Tradition and the Individual Talent (1917)." In *Selected Essays*, 13–22. London: Faber and Faber, 1932.

Emre, Merve. *Paraliterary: The Making of Bad Readers in Postwar America*. Chicago: University of Chicago Press, 2017.

Eribon, Didier. *Returning to Reims*. Translated by Michael Lucey. London: Allen Lane, 2018.

Farrar, Frederic W. *History of Interpretation*. London: Macmillan, 1886.

Felski, Rita. "Good Vibrations." *American Literary History* 32, no. 2 (2020): 405–15.

———. *Hooked: Art and Attachment*. Chicago: University of Chicago Press, 2020.

———. *The Limits of Critique*. Chicago: University of Chicago Press, 2015.

———. "Postcritical." In *Further Reading*, edited by Matthew Rubery and Leah Price, 135–43. Oxford: Oxford University Press, 2020.

———. "Recognizing Class." *New Literary History* 52, no. 1 (2021): 95–117.

———. "Remix: On Literature and Theory." Clark Lectures 2021. Online video

recording. YouTube, February 23, 2021. https://www.youtube.com/watch?v
=056TpkAbhKE.
Fenves, Peter. *Late Kant: Towards Another Law of the Earth*. London: Routledge, 2003.
Fichte, J. G. *Attempt at a Critique of All Revelation*. Edited by Allen Wood, translated by Garrett Green. Cambridge: Cambridge University Press, 2010.
———. *Early Philosophical Writings*. Translated and edited by Daniel Breazeale. Ithaca, NY: Cornell University Press, 1988.
———. *Foundations of Transcendental Philosophy*. Translated and edited by Daniel Breazeale. Ithaca, NY: Cornell University Press, 1998.
Fiddes, Paul S., and Günder Bader, eds. *The Spirit and the Letter: A Tradition and a Reversal*. London: Bloomsbury, 2013.
Foucault, Michel. "The Discourse on Language." In *"The Archeology of Knowledge" and "The Discourse on Language,"* translated by A. M. Sheridan Smith, 215–37. New York: Pantheon Books, 1972.
———. "What is Enlightenment?" translated by Catherine Porter, amended by Robert Hurley. In *Essential Works of Foucault 1954-1984*, vol. 1, *Ethics: Subjectivity and Truth*, 303–19, edited by Paul Rabinow. London: Penguin Books, 2000.
Franks, Paul W. *All or Nothing: Systematicity, Transcendental Arguments, and Skepticism in German Idealism*. Cambridge, MA: Harvard University Press, 2005.
Fraser, Nancy. "Rethinking Recognition." *New Left Review* 3 (2000): 107–20.
Fraser, Nancy, and Axel Honneth. *Redistribution or Recognition? A Political-Philosophical Exchange*. Translated by Joel Golb, James Ingram, and Christiane Wilke. London: Verso, 2003.
Freud, Sigmund. "Remembering, Repeating and Working-Through (Further Recommendations on the Technique of Psycho-Analysis II) (1914)." In *The Case of Schreber, Papers on Technique and Other Works*, vol. 12 of *The Standard Edition of the Complete Psychological Works of Sigmund Freud*, edited and translated by James Strachey, 145–56. London: Hogarth Press, 1958.
Geuss, Raymond. "A Response to Paul de Man." *Critical Inquiry* 10, no. 2 (1983): 375–82.
Goetschel, Willi. *Constituting Critique: Kant's Writing as Critical Praxis*. Translated by Eric Schwab. Durham, NC: Duke University Press, 1994.
Goh, Kien-how. "The Ideality of Idealism: Fichte's Battle against Dogmatic Kantianism." In *Fichte and Transcendental Philosophy*, edited by Tom Rockmore and Daniel Breazeale, 128–42. London: Palgrave Macmillan, 2014.
Guillory, John. *Professing Criticism: Essays on the Organization of Literary Study*. Chicago: University of Chicago Press, 2022.
Habib, M. A. R. *Hegel and the Foundations of Literary Theory*. Cambridge: Cambridge University Press, 201.
Hägglund, Martin. *This Life: Why Mortality Makes Us Free*. London: Profile Books, 2019.
Hamacher, Werner. *pleroma—Reading in Hegel*. Translated by Nicholas Walker and Simon Jarvis. London: Athlone Press, 1998.
Harman, Graham. "The Well-Wrought Broken Hammer: Object-Oriented Literary Criticism." *New Literary History* 43, no. 2 (2012): 183–203.
Hayles, N. Katherine. "How We Read: Close, Hyper, Machine." *ADE Bulletin* 150 (2010): 62–79.

Hegel, G. W. F. "Address on the Tercentenary of the Submission of the Augsburg Confession (25 June 1830)." In *Political Writings*, edited by Laurence Dickey and H. B. Nisbet, translated by H. B. Nisbet, 186–96. Cambridge: Cambridge University Press, 1999.
———. *Aesthetics: Lectures on Fine Art*, 2 vols. Translated by T. M. Knox. Oxford: Clarendon Press, 1988.
———. *Briefe von und an Hegel*, 4 vols. Edited by Johannes Hoffmeister. Hamburg: Felix Meiner, 1969.
———. *The Difference Between Fichte's and Schelling's System of Philosophy*. Translated by H. S. Harris and Walter Cerf. Albany: SUNY Press, 1977.
———. *Early Theological Writings*. Translated by T. M. Knox. Philadelphia: University of Pennsylvania Press, 1971.
———. *Elements of the Philosophy of Right*. Edited by Allen W. Wood, translated by H. B. Nisbet. Cambridge: Cambridge University Press, 2003.
———. *Encyclopedia of the Philosophical Sciences in Basic Outline*, part 1, *Science of Logic*. Translated by Klaus Brinkmann and Daniel O. Dahlstrom. Cambridge: Cambridge University Press, 2010.
———. *Enzyklopädie der philosophischen Wissenschaften im Grundrisse; Dritter Teil: Die Philosophie des Geistes*. In *Werke in zwanzig Bänden*, vol. 10, edited by Eva Moldenhauer and Karl Markus Michel. Frankfurt a.M.: Suhrkamp, 1986.
———. *Enzyklopädie der philosophischen Wissenschaften im Grundrisse; Erster Teil: Die Wissenschaft der Logik*. In *Werke in zwanzig Bänden*, vol. 8, edited by Eva Moldenhauer and Karl Markus Michel. Frankfurt a.M.: Suhrkamp, 1986.
———. *Grundlinien der Philosophie des Rechts*. In *Werke in zwanzig Bänden*, vol. 7, edited by Eva Moldenhauer and Karl Markus Michel. Frankfurt a.M.: Suhrkamp, 1986.
———. *Lectures on the History of Philosophy*, 3 vols. Translated by E. S. Haldane. Lincoln: University of Nebraska Press, 1995.
———. *Lectures on the Philosophy of History*. Translated by J. Sibree. London: H. G. Bohn, 1857.
———. *Lectures on the Philosophy of Religion: One Volume Edition; The Lectures of 1827*. Edited by Peter C. Hodgson, translated by R. F. Brown, P. C. Hodgson, and J. M. Stewart. Oxford: Oxford University Press, 2006.
———. *The Letters*. Translated by Clark Butler and Christiane Seiler. Bloomington, IN: Indiana University Press, 1984.
———. *Natural Law: The Scientific Ways of Treating Natural Law, Its Place in Moral Philosophy, and Its Relation to the Positive Sciences of Law*. Translated by T. M. Knox. Philadelphia, PA: University of Pennsylvania Press, 1975.
———. *Phänomenologie des Geistes*. In *Werke in zwanzig Bänden*, vol. 3, edited by Eva Moldenhauer and Karl Markus Michel. Frankfurt a.M.: Suhrkamp, 1986.
———. *The Phenomenology of Mind*, 2 vols. Translated by J. B. Baillie. London: Swan Sonnenschein, 191.
———. *The Phenomenology of Spirit*. Translated by Michael Inwood. Oxford: Oxford University Press, 2018.
———. *Phenomenology of Spirit*. Translated by A. V. Miller. Oxford: Oxford University Press, 1977.
———. *The Phenomenology of Spirit*. Translated by Terry Pinkard. Cambridge: Cambridge University Press, 2018.

———. "Philosophical Dissertation on the Orbits of the Planets (1801), Preceded by the 12 Theses Defended on August 27, 1801." Translated by Pierre Adler. *Graduate Faculty Philosophy Journal* 12 (1987): 269–309.

———. *Philosophy of Mind*. Translated by W. Wallace and A. V. Miller, revised by Michael Inwood. Oxford: Oxford University Press, 2017.

———. *Philosophy of Nature*. Translated by A. V. Miller. Oxford: Oxford University Press, 1970.

———. *The Philosophy of Spirit (1805–1806)*. In *Hegel and the Human Spirit: A Translation of the Jena Lectures on the Philosophy of Spirit (1805–6) with Commentary* by Leo Rauch, 83–183. Detroit: Wayne State University Press, 1983.

———. *The Science of Logic*. Translated by George di Giovanni. Cambridge: Cambridge University Press, 2010.

———. *"System of Ethical Life" and "First Philosophy of Spirit."* Translated by H. S. Harris and T. M. Knox. Albany: State University of New York Press, 1979.

———. "Über die wissenschaftlichen Behandlungsarten des Naturrechts, seine Stelle in der praktischen Philosophie und sein Verhältnis zu den positiven Rechtswissenschaften." In *Werke in zwanzig Bänden*, vol. 2, *Janaer Schriften*, 454–532, edited by Eva Moldenhauer and Karl Markus Michel. Frankfurt a.M.: Suhrkamp, 1986.

———. *Vorlesungen über die Ästhetik I*. In *Werke in zwanzig Bänden*, vol. 13, edited by Eva Moldenhauer and Karl Markus Michel. Frankfurt a.M.: Suhrkamp, 1986.

———. *Vorlesungen über die Geschichte der Philosophie I*. In *Werke in zwanzig Bänden*, vol. 18, edited by Eva Moldenhauer and Karl Markus Michel. Frankfurt a.M.: Suhrkamp, 1986.

———. *Vorlesungen über die Philosophie der Religion*, 3 vols. Edited by Walter Jaeschke. Hamburg: Felix Meiner, 1993.

Heidegger, Martin. *Hegel's Phenomenology of Spirit*. Translated by Parvis Emad and Kenneth Maly. Bloomington: Indiana University Press, 1988.

———. *Logic: The Quest of Truth*. Translated by Thomas Sheehan. Bloomington: Indiana University Press, 201.

Henrich, Dieter. *Between Kant and Hegel: Lectures on German Idealism*. Edited by David S. Pacini. Cambridge, MA: Harvard University Press, 2003.

The Holy Bible: New Revised Standard Version with Apocrypha. Oxford: Oxford University Press, 1995.

Honneth, Axel. *Pathologies of Reason: On the Legacy of Critical Theory*. Translated by James D. Ingram. New York: Columbia University Press, 2009.

———. *Recognition: A Chapter in the History of Ideas*. Translated by Joseph Ganahl. Cambridge: Cambridge University Press, 2021.

———. *The Struggle for Recognition: The Moral Grammar of Social Conflicts*. Translated by Joel Anderson. Cambridge: Polity Press, 2005.

Hortsmann, Rolf-Peter. "The Reception of the *Critique of Pure Reason* in German Idealism." In *The Cambridge Companion to Kant's "Critique of Pure Reason,"* edited by Paul Guyer, 329–45. Cambridge: Cambridge University Press, 2010.

Houlgate, Stephen. *The Opening of Hegel's "Logic": From Being to Infinity*. West Lafayette, IN: Purdue University Press, 2006.

———. "Phenomenology and *De Re* Interpretation: A Critique of Brandom's Reading of Hegel." *Hegel Bulletin* 29 (2015): 30–47.

———. Review of *A Spirit of Trust: A Reading of Hegel's "Phenomenology"* (2019), by

Robert B. Brandom. *Notre Dame Philosophical Reviews*, April 14, 2020. https://ndpr
.nd.edu/reviews/a-spirit-of-trust-a-reading-of-hegels-phenomenology/.
Hyppolite, Jean. *Genesis and Structure of Hegel's "Phenomenology of Spirit."* Translated by Samuel Cherniak and John Heckman. Evanston, IL: Northwestern University Press, 1974.
Inwood, Michael. "Glossary of Some Key Terms." In *The Phenomenology of Spirit*, translated by Michael Inwood, 323–30. Oxford: Oxford University Press, 2018.
Jacobi, Friedrich Heinrich. "David Hume on Faith, or Idealism and Realism: A Dialogue—Preface and also Introduction to the Author's Collected Philosophical Works." In *The Main Philosophical Writings and the Novel "Allwill,"* translated by George di Giovanni, 253–338. Montreal and Kingston: McGill-Queen's University Press, 1994.
Jameson, Fredric. "Criticism and Categories." *PMLA* 137 (2022): 563–67.
———. *The Hegel Variations: On the "Phenomenology of Spirit."* London: Verso, 2010.
———. "Itemised," review of *My Struggle*, vol. 6, *The End*. *London Review of Books* 40, no. 21, November 8, 2018.
———. *Marxism and Form: Twentieth-Century Dialectical Theories of Literature*. Princeton, NJ: Princeton University Press, 1974.
———. "Marxist Criticism and Hegel." *PMLA* 131 (2016): 430–38.
———. "Metacommentary." *PMLA* 86 (1971): 9–18.
———. *The Modernist Papers*. London: Verso, 2016.
———. *The Political Unconscious: Narrative as a Socially Symbolic Act*. London: Routledge, 2002.
———. *The Prison-House of Language: A Critical Account of Structuralism and Russian Formalism*. Princeton, NJ: Princeton University Press, 1972.
———. *Representing "Capital": A Commentary on Volume One*. London: Verso, 2011.
———. *Signatures of the Visible*. London: Routledge, 1992.
———. "Symptoms of Theory or Symptoms for Theory?," *Critical Inquiry* 30 (Winter 2004): 403–8.
———. *Valences of the Dialectic*. London: Verso, 2009.
Jarvis, Simon. "Prosody as Cognition." *Critical Quarterly* 40, no. 4 (1998): 3–15.
Kant, Immanuel. *"Critique of Practical Reason" and Other Works on the Theory of Ethics*. Translated by Thomas Kingsmill Abbott. London: Longmans, Green and Co., 1923.
———. *Critique of Pure Reason*. Translated by Paul Guyer and Allen W. Wood. Cambridge: Cambridge University Press, 1998.
———. *Religion within the Boundaries of Mere Reason*. Translated by Allen Wood and Georgie di Giovanni. Cambridge: Cambridge University Press, 1998.
Kierkegaard, Søren. *The Concept of Irony, with Continual Reference to Socrates*. In *Kierkegaard's Writings*, vol. 2, edited and translated by Howard V. Hong and Edna H. Hong. Princeton, NJ: Princeton University Press, 1989.
Knausgaard, Karl Ove. "865. Karl Ove Knausgaard," *Otherppl with Brad Listi*, podcast, September 2023, https://open.spotify.com/episode/ozOTUIpQoXGoqaobszMeYg?si=84c8081a64f64d7c.
———. "Karl Ove Knausgaard Became a Literary Sensation Exposing His Every Secret: Readers Love Him, He Hates Himself." Interview by Evan Hughes. *New Republic*. April 7, 2014.

———. *My Struggle*, vol. 2., *A Man in Love*. Translated by Don Bartlett. London: Vintage, 2013.

———. *My Struggle*, vol. 6., *The End*. Translated by Martin Aitken and Don Bartlett. London: Harvill Secker, 2018.

Knox, T. M. "Explanatory Notes." In *Outlines of the Philosophy of Right*, by G. W. F. Hegel, translated by T. M. Knox, edited and revised by Stephen Houlgate, 324-63. Oxford: Oxford University Press, 2008.

Kojève, Alexandre. *Introduction to the Reading of Hegel: Lectures on the "Phenomenology of Spirit."* Edited by Allan Bloom, translated by James H. Nichols Jr. Ithaca, NY: Cornell University Press, 1980.

Kornbluh, Anna. *Immediacy, or The Style of Too Late Capitalism*. London: Verso Books, 2024.

Kortian, Garbis. *Metacritique: The Philosophical Argument of Jürgen Habermas*. Translated by John Raffan. Cambridge: Cambridge University Press, 1980.

Kotsko, Adam. "Politics and Perversion: Situating Žižek's Paul." In *Žižek and Law*, edited by Laurent de Sutter, 31-41. Abingdon: Routledge, 2015.

Krell, David Farrell. "Of Pits and Pyramids." In *Of Memory, Reminiscence, and Writing: On the Verge*, 204-39. Bloomington: Indiana University Press, 1990.

Kristeva, Julia. *Julia Kristeva Interviews*. Edited by Ross Mitchell Guberman. New York: Columbia University Press, 1966.

Lacan, Jacques. "Kant with Sade." In *Écrits*, translated by Bruce Fink, 645-68. London: W. W. Norton, 2006.

———. "The Mirror Stage as Formative of the *I* Function as Revealed in Psychoanalytic Experience." In *Écrits*, translated by Bruce Fink, 75-81. London: W. W. Norton, 2006.

Latour, Bruno. "The Politics of Explanation: An Alternative." In *Knowledge and Reflexivity: New Frontiers in the Sociology of Knowledge*, edited by Steve Woolgar, 155-77. London: Sage, 1988.

———. *Reassembling the Social: An Introduction to Actor-Network-Theory*. Oxford: Oxford University Press, 2005.

———. "Why Has Critique Run out of Steam? From Matters of Fact to Matters of Concern." *Critical Inquiry* 30 (2004): 225-48.

Lenin, V. I. *Imperialism: The Highest Stage of Capitalism*, translated by Yuri Sdobnikov. In *Lenin: Collected Works*, vol. 22. Moscow: Progress Publishers, 1974.

Lerner, Ben. "Each Cornflake," review of *My Struggle*, vol. 3, *Boyhood Island* by Karl Ove Knausgaard. *London Review of Books* 36, no. 10, May 22, 2014.

Lotze, Rudolf Hermann. *Microcosmos: An Essay Concerning Man and His Relation to the World*, 2 vols. Translated by Elizabeth Hamilton and E. E. Constance Jones. Edinburgh: T. & T. Clark, 1894.

Love, Heather. "Close Reading and Thin Description." *Public Culture* 25, no. 3 (2013): 401-34.

Lukács, Georg. *History and Class Consciousness: Studies in Marxist Dialectics*. Translated by Rodney Livingstone. Cambridge, MA: MIT Press, 1971.

Luther, Martin. *Luther's Works*, vol. 39, *Church and Ministry*, edited by Eric W. Gritsch. St Louis, MO: Concordia; and Philadelphia: Fortress Press, 1970.

———. *An Open Letter on Translating*. Translated by Howard Jones. Oxford: Taylor Institution Library, 2017.

Malabou, Catherine. *The Future of Hegel: Plasticity, Temporality and Dialectic.* Translated by Lisabeth During. London: Routledge, 2009.

———. "'Idealism': A New Name for Metaphysics; Hegel and Heidegger on *a priori* Synthesis." In *German Idealism Today*, edited by Markus Gabriel and Anders Moe Rasmussen, 189-202. Berlin: De Gruyter, 2017.

Marasco, Robyn. *The Highway of Despair: Critical Theory after Hegel.* New York: Columbia University Press, 2015.

Marx, Karl. *Capital: A Critique of Political Economy.* Translated by Ben Fowkes. London: Penguin Books, 1982.

———. *Das Kapital.* 2nd German edition, 1872. In *Marx-Engels-Gesamtausgabe.* Berlin: Dietz, 1989 (1975).

———. *Grundrisse: Foundations of the Critique of Political Economy (Rough Draft).* Translated by Martin Nicolaus. London: Penguin Books, 1993.

———. "Theses on Feuerbach [Original Version]." In *Marx/Engels Collected Works (MECW)*, vol. 5. London: Lawrence & Wishart, 1976.

Marx, Karl, and Friedrich Engels. *The Holy Family, or Critique of Critical Criticism,* translated by Richard Dixon and Clemens Dutt. In *Marx/Engels Collected Works (MECW)*, vol. 4. London: Lawrence & Wishart, 1975.

McGowan, John. *Postmodernism and Its Critics.* New York: Cornell University Press, 1991.

Milbank, John. "The Theological Critique of Philosophy in Hamann and Jacobi." In *Radical Orthodoxy: A New Theology*, edited by John Milbank, Catherine Pickstock, and Graham Ward, 21-37. London: Routledge, 1999.

Miller, Andrew H. "Implicative Criticism, or The Display of Thinking." *New Literary History* 44, no. 3 (2013): 345-60.

Milne, Drew. "The Beautiful Soul: From Hegel to Beckett." *Diacritics* 32, no. 1 (2002): 63-82.

———. "Introduction: Criticism and/or Critique." In *Modern Critical Thought: An Anthology of Theorists Writing on Theorists*, edited by Drew Milne, 1-22. Hoboken, NJ: Blackwell, 2003.

Moggach, Douglas. "Hegel and Habermas." *The European Legacy* 2, no. 3 (1997): 550-56.

Moi, Toril. *Revolution of the Ordinary: Literary Studies after Wittgenstein, Austin, and Cavell.* Chicago: University of Chicago Press, 2017.

Moretti, Franco. "Conjectures on World Literature." *New Left Review* 1 (2000): 54-68.

———. *Distant Reading.* London: Verso, 2013.

Moshenska, Joe. "Why Can't Spenserians Stop Talking About Hegel? A Response to Gordon Teskey." *Spenser Review* 44 (2014).

Muella, Gustav E. "The Hegel Legend of 'Thesis-Antithesis-Synthesis.'" In *The Hegel Myths and Legends*, edited by Jon Stewart, 301-5. Evanston, IL: Northwestern University Press, 1996.

Nersessian, Anahid. *Keats's Odes: A Lover's Discourse.* Chicago: The University of Chicago Press, 2021.

Ng, Karen. *Hegel's Concept of Life: Self-Consciousness, Freedom, Logic.* Oxford: Oxford University Press, 2020.

———. "Ideology Critique from Hegel and Marx to Critical Theory." *Constellations* 22, no. 3 (2015): 393-404.

Nietzsche, Friedrich. *Daybreak: Thoughts on the Prejudices of Morality*. Translated by R. J. Hollingdale. Cambridge: Cambridge University Press, 2003.
Nuzzo, Angelica. *Approaching Hegel's Logic, Obliquely: Melville, Molière, Beckett*. New York: SUNY Press, 2018.
———. *Memory, History, Justice in Hegel*. London: Palgrave Macmillan, 2012.
"Oldest System Programme of German Idealism (1796)," translated by Andrew Bowie. In *Aesthetics and Subjectivity: From Kant to Nietzsche*, by Andrew Bowie, 2nd ed., 334-35. Manchester: Manchester University Press, 2006.
Olson, Alan M. *Hegel and the Spirit: Philosophy as Pneumatology*. Princeton: Princeton University Press, 1992.
Osborne, Peter. "Hegelian Phenomenology and the Critique of Reason and Society." *Radical Philosophy* 32 (1982): 8-15.
Pahl, Katrin. *Tropes of Transport: Hegel and Emotion*. Evanston, IL: Northwestern University Press, 2012.
Piché, Claude. "The Letter is Particularly Lethal in the *Wissenschaftslehre*." In *Fichte and Transcendental Philosophy*, edited by Tom Rockmore and Daniel Breazeale, 85-102. London: Palgrave Macmillan, 2014.
Pinkard, Terry. *German Philosophy 1760-1860: The Legacy of Idealism*. Cambridge: Cambridge University Press, 2002.
———. *Hegel: A Biography*. Cambridge: Cambridge University Press, 2000.
———. "Translator's Note." In *The Phenomenology of Spirit*, by G. W. F. Hegel, translated by Terry Pinkard, pp. xxxvii-xlv. Cambridge: Cambridge University Press, 2018.
Piper, Andrew. *Enumerations: Data and Literary Study*. Chicago: University of Chicago Press, 2018.
Pippin, Robert B. *After the Beautiful: Hegel and the Philosophy of Pictorial Modernism*. Chicago: University of Chicago Press, 2015.
———. "Hegel, Modernity, and Habermas." *The Monist* 74, no. 3 (1991): 329-57.
———. "Reconstructivism: Honneth's Hegelianism." *Philosophy and Social Criticism* 40, no. 8 (2014): 725-41.
———. "The Status of Literature in Hegel's *Phenomenology of Spirit*: On the Lives of Concepts." In *Philosophy by Other Means: The Arts in Philosophy and Philosophy in the Arts*, 39-55. Chicago: University of Chicago Press, 2021.
Plato. *Meno*. In *"Meno" and "Phaedo,"* edited by David Sedley and Alex Long, 1-41. Cambridge: Cambridge University Press, 2011.
———. *Phaedrus*. Edited by Harvey Yunis. Cambridge: Cambridge University Press, 2011.
Proust, Marcel. *In Search of Lost Time*, translated by C. K. Scott Moncrieff and Terence Kilmartin, revised by D. J. Enright, vol. 1, *Swann's Way*. New York: Modern Library, 1992.
Reid, Jeffrey. *The Anti-Romantic: Hegel against Ironic Romanticism*. London: Bloomsbury, 2014.
———. *L'anti-romantique: Hegel contre le romantisme ironique*. Laval: Presses de l'Univeristé Laval, 2007.
Ricci, Valentina, and Federico Sanguinetti, eds. *Hegel on Recollection: Essays on the Concept of "Erinnerung" in Hegel's System*. Newcastle: Cambridge Scholars Publishing, 2013.

Rickel, Laurence A. *Aberrations of Mourning*. Minneapolis: University of Minnesota Press, 2011.

Ricoeur, Paul. *Freud and Philosophy: An Essay on Interpretation*. Translated by Denis Savage. New Haven: Yale University Press, 2008.

Robbins, Bruce. "Not So Well Attached." *PMLA* 132 (2017): 371–76.

Robertson, Lisa. "Lastingness: Réage, Lucrèce, Arendt." In *Nilling: Prose Essays on Noise, Pornography, The Codex, Melancholy, Lucretius, Folds, Cities and Related Aporias*, 19–40. Toronto: Bookthug, 2012.

Robson, Leo. "Jameson after Post Critique." *New Left Review* 144 (November/December 2023).

Rorty, Richard. *Consequences of Pragmatism (Essays: 1972–1980)*. Minneapolis: University of Minnesota Press, 1994.

Rose, Gillian. *The Broken Middle: Out of our Ancient Society*. Oxford: Blackwell, 1992.

———. *Dialectic of Nihilism: Post-Structuralism and Law*. Oxford: Blackwell, 1984.

———. "Does Marx Have a Method?" unpublished lecture recording, University of Sussex, 1987.

———. *Hegel Contra Sociology*. London: Verso, 2009.

———. "Interview with Gillian Rose." Transcribed and edited by Vincent Lloyd. *Theory, Culture & Society* 25 (2008): 201–18.

———. *Judaism and Modernity: Philosophical Essays*. London: Verso, 2017.

———. *Marxist Modernism: Introductory Lectures on Frankfurt School Critical Theory*. Edited by Robert Lucas Scott and Gordon Finlayson. London: Verso, 2024.

———. *The Melancholy Science: An Introduction to the Thought of Theodor W. Adorno* London: Verso, 2014.

———. *Mourning Becomes the Law: Philosophy and Representation*. Cambridge: Cambridge University Press, 1996.

Rose, Jacqueline. "This Is Not a Biography." *London Review of Books* 24, no. 16 (August 22, 2002).

Rousseau, Jean-Jacques. *Emile; or, Education*. Translated by Barbara Foxley. London: J. M. Dent, 1911.

Royce, Josiah. *Lectures on Modern Idealism*. New Haven: Yale University Press, 1919.

Ruda, Eva, ed. *Beckett and Dialectics: Be It Something or Nothing*. London: Bloomsbury Academic, 2021.

Ruda, Frank. *Abolishing Freedom: A Plea for Contemporary Fatalism*. Lincoln: University of Nebraska Press, 2016.

Rupp, E. Gordon, and Philip S. Watson, eds. *Luther and Erasmus: Free Will and Salvation*. Louisville, KY: Westminster, 1996.

Rush, Fred. *Irony and Idealism: Rereading Schlegel, Hegel, and Kierkegaard*. Oxford: Oxford University Press, 2016.

Sallis, John. "Ending(s): Imagination, Presentation, Spirit." In *Spacings: Of Reason and Imagination in Texts of Kant, Fichte, and Hegel*. Chicago: University of Chicago Press, 1987.

Schelling, F. W. J. "Lectures on the Method of Academic Study (1803)," translated by E. S. Morgan. In *The Schelling Reader*, edited by Benjamin Berger and Daniel Whistler, 361–70. London: Bloomsbury, 2020.

———. *System of Transcendental Idealism*. Translated by Peter Heath. Charlottesville: University Press of Virginia, 2001.

Schick, Kate. "Re-recognizing Recognition: Gillian Rose's 'Radical Hegel' and Vulnerable Recognition." *Telos* 173 (2015): 87–105.
Schlegel, Friedrich. "Ideas." In *The Early Political Writings of the German Romantics*, edited and translated by Frederick C. Beiser, 123–40. Cambridge: Cambridge University Press, 1999.
Schleiermacher, Friedrich. *On Religion: Speeches to its Cultured Despisers*. Translated by Richard Crouter. Cambridge: Cambridge University Press, 2010.
Schwartz, Regina M. "Introduction: On Biblical Criticism." In *The Book and the Text: The Bible and Literary Theory*, edited by Regina M. Schwartz, 1–15. London: Basil Blackwell, 1990.
Scott, Robert. "Suffering and the Feeling of Suffering in Marx's *Capital*." *Textual Practice* 36 (2022): 76–93.
Sedgwick, Eve Kosofsky. "Paranoid Reading and Reparative Reading, or, You're So Paranoid, You Probably Think This Essay is About You." In *Touching Feeling: Affect, Pedagogy, Performativity*, 123–52. Durham, NC: Duke University Press, 2003.
Sedgwick, Sally. *Hegel's Critique of Kant: From Dichotomy to Identity*. Oxford: Oxford University Press, 2012.
Shakespeare, William. *The Tempest*. In *The Oxford Shakespeare: The Complete Works*, 2nd ed., edited by W. J. Craig, 1–23. London: Oxford University Press, 1966.
Smith, John H. *The Spirit and Its Letter: Traces of Rhetoric in Hegel's Philosophy of "Bildung."* New York: Cornell University Press, 1988.
Speight, Allen. *Hegel, Literature and the Problem of Agency*. Cambridge: Cambridge University Press, 2001.
Stace, W. T. *The Philosophy of Hegel: A Systematic Exposition*. New York: Dover, 1955.
Stanglin, Keith D. *The Letter and Spirit of Biblical Interpretation: From the Early Church to Modern Practice*. Grand Rapids, MI: Baker Academic, 2018.
Stein, Gertrude. *Tender Buttons*. New York: Claire Marie, 1914.
Sullivan, David. "Hermann Lotze." In *The Stanford Encyclopedia of Philosophy*. First published January 12, 2005; substantive revision November 2, 2018. https://plato.stanford.edu/archives/win2018/entries/hermann-lotze/.
Suther, Jensen. "Back to Life? The Persistence of Hegel's Idealism (A Response to Karen Ng, *Hegel's Concept of Life: Self-Consciousness, Freedom, Logic*)." *boundary 2* 23 (September 2020).
———. "Spirit Disfigured: The Persistence of Freedom in the Modernist Novel" (PhD diss., Yale University, 2019).
Sutherland, Keston. "Marx in Jargon." In *Stupefaction: A Radical Anatomy of Phantoms*, 26–90. London: Seagull Books, 2011.
———. "Marx's Defence of Poetry." *World Picture* 10 (Spring 2015): 1–15.
———. "The Poetics of *Capital*." In *Capitalism: Concept, Idea, Image*, edited by Peter Osborne, Éric Alliez, and Eric-John Russell, 203–18. London: CRMEP Books, 2019.
———. "Poetry and Subjective Infinity." Online video recording, Vimeo, April 7, 2014. https://vimeo.com/91328990.
———. "Statement for 'Revolution and/or Poetry.'" *Revolution and/or Poetry*, October 15, 2013. https://revolutionandorpoetry.wordpress.com/2013/10/15/keston-sutherlands-statement-for-revolution-andor-poetry/.
———. "*Sub Songs* versus the Subject: Critical Variations on a Distinction between

Prynne and Hegel." In *On the Late Poetry of J. H. Prynne*, edited by Joe Luna and Jow Lindsay Walton, 123-42. Brighton: Hi Zero & Sad Press, 2014.

———. "Wrong Poetry." In *Stupefaction: A Radical Anatomy of Phantoms*, 91-158. London: Seagull Books, 2011.

Tally, Robert T., Jr. "Reading Adorno by the Pool; or, Critical Theory in a Postcritical Era." *symploke* 27 (2019): 281-89.

Taylor, Charles. "The Politics of Recognition." In *Multiculturalism: Examining the Politics of Recognition*, edited by Amy Gutmann, 25-73. Princeton, NJ: Princeton University Press, 1994.

Tolstoy, Leo. *War and Peace*. Translated by Anthony Briggs. London: Penguin Books, 2007.

Verene, Donald Phillip. *Hegel's Recollection: A Study of Images in the "Phenomenology of Spirit."* Albany: SUNY Press, 1985.

Ward, Graham. "How Hegel Became a Philosopher: Logos and the Economy of Logic." *Critical Research on Religion* 1, no. 3 (2013): 270-92.

Willey, Thomas E. *Back to Kant: The Revival of Kantianism in German Social and Historical Thought, 1860-1914*. Detroit: Wayne State University Press, 1978.

Wittgenstein, Ludwig. *Tractatus Logico-Philosophicus*. Translated by D. F. Pears and B. F. McGuinness. London: Routledge, 2001.

Wohlfart, Günter. *Der spekulative Satz: Bemerkungen zum Begriff der Spekulation bei Hegel*. Berlin: Walter de Gruyter, 1981.

Žižek, Slavoj. *Absolute Recoil: Towards a New Foundation of Dialectical Materialism*. London: Verso, 2014.

———. *Disparities*. London: Bloomsbury, 2016.

———. *First as Tragedy, Then as Farce*. London: Verso, 2009.

———. "Hegel and Shitting: The Idea's Constipation." In *Hegel's Infinite: Religion, Politics, and Dialectic*, edited by Slavoj Žižek and Creston Davis, 221-35. New York: Columbia University Press, 2011.

———. "Hegel: The Spirit of Distrust." In *Reading Hegel*, by Slavoj Žižek, Frank Ruda, and Agon Hamza, 13-100. Cambridge: Polity, 2022.

———. "Kant and Sade: The Ideal Couple." *Lacanian Ink* 13 (1998): 12-25.

———. *Less Than Nothing: Hegel and the Shadow of Dialectical Materialism*. London: Verso, 2013.

———. *The Parallax View*. Cambridge, MA: MIT Press, 2006.

———. "A Short Note on Hegel and the Exemplum of Christ." *Crisis & Critique* 82 (2021): 432-41.

———. *The Sublime Object of Ideology*. London: Verso, 2008.

Index

Abrams, M. H., 47
absolute, the, 2, 15, 27, 36, 46, 104-5, 110, 175n48, 195n126
absolute ethical life, 141-42, 194n105. *See also* communism; ethical life
absolute knowing, xviii, 11-13, 24, 26, 34, 46-48, 56-57, 62, 64-70, 73, 75, 141
absolute recoil, 176n54
absolute spirit, 56, 62, 64, 67, 69, 73-74, 147
abstraction, xi-xiii, xxi, 4, 7-8, 10, 15, 25, 29, 34-38, 40, 48-50, 52, 63, 65, 78, 80, 85, 87, 101-2, 106-8, 124-26, 143, 158, 161, 190n23, 195n126; abstract experience, 124; abstract identity, 10, 35, 37-38, 40, 43, 83, 106, 125, 139; real, 14-16, 144-45, 157, 160
Achella, Stefania, 99
activity, xvi-xvii, xix, 30, 50-51, 54, 57. *See also* passivity
Adorno, Theodor W., 1-2, 9-10, 15, 25, 41-43, 45, 50, 56, 84, 86-87, 103, 122, 137, 142, 145, 152, 160, 165, 170n12, 171n4, 178n16, 187n44; and Horkheimer, 93, 103, 185n14
Agamben, Giorgio, 153
Aira, César, 169n5
Alexandrian school, 110, 113
Alexie, Sherman, 169n5

alienation, 15, 44, 141-42, 144, 151, 160-61, 165, 185n12. *See also* relinquishment/kenosis (*Entäußerung*)
allegory, 65, 84, 113, 115, 177n14
Althusser, Louis, 2, 79, 122, 138, 140
Anderson, Amanada, 137
Antigone (Sophocles), 6, 42
antinomianism, 107, 113-14
antinomies, 102-7, 121, 127, 131, 135, 140
Antioch, school of, 113
antisemitism, 77, 92, 185n12
a priori, 122-23, 131-32, 149; synthesis, 62-63, 78, 98. *See also* Kant, Immanuel
Aquinas, Thomas, 113
Arendt, Hannah, 77, 177n80
Aristotle, 8, 71, 96, 111, 116, 181n71
Armstrong, Isobel, 47
art, xi, xiii, 33, 60-61, 64-65, 83, 105, 124, 135, 147, 149, 160, 180n46
atheism, 109-10
Augustine, Saint, 94, 113-14
authorial intention, xvii, 51, 89, 98, 117-18
autofiction, xiii-xiv, 162. *See also* Knausgaard, Karl Ove

Badiou, Alain, 43, 103, 114, 188n81
Bahti, Timothy, 55, 178n14
Baillie, J. B., 178nn16-18, 179n36, 180n55

Barth, Karl, 117
Bates, Jennifer Ann, 71, 172n28, 180n62
Bayard, Pierre, 182n91
Baynes, Kenneth, 172n14
beautiful soul, 59, 73, 77-78, 85; possible sources, 77
Beck, Jakob Sigismund, 96
Beckett, Samuel, 6, 35
beginning, xxi-xxii, 7, 11, 22, 26-29, 47, 70, 82, 133, 158, 162
Beiser, Frederick, 90
Benjamin, Walter, 137, 144-45, 178n16
Bernstein, J. M., 170n19, 171n23
Best, Stephen, 13, 131, 150-51, 190n34
Bewes, Timothy, 130, 191n38
Bhabha, Homi, 6
Bible, 48, 56, 65-66, 99-100, 109-10, 112-17, 178n9, 178n13, 185n18; biblical hermeneutics, 90-91, 100, 108-9, 111, 113, 115-17, 187n43, 188n75
Bildung, 55, 75, 81, 134, 178n16
bildungsroman, 47, 126
biography, 50, 110, 159
Bishop, Elizabeth, 6
Björk, 162
Blanchot, Maurice, 1
Bloch, Ernst, 80-81, 83, 137, 145
Boltanski, Luc, 142
Bonney, Sean, 159, 161, 197n190
Boyer, Anne, 161-62, 169n5
Brandist, Craig, 192n66
Brandom, Robert, xv, 4-5, 13, 21, 30-34, 38, 51-52, 64, 70, 85-87, 170n15, 172n14, 177n85, 183n133, 184n6. See also *de re/de dicto*
Buck-Morss, Susan, 9, 181n86
Butler, Judith, 2, 21-22, 46

capital, 15, 44, 79, 87, 142, 144-45, 152, 157, 159-60
capitalism, xiii, 14-15, 79, 123-24, 142-43, 162
capitalist realism, 163
caricature, 21, 57, 84, 89, 183n120
Catholicism, 99-100, 111, 186n39
Celikates, Robin, 136
Christ, Jesus, 56-57, 65-66, 77, 83, 94, 106, 108-12, 114-16; historicity, 7, 110, 112. See also God
Christianity, 7, 90-92, 94, 99, 109-12, 185n12; Christian atheism, 109-10; historicity of, 109-12, 117. See also Catholicism; Christ, Jesus; God; holy spirit; Luther, Martin; Protestantism; Reformation; religion; Trinity
Cixous, Hélène, 6
class, 138, 143-44, 151, 194n105. See also labor/work; property
climate crisis, 15, 86
Coetzee, J. M., 169n5
Cole, Andrew, 7-8
Cole, Teju, 169n5
Colebrook, Claire, 21
Coleridge, Samuel Taylor, 173n28
Colston, Edward, 87, 184n138
Comay, Rebecca, xviii, 3, 47, 53, 67, 75-76, 84, 93, 100, 108, 172n27, 173n28, 183n120, 185n14
commodity fetish, 15, 79-80, 142, 149, 152-57, 160, 194n106, 196n150
communism, 9, 44, 194n105. See also absolute ethical life
concept (*Begriff*), 13, 26, 31, 34, 47, 51-52, 55, 57, 60-65, 67, 70-72, 74, 77-80, 104-5, 107, 109, 153-54, 156, 190n23
Conrad, Joseph, 147
consciousness, 10, 24-26, 29-34, 36, 51-52, 64-65, 68-69, 73-75, 95, 99-100, 111, 124, 149-50. See also unhappy consciousness
containment strategies, 147-48, 157, 160-61, 195n126. See also ideology; Jameson, Fredric
contingency, xvi-xvii, 12-13, 40, 43, 48, 55, 57, 63, 67, 74, 132-33
contradiction, xiv, xvi-xvii, xix, xxi, 14-16, 24-25, 29, 33, 35, 37-38, 42, 45-46, 49, 51, 57, 104-5, 144-45, 147-48, 156-57, 160-61, 165
critique, xii-xiv, xvi, xx, xxi, 13-14, 20, 38, 121-37, 142, 144-45, 151-52, 155, 157, 160, 162; critical attachment/intimacy, xiii-xiv, xviii, xx, 57; critical detachment, xiii, xviii, xx, 13-14, 57,

136, 145, 147, 149, 152, 154–56, 163; critical theory, xiii, 121–22, 127–28, 131–32, 136–37, 143, 145. *See also* postcritique
Croce, Benedetto, xviii–xix, 1, 3, 9, 171n4
Culler, Jonathan, 148, 197n177
Cusk, Rachel, 162, 169n5

Deakin, Wayne, 172n28
de Boer, Karin, 172n15
de Brosses, Charles, 153–54, 196n163
Deleuze, Gilles, 3, 6, 8, 132
de Man, Paul, xi, 20–21, 23, 70, 174n18, 180n62
de re/de dicto, 4–5, 38, 51–53, 70, 86, 184n6. *See also* Brandom, Robert
Derrida, Jacques, xi, xviii–xix, 1–2, 6, 10, 48, 67, 70, 78, 81–83, 87, 180n62, 180n86, 183n115
Descartes, René, 10, 26–27, 50
dialectic, xii, xiv–xvii, xix–xx, 1, 6–9, 15, 21, 24, 28–29, 37–38, 41, 43, 46–49, 51–52, 55, 57, 69–70, 77, 79, 81–82, 85, 87, 90, 101–3, 105–10, 116, 145–50, 154, 175n34, 185n12; dialectical criticism, 145–48; transcendental, 101–8, 146
Di Cesare, Donatella, 185n12
difference, xi, xix, 1–2, 7, 10, 39, 44, 62–63, 82
difficulty, 9–10, 25, 50, 65, 68, 80, 84–85, 102, 104, 121, 126, 145
Dionysius the Areopagite, 115
Döderlein, Ludwig, 101
dogmatism, 90–91, 93–96, 101–4, 109, 132
Dolar, Mladen, 45, 69
Durkheim, Émile, 2, 122–23

Eichmann, Adolf, 77
Eliot, T. S., 170n16
Emezi, Akwaeke, 169n5
Emre, Merve, 191n54
Emser, Hieronymus, 115
Enlightenment, 131, 137
epistemology, 25, 30, 62, 131
Erasmus, 189n89
Eribon, Didier, 137–39, 143–44
ethical life, 126, 141, 154, 161, 194n105; absolute, 141–42, 194n105

Eucharist, 56, 111
experience, xiii, xvi, xviii, xxi, 10, 12–14, 22–23, 26, 32, 36–37, 40, 46–48, 50–52, 54, 57, 74, 87, 103, 122–24, 126, 133–38, 145, 148–51, 155, 157–59, 161, 164–65; historical, 75–76, 81; lived, xiii, 137–39, 142–43, 159, 161; reading, xx, 37, 46, 54, 127, 152–53, 157; sensory/intuitive, 71, 73. *See also* speculative: experience
expression (*Äußerung*), 57, 82–84, 157–61, 163. *See also* relinquishment/kenosis (*Entäußerung*)

fascism, 44, 144, 155–57
Felski, Rita, 13, 127, 130, 132, 135–40, 142–44, 150–52, 172n15, 191n40, 191n47, 191n54, 193n83
feminism, 42, 126
fetishistic disavowal, 28, 195n126
Fichte, J. G., 2, 20, 23, 26, 60, 62, 90–91, 95–99, 101, 107–9, 117, 178n16, 186n26, 187n63, 195n126
finitude, 12, 19–20, 70, 99, 103, 128, 159, 165. *See also* infinity
first person/"I," xiv, 160–64. *See also* third person
Fleabag (television series), xiii
Fosse, Jon, 165
Foucault, Michel, 1, 3, 6, 132–34, 136, 192n66
Frankfurt School, 121, 130, 135–38, 143, 145
Franks, Paul, 90
Fraser, Nancy, 140
freedom, 9, 15, 59, 61, 71, 82, 91, 95, 97, 100–101, 108, 112, 116, 118, 121, 125, 128, 139, 144, 157, 161, 165, 190n21; as necessity/fate, 116–17, 189n89
Freud, Sigmund, 53, 84, 127–28, 130–31, 155, 186n37

Geuss, Raymond, 180n62
Gleason, Randall C., 188n83
God, xviii, 38–40, 44, 56, 59, 62, 65–66, 83, 92, 95, 99, 104–7, 110–11, 114–15, 150, 187n43; as coal, 105–6, 116. *See also* Christ, Jesus; holy spirit; Trinity

Goethe, Johann Wolfgang von, 77, 80, 103
Goetschel, Willi, 129, 131
Goldman, Francisco, 169n5
Gregory of Nyssa, 113
Guillory, John, 130

Habermas, Jürgen, 2-4, 122, 136-37, 140, 172n14
Habib, M. A. R., 6-8, 126
Hägglund, Martin, 166, 170n19
Hamacher, Werner, xviii, 1, 44, 46, 81-83
Harman, Graham, 191n41
Hartmann, Geoffrey, 6
Hayles, N. Katherine, 191n36
Hegel, G. W. F., works of: "Address on the Tercentenary of the Submission of the Augsburg Confession," 112; correspondence, 40-41, 68, 90-91, 93-95, 100-108, 111-12, 116-17; *Difference Between Schelling's and Fichte's Systems of Philosophy*, 98, 175n48; *Encyclopedia Logic*, 27, 36, 63-65, 82-83, 85, 104, 117-18, 179n44, 180n62; *Faith and Knowledge*, 61-62, 78, 98; lectures on aesthetics, 19-20, 78, 158-60, 179n46; lectures on history of philosophy, xvi, 37; lectures on philosophy of religion, 65, 90, 109; lectures on philosophy of spirit, 72; *Natural Law*, 61, 78; "On the Orbits of the Planets," xiv, xvi, xxi, 34; *Phenomenology of Spirit*, xii, xv-xvi, xix-xxi, 4-6, 10-13, 16, 20, 26-52, 55-57, 60-64, 66-70, 72-79, 82-83, 85, 99-100, 106, 108, 110, 116, 125, 128, 139-40, 150, 158-59, 164-65, 185n12, 185n17, 187n43; *Philosophy of Mind*, 64, 70-74, 76, 177n2, 184n1; *Philosophy of Nature*, xix; *Philosophy of Right*, 42, 44, 80-81, 83, 118, 121, 133, 190n21; "The Positivity of the Christian Religion," 92; *Science of Logic*, xix, xxi, 28, 30, 34, 63, 65, 68, 74-75, 82, 91, 100, 105, 112-13, 136, 152, 158, 170n19, 185n17; "The Spirit of Christianity," 92, 114; *System of Ethical Life*, 139-42, 194n105

Hegelianism, xvii-xviii, 3, 7, 52; anti-Hegelianism, 1, 6, 8
Heidegger, Martin, 2, 10-12, 51, 81, 163, 189n9
Henrich, Dieter, 186n26
Henry, Michel, 51
hermeneutics of suspicion, 127-28, 131-32, 191n54
Heti, Sheila, 162
Hiraide, Takashi, 169n5
historicism, 7, 52, 111-12, 132-33, 147
history, xi, 7, 9, 33, 55-58, 67, 73-76, 79, 85-87, 89, 105-6, 110-12, 116, 126, 132, 148, 151, 185n12
history of philosophy, xviii, xx, 133
Hitler, Adolf, 87
Hölderlin, Friedrich, 61
Holocaust, 86, 155
holy spirit, 56, 83. *See also* God; Trinity
Honneth, Axel, 4, 136-43, 172n15
Horkheimer, Max, 93, 103
Houlgate, Stephen, 5, 23, 52, 172n23
Husserl, Edmund, 51, 189n9
Hyppolite, Jean, 47, 68

identity, xix-xx, 10, 13, 35-39, 43, 46, 48, 62-63, 78, 80, 82-83, 98, 105, 125-26, 141, 148, 150, 175n48; abstract, 10, 35, 37-38, 40, 43, 83, 106, 125, 139; non-/lack of, 9-10, 36, 39-40, 48, 63, 80, 83, 105, 125, 141-42, 148, 150, 175n48, 194n105. *See also* difference; "is"; speculative: identity
ideology, xiv, 14, 139-40, 147, 150-51, 156-57, 161-62. *See also* containment strategies
image (*Bild*), 57-58, 61-63, 65-67, 69-80, 83, 85, 88, 98, 147; translations of *Bild*, 178n16
imagination (*Einbildungskraft*), 70-72, 105, 107, 160, 178n16
immediacy, xii-xiv, xviii, xxi, 21, 25, 28-30, 36-37, 45, 47, 55, 62, 64-66, 71, 73, 80, 87, 100, 124, 145, 149-52, 154, 157-64, 169n8, 185n12. *See also* mediation
infinite judgment, 45, 57, 69, 106. *See also* God: as coal; spirit (*Geist*): as bone

infinity, 12, 15, 19-20, 70, 106, 159-60, 165; bad infinite, 12, 15, 55. *See also* finitude
interpretation, 51-53, 70, 90, 93, 97, 99, 101, 113, 115-16, 130, 148, 150-51, 160; reinterpretation, 87. *See also* Bible: biblical hermeneutics
intuition, 60-61, 65-66, 71, 73, 76, 89, 117, 194n117
Inwood, Michael, 178nn16-18, 179n36, 180n55, 183n115
irony, xii, xiv-xvii, xx-xxi, 1, 4-5, 8-10, 12-15, 19-29, 34-44, 46-55, 57, 69, 80, 82-83, 87, 89, 93, 95-96, 106, 108, 116-17, 125, 133, 145, 147, 154-55, 157, 160-61, 164; dramatic, xvi, 46, 155; ironic distance/detachment, xvi, xviii, 22, 28, 35-36, 43, 49, 53; postmodern, xv, 22, 48; Romantic, xv-xvi, 19-24, 43, 49, 53-54; Socratic, 37; woman as irony of the community, 41-44. *See also* truth
"is," xix-xx, 35-40, 43-44, 46, 159, 162. *See also* identity; speculative: identity
Ishiguro, Kazuo, 155-57
Israel, 43-44
Ivory, James, 155

Jacobi, Friedrich Heinrich, 77, 96, 186n26
Jaeggi, Rahel, 136
Jameson, Fredric, 64-65, 67, 79, 125-26, 145-52, 164-65, 194n122, 195n126, 195n139, 196n150
Jerome, Saint, 115
Jojo Rabbit (film), 196n163
Judaism, 92, 99-100, 185n12

Kafka, Franz, 6
Kanehara, Hitomi, 169n5
Kant, Immanuel, 2, 10, 20, 27, 30-31, 34, 37, 60-62, 75, 90-93, 95-98, 102-4, 107, 109, 121-22, 124-25, 128, 130-36, 139-40, 149-52, 178n16, 183n120, 185n14, 186n26, 195n126; categorical imperative, 93, 97; *Critique of Judgment*, 60-61; *Critique of Practical Reason*, 185n13; *Critique of Pure Reason*, 61-62, 96-97, 102-3, 184n10, 194n117; *Religion within the Boundaries of Mere Reason*, 184n10. *See also* antinomies; a priori; neo-Kantianism; transcendental
Keats, John, 158, 160-61, 197n190
Kierkegaard, Søren, xv, 3, 19-21, 23
Knausgaard, Karl Ove, xiv, 162-65, 169n5
Knebel, Karl Ludwig von, 40
knowledge, xxii, 22, 26-31, 40, 47-49, 51, 55, 81, 102-4, 150; wrong, 47, 102, 128. *See also* absolute knowing
Knox, T. M., 80, 185n13
Kojève, Alexandre, 181n86
Kompridis, Nikolas, 136
Kornbluh, Anna, xiii-xiv, 161-63, 169n5, 170n8
Kortian, Garbis, 172n14
Kotsko, Adam, 188n81
Kraus, Chris, 169n5
Krell, David Farrell, 180n62
Kristeva, Julia, 42-43
Kürnberger, Ferdinand, 15

labor/work, 15, 79, 141-42, 160
Lacan, Jacques, 45, 138, 185n14
Laing, Olivia, 162, 169n5
language, 9-10, 35, 105-6, 126
lateness, xvi, 46, 80, 130-31, 155, 157
Latour, Bruno, 131, 134-35, 151-52, 191n40
law, 91-92, 94-95, 97, 100, 102-3, 105, 107-9, 113-15, 185n18, 187n43, 188n81
Leibniz, Gottfried Wilhelm, 87
Lenin, Vladimir, 15, 80
Leopardi, Giacomo, 6
Lerner, Ben, 162
liberal democracy, 3-5, 44
life, xviii-xix, 12, 15, 44, 54, 80, 83, 100, 106, 108, 114-16, 125-26, 128, 144-45, 157, 159-61, 163-64, 170n19
Lin, Tao, 162, 169n5
literalism, xviii, 37, 47, 66, 89, 91, 96, 99-100, 108, 113
literary theory/criticism, xi-xv, xx, 5-7, 13-14, 70-71, 121, 126-31, 132, 134-38, 145-52, 157; Marxist literary criticism, 14-15, 145-52, 157

literature, xiii, 6, 21, 65–66, 128, 148–49
Locke, John, 27
Lotze, Rudolf Hermann, 122, 152, 189n9
love, 92–93, 108, 114, 156–57, 160–61, 165
Love, Heather, 13, 131, 151, 191n37
Lukács, György, xi, 2, 103, 122, 137, 145, 152
Luther, Martin, 56–57, 83, 87, 89, 91–92, 94, 99–101, 108–9, 111–17, 187n43, 189n89
lyric, xiv, 158–61. *See also* poetry

Malabou, Catherine, 2, 11–13, 38, 44, 61, 84–85. *See also* plasticity
Mann, Thomas, 6
Marasco, Robyn, 128
Marcion of Sinope, 94, 185n18
Marcus, Sharon, 13, 131, 150–51, 190n34
Marcuse, Herbert, 145
Marx, Karl, 14–16, 79–81, 127–28, 130–31, 140, 142–45, 149, 152–56, 159, 161, 173n48, 173n50, 183n109. *See also* commodity fetish
Marxism, 14–15, 80, 83, 124, 126, 143–45, 148, 153, 155, 157; critical, 122. *See also* literary theory/criticism: Marxist literary criticism; Marx, Karl
master-slave dialectic, 9, 58, 77–78, 85, 139, 156; possible sources of, 77, 181n86
McGowan, John, 21–22
meaning, xvii–xix, 10, 12, 24–25, 40, 45, 48, 50, 52, 54, 65, 87, 112–13, 116–17, 125, 127, 130, 151–52, 158–59
mediation, xii–xiv, xxi–xxii, 21–22, 28, 31, 47, 55, 61–62, 71, 87, 111, 124, 138, 141, 149, 152, 154, 158–65, 170n8, 170n12. *See also* immediacy
melancholia, 48, 73–74, 100, 159
Melville, Hermann, 6
memory (*Gedächtnis*), 70, 180n62. *See also* recollection (*Erinnerung*)
Merleau-Ponty, Maurice, 51
metaphor, 35, 47–48, 56, 63, 65–66, 72, 78, 84
metaphysics, xviii
method, xii, xiv, xxi, 7–9, 22, 24, 26–34, 38–39, 46, 49–50, 89, 111, 113, 121, 123, 127, 131, 134–36, 140, 142, 145, 147, 150, 152, 155, 162, 175n34; *meta-hodos*, xii, 28, 38, 127
Milbank, John, 111
Miller, Andrew H., 191n42
Miller, A. V., 178nn16–18, 179n36, 180n55
Miller, J. Hillis, 6
Milne, Drew, 77, 131–32, 181n87
modernity, 21–22, 148, 185n12
Moggach, Douglas, 172n14
Moi, Toril, 191n39
Molière, 6
morality, 33–34, 127, 132, 142, 147, 158, 162, 183n120
Moretti, Franco, 130, 191n35
Moshenska, Joe, 172n28
mourning, 48, 74, 84–85, 100
Mueller, Gustav E., 175n34

Napoleon, 68
negativity, 10, 33–35, 45, 48, 53–54
Nelson, Maggie, 162, 169n5
neo-Kantianism, xx, 122–24, 127–29, 134, 145, 149, 152, 157, 189n9, 192n66, 194n117. *See also* Kant, Immanuel
Nersessian, Anahid, 160–61
New Age, 53, 163
Ng, Karen, 170n19
Nicholas of Cusa, 8
Nicholas of Lyra, 113
Niethammer, Friedrich Immanuel, 68, 100–101
Nietzsche, Friedrich, 3, 8, 114, 127–28, 130–31
Novalis, 19–20, 49, 60, 77, 84
Nuzzo, Angelica, 170n15, 173n28

object, 22, 30–35, 62, 122–23, 131, 155
objectivity, 12–13, 20, 22, 31, 123–27, 129, 134, 138–39, 141, 143, 150, 155, 157–58, 161, 165
"Oldest System Programme of German Idealism," 61
Olson, Alan M., 116
ontology, 30, 43, 62, 98
Origen, 113, 115

Osborne, Peter, 121
ought (*Sollen*), xix, 80, 91, 93, 184n10, 190n23, 195n126
outline (*Grundriss*), 60, 78, 84–85, 89, 126
owl of Minerva, 80, 83, 131

Pahl, Katrin, 6
Palestine, 43–44, 86
passivity, xvii, 30, 50–51, 53–55, 57
Paul, Saint, 89–90, 93–94, 107–9, 112, 114, 117, 185n18, 187n43, 188n75, 188n81, 189n89
phenomenology, twentieth-century, 50–51, 73
philology, 100–101, 116, 182n87
Pinkard, Terry, 40, 56, 68, 90, 178nn16–18, 179n36, 180n50, 180n55
Piper, Andrew, 191n43
Pippin, Robert, 61, 172nn14–15, 172n27
plasticity, xix–xx, 2, 12–13, 33, 36–38, 46. *See also* Malabou, Catherine
Plath, Sylvia, 159
Plato, 8, 21, 81, 104, 111; neoplatonism, 110. *See also* Socrates
Plotinus, 8
poetry, 59–61, 67, 69, 98, 159, 180n46. *See also* lyric
postcritique, xiv, xx, 13–14, 127, 129–31, 134–36, 145, 150–51, 172n15, 191n54, 193n83; ANT (actor-network theory), 129–30, 191n40; surface reading, 129, 150–51. *See also* Felski, Rita
postmodernism, 22, 48. *See also* irony: postmodern
poststructuralism, xviii, 80, 126. *See also* Derrida, Jacques; Hamacher, Werner
presuppositions/presuppositionlessness, xii, xxii, 4, 7–8, 10, 25–26, 29, 36, 39, 51–54, 75, 112, 115, 122, 136, 140, 159, 162–63
proletariat, 44, 143–44. *See also* class; labor/work
property, 141–42, 144, 194n105
propositional form, 22–23, 35–40, 44–46, 50, 54, 62, 83, 116. *See also* speculative: proposition

Protestantism, 99, 112; Protestant ethic, 123. *See also* Luther, Martin; Reformation
Proust, Marcel, 53, 55, 71
Prynne, J. H., 6
psychoanalysis, 53, 84, 126, 149. *See also* Freud, Sigmund; Lacan, Jacques

Rameau's Nephew (Diderot), 6, 59
reading, xii–xiv, xviii, 8–14, 23, 36–41, 44–46, 49–53, 57, 108–9, 113, 116, 126–27, 157–59, 163, 165; de re/de dicto, 4–5, 38, 51–52; experience of, xx, 37, 46, 54, 127, 152–53, 157; misreading, xix, 38, 40, 44, 47, 49, 57, 69–70, 150; paranoid, 191n47, 191n54; rereading, 10–14, 38, 40–41, 47, 57, 69, 87, 118, 160, 165; transcendental, 46. *See also* speculative: reading
Réage, Pauline, 177n80
reason (*Vernunft*), 64–65, 86, 92–93, 103–5, 108, 126, 135
recognition, xi, 4–5, 7, 77, 126, 138–44, 146, 164, 190n23, 193n100; misrecognition, 124–25, 138, 141–44, 146, 194n105
recollection (*Erinnerung*), xiv, xvi–xvii, xx, 4, 10–11, 14, 54–58, 60, 67, 70–89, 100, 107, 110, 112, 116–18, 121, 128, 130–31, 157, 159, 165, 170n15, 183n115; and *anamnesis*, 11, 81, 182n106
Reformation, 112, 114. *See also* Luther, Martin; Protestantism
Reid, Jeffrey, 19–21, 174n6
Reinhold, Karl Leonhard, 90
religion, 33–34, 64–65, 69, 91–92, 99, 102, 105, 110–12, 117, 124–25, 147. *See also* Christ, Jesus; God
relinquishment/kenosis (*Entäußerung*), 55–57, 82–85, 87–88, 110, 159, 165, 183n115, 185n12
Remains of the Day, The (film), 155–57. *See also* Ishiguro, Kazuo
representation/picture-thinking (*Vorstellung*), 6, 46, 57, 62–79, 82–85, 89, 104–7, 109–10, 112, 116, 122, 155–56, 159, 162, 180n46; nonrepresentability, 156; translations of *Vorstellung*, 179n36

resolve (*Entschluß*), xvii, 10, 14, 57, 82–83, 87, 97, 118
revolution, 15, 48, 145, 155, 159
Rickels, Laurence A., 186n37
Ricoeur, Paul, 130–31. *See also* hermeneutics of suspicion
Robbins, Bruce, 191n54, 193n83
Robertson, Lisa, 177n80
Robson, Leo, 150, 195n139
Romanticism, xvi, 19–24, 43, 49, 53–54, 59–60, 78, 87, 107, 160. *See also* irony: Romantic
Rorty, Richard, 21–22
Rosa, Hartmut, 136
Rose, Gillian, xx, 2, 14–15, 21–22, 29, 40, 48, 83, 104, 128, 143, 152–53, 155–56, 185n12, 186n37, 187n44, 192n63, 192n66, 193n100, 194n106; *Hegel Contra Sociology*, 14, 121–27, 129, 134–36, 138, 140–42, 144–45, 152, 154, 162, 190n23, 194n105, 194n117, 195n126, 196n160, 197n188
Rose, Jacqueline, 159, 163
Rousseau, Jean-Jacques, 181n86
Royce, Josiah, 47
Ruda, Frank, xviii, 3, 53, 75, 108, 116, 189n89
Rush, Fred, 21, 24–25, 30, 34, 47
Russian Formalism, 194n122

Sade, Marquis de, 93, 185n14
Sallis, John, 180n62
Sartre, Jean-Paul, 145
satire, 42, 80, 153–55
Schelling, F. W. J., 60–61, 77, 91, 93–94, 178n16
Schick, Kate, 193n100
Schiller, Friedrich, 6, 60, 67, 95, 107, 179n45, 187n43, 187n63
Schindler's List (film), 155
Schlegel, Friedrich, 20, 24, 49, 60–61, 77, 84
Schleiermacher, Friedrich, 49, 111, 113, 188n69
Schopenhauer, Arthur, 3
Schwartz, Regina, 188n75
Sedgwick, Eve Kosofsky, 191n47, 191n54
Sedgwick, Sally, 132–33
sensuous certainty, 35, 100
Shaftesbury, Lord (Anthony Ashley Cooper), 77
Shakespeare, William, 6, 68
Shelley, Mary, 173n28
Shelley, Percy Bysshe, 173n28
Simmel, Georg, 2, 122
simplification, 57, 71–72, 74–75, 77, 79–80, 84–85. *See also* caricature
Smith, John, 89–90
sociology/social theory, 14, 121–27, 130–31, 134–42, 150, 192n66, 194n117
Socrates, 37, 101, 182n106. *See also* irony; Plato
sola scriptura/sola fide, 99, 114
speculative, 101, 104–7, 143, 152–53, 160; experience, xii, xxi, 2, 5, 8–9, 14–16, 22, 52, 121–22, 125–29, 133, 135–36, 140, 144–46, 149, 152–55, 157–58, 161, 165 (*see also* experience); identity, xx, 32, 40, 43, 56, 70, 74, 80, 105, 107, 125, 133, 140, 150 (*see also* identity; "is"); naivete, xiii, 4, 7, 53; proposition, xix–xx, 11–13, 23, 36–40, 44–46, 48, 53–54, 58, 62, 69, 83, 106, 116, 125 (*see also* propositional form); reading, xii, xiv, xix–xxi, 7, 9–10, 23, 37–41, 45–46, 51–52, 54, 57, 83, 115–16, 148, 150, 158, 160–61, 165 (*see also* reading); thinking, xvii–xviii, 3, 5, 7–8, 11–12, 14, 25, 36–37, 42, 46, 48–49, 51, 54, 64, 74, 76, 89, 106–7, 157, 159; truth, 23, 38, 45, 48; words, 36, 106 (*see also* truth)
Speight, Allen, 6, 68
Spenser, Edmund, 6
spirit (*Geist*), xvii, 4, 14–15, 24, 34, 50, 55–56, 58, 73, 78–85, 89, 99, 105, 107–8, 110–11, 139, 158–59, 180n46; as bone, 45, 57, 60, 106; shape (*Gestalt*) of, xxi, 60, 74, 79, 82–85, 87, 89, 150. *See also* holy spirit
spirit and the letter, xiv, xviii, xx, 9, 12–14, 57, 62, 76, 83, 87–118, 121, 159, 165, 188n75. *See also* Fichte, J. G.; Paul, Saint
Stace, W. T., 175n34

Stein, Gertrude, 164
style, xiii–xiv, 8, 13, 23, 36, 79, 84, 137, 151, 160–62
subject, 12–13, 21–22, 31, 34, 38, 40, 45–47, 56, 62–63, 121, 131, 148, 160–61; and substance, xx, 13, 34, 107–8, 125, 148, 152, 155, 157, 161, 190n21
subjectivism, 12–13, 135, 137, 145
subjectivity, xv, 12–13, 22, 38, 41, 45, 90, 111, 124–28, 134, 136, 138–39, 141, 143–45, 148, 150, 155, 157–58, 160–61, 164–65, 190n21, 195n126
sublation (*Aufhebung*), xvii–xviii, 1–2, 10, 36–37, 45, 60, 62, 64, 73, 75, 78, 85, 108, 110, 165, 178n14, 185n12
Sullivan, David, 189n9
Suther, Jensen, 170n19, 173n28
Sutherland, Keston, 15, 49, 79, 153–56, 160, 172n28, 173n48, 173n50, 174n54, 196n150, 196n163, 197n180

Tally, Robert T., Jr., 193n83
theology, 90–91, 98, 109–11, 114
third person, 161–62. *See also* first person/"I"
Tholuck, August, 111
Tolstoy, Leo, 165
transcendental, 5, 46, 127, 131, 133–34, 139, 146, 165; critique, 103; dialectic, 101–8, 146; idealism/philosophy, 96, 104, 122, 140; justification, 125, 132–33; imagination, 62; logic, 123; quasi-transcendental, xi, 4, 7, 122–24, 126–27, 131, 133, 140, 142–43, 149; reading, 46; subject, 133

translation, 117–18, 187n43
Trinity, 109–11. *See also* Christ, Jesus; God; holy spirit
Trump, Donald, 196n163
truth, xiv–xviii, xix–xx, 1, 6–10, 12, 14–15, 19, 23, 26, 29–31, 34–36, 38, 40–41, 44–47, 49, 51–54, 57, 61, 63–67, 74, 78, 82–84, 87, 89, 93, 95–96, 101, 104–5, 107–12, 116–17, 121, 132–33, 145, 155, 157, 161; post-truth, 108. *See also* irony

understanding (*Verstand*), 64
unhappy consciousness, 59–60, 77, 85, 99–100
universality, xvi, xix, 9, 12, 15, 37, 41–44, 71–72, 114, 132–33, 158–61, 166

validity/values, 122–25, 127, 145, 149, 152, 157, 189n9
Verene, Donald Phillip, 28, 69–70, 72, 178n17

Ward, Graham, 110
Weber, Max, 2, 122–23
Wieland, Christoph Martin, 77
Willey, Thomas E., 189n9
Wittgenstein, Ludwig, 75
Wohlfart, Günter, 23, 36
woman, xx, 41–44
Wordsworth, William, 6, 159, 173n28

Žižek, Slavoj, 1, 3, 9, 45, 77, 169n8, 170n16, 176n54, 182n91, 183n116, 183n133, 185n14, 186n26, 187n57, 188n81

www.ingramcontent.com/pod-product-compliance
Lightning Source LLC
Chambersburg PA
CBHW022050290426
44109CB00014B/1050